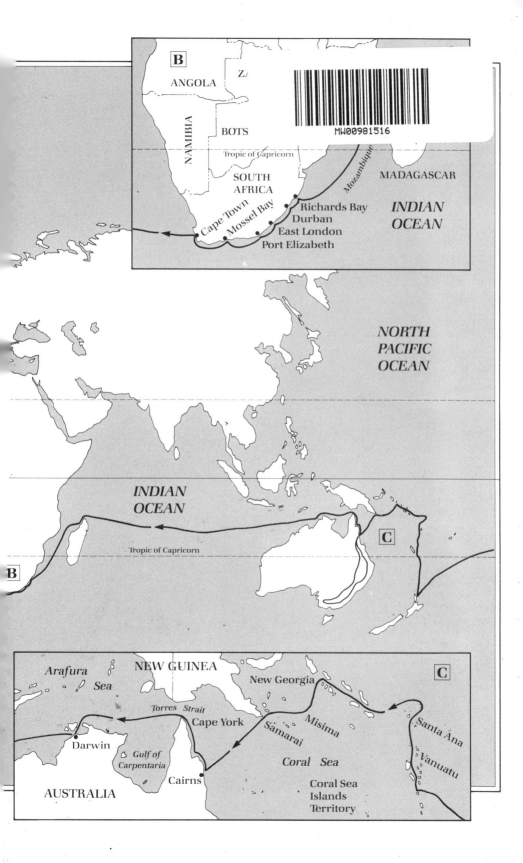

B

ANGOLA

Z...

NAMIBIA

BOTS

Tropic of Capricorn

SOUTH
AFRICA

MADAGASCAR

*INDIAN
OCEAN*

Cape Town

Mossel Bay

Richards Bay
Durban
East London
Port Elizabeth

Mozambique

*NORTH
PACIFIC
OCEAN*

*INDIAN
OCEAN*

C

Tropic of Capricorn

B

C

Arafura
Sea

NEW GUINEA

New Georgia

Torres Strait

Cape York

Samarai

Misima

Santa Ana

Darwin

*Gulf of
Carpentaria*

Coral Sea

Vanuatu

AUSTRALIA

Cairns

Coral Sea
Islands
Territory

STILL IN THE SAME BOAT

STILL IN THE
SAME BOAT

Fiona McCall and Paul Howard

M&S

Endpaper map: James Loates Illustrating

Canadian Cataloguing in Publication Data

McCall, Fiona
    Still in the same boat

ISBN 0-7710-5440-8

1. Yachts and yachting – Pacific Ocean.
2. Voyages and travels. 3. Lorcha (Yacht).
I. Howard, Paul. II. Title.

G530.M33 1989   910'.09164   C89-094360-5

Printed and bound in Canada

McClelland & Stewart Inc.
The Canadian Publishers
481 University Avenue
Toronto, Ontario
M5G 2E9

"Around the world and home again. That's the sailor's way."
Richard Allingham, *Homeward Bound*

CONTENTS

INTRODUCTION

On July 1, 1983, our family of four packed what we could aboard our nine-metre (thirty-foot) sailboat, *Lorcha*, and cast off from our downtown Toronto marina berth. Penny was six years old and Peter was four. Before either of them had been born, Fiona and I had made a two-year sailing trip, and now, six years later, we were ready once more to give up city living for the peripatetic ocean-cruising way of life.

Our six-week sail down the historic St. Lawrence Seaway, sailing during the day and mooring in different harbours at night, was a good introduction to life aboard a cruising vessel for our two youngsters.

We were all dreadfully seasick on our first ocean crossing from St. John's, Newfoundland, to the Azores. At times we wondered whether we would be able to complete this first passage, let alone any further voyaging. *Lorcha*'s seaworthiness was tested in a full gale, and she buoyantly rose to the big waves and remained unbowed by the high winds in a way that inspired confidence, rather than causing fright. We cheered ourselves when Flores, the western-most island of the Azores, came into sight on our eleventh day at sea.

When we reached Madeira we began to meet European cruising boats, many with children on board. We were all more or less heading west and we anchored with the same boats and people at various times and places around the world over the next few years.

The Canary Islands were crowded at Christmas and the New

1

Year, the season when most boats make the east-to-west North Atlantic Ocean crossing. We made some modifications to *Lorcha*'s interior appointments to allow more stowage space for food supplies, refining our vessel to incorporate lessons learned so we could truly be at home at sea.

We sailed towards the Cape Verde Islands at the height of the winter-time trade winds, battling near-gale conditions for most of the passage. With strong winds and a sky full of dust blowing off the Sahara Desert we found it difficult to identify our island landfall, but when we found it, in a never-to-be-forgotten experience, we slid down the face of twenty-foot waves, looking back over our shoulders to see dolphins and flying fish high above us as we surfed into harbour.

Lorcha made her first equatorial crossing when sailing from the Cape Verde Islands to Brazil. A school of sharks accompanied us across that theoretical line, just as Fiona was planning her first dip in the waters of the southern hemisphere.

Fiona often describes Brazil as the country most lacking in sanitation that we have visited, but we enjoyed our four months spent cruising her northern coast, as well as fighting our way up the mighty Amazon River to visit the rain forest of that enormous watershed.

We never could decide which was the most memorable of our experiences in French Guiana – visiting the former French penal colony at Devil's Island, or watching the giant luth turtles drag themselves onto the beach at Les Hattes to lay their eggs.

At the offshore islands of Venezuela we found pristine tropical reefs, and were entranced by the abundance and variety of sea creatures inhabiting them. We were by this time practised fishermen, and we enjoyed the bounty of the sea. At age five, Peter was able to help us forage for food by diving for conch and struggling to the surface with the heavy shell.

Bonaire, in the Netherlands Antilles, brought diving experiences with a difference. Dive guide Dee Scarr introduced Peter and Penny to sea creatures they could relate to in a

2

personal way. The children hand-fed tame ocean fish with hot dogs, and Peter made friends with a small moray eel.

At the San Blas Islands of Panama we were to meet the last remaining Caribe Indians, the Kuna Indians, in their autonomous territory. These gentle people of diminutive stature (few are more than one and a half metres, or five feet, tall) showed us their hand-stitched layered *molas* and their way of life.

By the time we arrived at the Panama Canal we had been travelling for twenty months and had sailed 12,000 miles. Our small family had learned a great deal about ocean voyaging, sea creatures, and the people who inhabit coastal areas of the world. Our first book, *All in the Same Boat*, told of our adventures to this point.

We had originally planned to be away from Toronto for two to three years, but we had also hoped to do some sailing in the Pacific Ocean. At Panama we had to make a family decision: should we turn north and island-hop through the Caribbean chain of islands on our way up to the east coast of the United States and back to our home in Canada? Or should we transit the Panama Canal, crossing from the Caribbean Sea to the Pacific Ocean and continue heading west?

The whole family agreed that we were not ready to give up our ocean voyaging way of life. Penny and Peter were healthy and happy shipmates and daring adventurers. *Lorcha* had proven her seaworthiness whenever it was tested, and we had no doubt she would carry us wherever we chose to point her bow. We chose to head west, setting *Lorcha*'s sail to run before the trade winds of the southern hemisphere.

In our previous book, Fiona and I took turns telling our stories, and we have continued to do that in this book. We hope it will not be confusing to find *I* sometimes referring to Fiona, sometimes to myself. We have also tried to eliminate any confusion over metric and imperial usage in measurements by sticking to metric almost exclusively. When we refer to "miles" in the book, we mean nautical miles, rather than imperial miles.

Think of yourself as settling into a cushioned corner of

Lorcha's cockpit, with Fiona and I ready to share our experiences, each of us giving our impressions of places visited or people met.

If you're comfortable, we will get started, as we have oceans to cross, islands to visit, and many adventures to share.

THE CHALLENGE OF THE PANAMA CANAL

1

The Cristobal Yacht Club, at the town of Cristobal on the northern end of the Panama Canal Zone, is the main staging area for yachts crossing through the Panama Canal from the Atlantic to the Pacific Ocean.

Sailing through the breakwater towards the club, we all made bets on how many yachts would be there waiting to transit. Peter's guess of twenty-two was nearest to the mark; mine of five was farthest off. Perhaps, as a nervous skipper with a full realization of the effort involved in transiting the canal, and the long crossing of the Pacific Ocean immediately thereafter, I assumed that others too would be hesitant to make that commitment. There were thirty-two yachts at Cristobal, twenty of them anchored at no charge in an area called the Flats and twelve moored at the yacht club docks. Three to seven yachts were transiting every day, with about the same number also arriving daily. It was April, one of the peak months for yacht traffic through the canal.

The history of Panama centres on the trans-isthmus route, beginning in 1513 when Vasco Nuñez de Balboa first glimpsed the Pacific Ocean "silent upon a peak in Darien." Panama City, on the Pacific coast, was founded in 1519 when a trail was discovered leading from there to the Caribbean coast.

Arrival at Colon . . . history of Panama . . . line handlers . . .
arrival of our pilot . . . rafting up . . . dangerous cargo
delays transit . . . sideways swing . . . across Lake Gatun . . .
"down" locks . . . the monkey's fist falls short . . .
the Pacific Ocean.

Spaniards transported the wealth of their Pacific coast colonies across the isthmus to the Caribbean coast, where it was loaded on ships for transport to the mother country.

Nearly two hundred years later, the trail became a crowded route when the Forty-niners trooped across it *en route* to the gold fields of California. A railroad, which is still operating, was opened in 1853 and was a huge financial success, although its importance lessened after 1869 when the transcontinental railroad was completed across the United States.

Ferdinand de Lesseps, the same engineer who had successfully completed the Suez Canal, was in charge of the first attempt at building a trans-isthmus canal in 1881. This was abandoned, however, in 1893, and an American government agency purchased the rights and properties of the failed company. The residents of this region of Colombia were then encouraged to declare independence, and the United States recognized the independent country of Panama in 1903. Work was begun on the canal after the establishment of the Panama Canal Zone, originally a sixteen-kilometre-wide ribbon of land which included the cities of Cristobal and Balboa. The canal, an engineering marvel of its time, was built at a cost of roughly $639 million (U.S.) and 25,000 lives. The first ship passed through the canal in 1914, with about 12,000 vessels per year now making that same passage.

We headed for the dock at the Cristobal Yacht Club where we planned to stay for ten days. There was much to do: we had to arrange for *Lorcha* to be measured for her canal transit permission, buy four months' provisions, find replacement stove parts, and do the paperwork for a Panamanian Cruising Permit. The daily berthing charge was reasonable, and the club had hot showers, washers, and dryers, as well as a twenty-four-hour bar and restaurant.

Perhaps best of all, there was a twenty-four-hour security guard at the gate, with guards patrolling the grounds all night. Colon, Panama's second-largest city, begins about a hundred metres from the gates. It has a bad reputation for pickpockets and muggers. Fellow yachtsmen told us of having their pockets slashed by gangs of youths with straight razors, and their wallets snatched. The problem had gotten so out-of-hand that the National Guard was called out to patrol the streets when the cruise ships stopped so that their passengers could browse through the many duty-free shops.

Lying alongside a dock is a treat for long-distance sailors, and we knew that this would be the last chance for a long time for Penny and Peter to be able to step ashore to run and play without having to be ferried ashore in the dinghy. (It wasn't until eight months later that we were again able to lie alongside a dock.)

Many other family boats with children on board were also preparing to transit the canal. We took turns minding each others' children; we never took Penny or Peter into Colon when we had reason to go into town. They happily played on the club grounds with the other children, and pitched their tent under a palm tree just off *Lorcha*'s bow. Peter and a small friend were determined to sleep overnight in the tent, but at about midnight they got spooked by some noise and came clambering back on board for the remainder of the night.

Just two boats down the dock from *Lorcha* lay New Zealand-registered *Mainstay* with Larry and Fleur Rayner on board. We had met them while cruising among the San Blas Islands a couple of weeks earlier.

"We're short a line handler for tomorrow," Larry told me the following day. "A crew on another kiwi boat who had promised to help us just told me he couldn't make it. Would you like to come through with us?"

"Sure," I said. "It'll be good to see what it's like."

Perhaps I shouldn't have been so eager to volunteer. The transit of the canal can take from ten to fifteen hours, and Larry and Fleur wouldn't be able to reciprocate and come through with us as line handlers, as they were leaving almost immediately for the Galapagos Islands.

Each boat must have four line handlers and a helmsperson (as well as a pilot) on board for the transit, and children don't count.

I was aboard *Mainstay* at 0530, and the pilot showed up soon after. It was an entertaining day, with periods of hard work followed by plenty of time to swap stories with Larry and Fleur. This was the final stage of Larry's second circumnavigation. They dropped me at the docks at Balboa about twelve hours later, and, along with their other line handlers, I took a cab to the train station, and a one-and-a-half-hour journey on the rickety old narrow-gauge train back across the isthmus to Colon.

The following day *Lorcha* was measured for her tonnage according to a rule of volume, a theoretical amount of cargo she might carry if she were a cargo ship. Our Canadian Registered Tonnage, also a measure of volume, but under a different formula, is 7.19 tonnes. Our Panama Canal tonnage was 10.28 tonnes. The fee for the transit is based on this tonnage measurement, in addition to the $50 (U.S.) measurement fee, in total less than $100.

Fiona and I visited a ship chandler, a company which supplies foodstuffs to the ships who pass through the canal. They also supplied yachts, but we had to buy in case lots to get the wholesale discount. We bought canned goods – cases of milk, fruit, corned beef, tuna fish, roast beef, corn, beans, cooking oil – and sacks of flour, sugar, rice, pasta, a box of chocolate bars, a sack of potatoes and one of onions. All this created a huge pile on the dock when it was delivered the following day.

We packed the provisions away in the lockers in roughly the order that we would be using them. *Lorcha* settled a couple of inches lower in the water, and even we were amazed to see it all stowed away.

Armed with *Lorcha*'s measurement certificate I went to the port captain's office to schedule our transit. Fi and I had agreed to try for a date five days hence, allowing time for some additional maintenance and shopping, as well as time to arrange for our line handlers. Commercial shipping takes precedence over pleasure craft, but I found that our chosen date was available.

While Fi did some shopping at local supermarkets and looked for books and games for the kids, I wandered around the yacht club and spoke to crews from boats at anchor. We needed an additional three line handlers for our transit. I met Warrick Clark, skipper on the Australian boat *Sounion*. He was also seeking line handlers, as he was scheduled to go through the day before we were. We wandered back to *Lorcha* to discuss arrangements and were surprised to find his crew, Toni Woodman, speaking to Fiona, Penny, and Peter.

Toni, a grandmother hitch-hiking her way around the world on boats, was missing her own grandchildren.

"Only I will be able to go through as a line handler on your boat," I told Warrick. "Fiona has to stay here to look after the kids."

"That's just fine," said Toni. "You come through with us, we'll leave *Sounion* anchored at the other end of the canal, and the two of us will come back with you to take *Lorcha* through next day. Okay, Warrick?" He shrugged, knowing I was getting a good deal – two line handlers for *Lorcha* in exchange for one for *Sounion*.

The following day I spoke to Wim van Blaricum, a single-hander on Dutch-flagged 7.5-metre *Anna*. We had first met Wim in Bonaire, Netherlands Antilles, several months earlier. He was scheduled to transit the canal two days after us, and needed another line handler. We agreed to exchange services, so *Lorcha* had her full complement arranged.

At 0500 the day before *Lorcha*'s transit I boarded *Sounion*. My head was spinning with details I hoped I had seen to on our vessel, as I wouldn't have time to do any more shopping before our transit the following day. I left Fiona still fuzzy with sleep, but already planning her busy day. Penny and Peter were asleep, but I knew they were going to be seeing their recently made friends for the last day.

Fourteen hours later we anchored *Sounion* on the west side of the channel below the last canal lock and went ashore to catch the train and return to the yacht club at Cristobal. Toni and Warrick slept overnight in a tent on the club lawn to be ready for *Lorcha*'s early-morning departure.

Wim arrived in his dinghy from his vessel anchored in the Flats just before 0500, just as I was rousing Toni and Warrick.

Our pilot, Lauro Gonzales arrived just after 0500 hours.

"Got all your line handlers?" he asked. "Let me see your lines."

Too few crew members or lines less than thirty metres in length or judged not robust enough to hold the boat in the turbulence of the rushing waters in the locks can mean a polite refusal to transit that day – and a $200 penalty. But all was in order on our little ship, and we headed for the main channel.

It was still dark and we could see the lights of cargo ships lined up to go through, as well as the twinkling green lights at the first lock. We would be raised up twenty-six metres in three locks on this side, cross the thirty-seven-kilometre Lake Gatun, and then be lowered down the three locks on the other side. The total distance from shore to shore across the isthmus is sixty-seven and a half kilometres. The mean level of the Pacific Ocean is about twenty centimetres higher than the Atlantic Ocean.

Our pilot nodded towards a large orange tanker coming up the main channel about one kilometre away. "A tug will take that tanker into the lock and once he's past us, we'll follow him in. We'll centre-lock [hold the boats in the centre of the lock with four lines, spider-web fashion] with that yacht just

11

ahead," Gonzales explained to us, indicating a twelve-metre (forty-foot), fifteen-tonne displacement motorsailer named *Joan D* III. "Have your bow and stern lines ready to attach *Lorcha* to his starboard side," he continued. "We'll enter the lock together."

I was not eager to raft up to *Joan D* III, as our own vessel is only nine metres long, displacing five tonnes. With the much heavier boat lying alongside, we were likely to have more stress and pull when handling the lines than we were ready to handle.

"You have the right to refuse to go through rafted up," Gonzales told me, "but you would have to be rescheduled for another day. Yours is a strong steel boat, and I'll help if necessary."

"Okay, crew," I said. "We're going through with *Joan D*. We'll only need the thirty-metre lines on the starboard side. Wim, can you take the bow and Warrick and Toni, can you handle the stern?"

Quickly we made fast to the other yacht, which had an all-male crew, then steered aside to let the large tanker past. While we waited, Gonzales took a call on his hand-held VHF radio from Canal Control. Signing off, he turned to me. "Relax," he said. "This ship's got explosives on board. It's going through on its own, and we have to wait for the next one."

The sky was just beginning to lighten and, though it was an anti-climax, the wait would give us time for breakfast.

There was a cheer from *Lorcha*'s crew as the aromas of frying bacon and eggs, toast, and perking coffee began wafting up from the galley. A quick look over at *Joan D* III showed several twitching noses; no inviting vapours drifted from her galley. The Panamanian pilot sidled over and begged, "Please pass me a plate of that or I'll go crazy!"

It was still only about 0700 hours when the next cargo ship to go through, the container ship *Ludwigshafen Express* of Hamburg, manoeuvred into the 305-metre lock, leaving about 45 metres behind her for us.

12

"Engines forward," said Gonzales. "Motor in slowly and tell your line handlers to be ready."

High above us, the onshore line handlers expertly twirled their monkey's fists (a heavy ball on the end of a line) and sent them whizzing down to the two yachts. Wim caught one and deftly tied it around the loops of our bow and stern lines.

"Ready to go," he yelled, and our lines were hauled ashore and the loops dropped over the big bollards. We took in the slack, working in concert with the crew on *Joan D* to position the paired vessels in the centre of the lock.

The two-metre-thick lock gates closed behind us; water rushed around *Lorcha* as the four 2.2-metre-diameter feeder tubes at the bottom of the chamber opened to fill the lock. Suddenly our bow line pulled so taut that it actually hummed. The rushing turbulence brought all the tension to bear on that one line. Wim had two turns of line around the forward cleat, but he couldn't hold it. It was racing through his hands.

The rafted boats swung sideways in the lock. Even with the other three lines attached, we were out of control and in danger of being slammed into the wall on our port side.

Lauro and I ran forward to help Wim. With all three of us straining mightily we slowly pulled the boats back to the centre of the lock. We had saved the yachts, but Wim's hands were painfully rope-burned.

Lauro and I tended the bow line as Fiona hastily applied some cream and gauze dressing to Wim's hands, and Penny rummaged in one of the lockers for a pair of leather mittens to protect his hands for the upcoming rope-handling. Hardly was Fiona's first-aid finished than the lock was full.

"Good work," said Gonzales as the forward lock gates opened. "Keep your lines fast while the container ship moves forward. She'll throw a lot of water towards us when she engages her engines."

The mules, electric locomotive-type vehicles, are attached to a freighter's cables to tow her from one lock chamber to the next. There are usually four mules working in unison for a

13

medium-sized ship, but there may be more. The ship engages her engines, turning her propellers, to help the mules get the ship moving. We were tied so close under the ship's stern that the propeller wash shot back to us as a fast current. Had we released our lines too soon we would have been driven back into the lock gate behind us. But once the ship starts to move she disengages her propellers, letting the mules control her forward movement, and we could safely cast off and follow her.

There was no time for coffee as we worked our way through the remaining two rising locks. It takes about half an hour to go through each chamber, and it is a busy half-hour of constant work, adjusting the lines and manoeuvring the boat. Once out of the third lock, we released *Lorcha* from *Joan D* and, making the sail, we prepared to enjoy our thirty-seven-kilometre sail before we entered the next canal locks.

The Chagres River was dammed to create Lake Gatun as a reservoir and source of water for the locks. About 3,800 millimetres of rain falls each year, so the vegetation is lush and green. The lake is a flooded river valley, so the channel twists and turns around islands which are the tops of the hills of the continental divide. The largest island, Barro Colorado, is a biological reserve with a research station on it run by the Smithsonian Institution. It was to this island that most of the animals fled when the original river valley was flooded.

"Hot coffee, tea, cookies, and more toast coming right up," sang out Fiona, the cook. We had also filled a cooler with ice, a rare treat on *Lorcha*, and had cold soft drinks and beer on hand.

The pilot can elect to take the yacht through the regularly buoyed main shipping channel, or through the narrower and unmarked "Banana Cut," so named because the small banana boats used to use it as it is slightly shorter than the main channel.

"We'll take the main channel," said Gonzales. "That's a rookie pilot aboard *Joan D* so I'd prefer to take the marked channel. There are some quite narrow passages between a

14

maze of small islands and no markers for reference in the Banana Cut. If you get confused and make a wrong turn you can run aground."

Buoys clearly mark the route around the lush, tropical, heavily forested islands in the main channel. We had a clear sunny day with the trade winds blowing briskly as *Lorcha* sailed smoothly through the mountain tops, with steep-sided Cordillera de Talamanca, an extinct volcano at one side, and the San Blas range of mountains at the other. She dipped her sails graciously to the many cargo and passenger ships heading towards the Caribbean Sea, and everyone took a turn at the helm as we exchanged voyaging stories.

Lunch was a cold one: crispy deep-fried chicken breasts, soy-sauced garlic beef with noodles, a rice and pepper salad, with chilled sliced tomatoes and cucumbers and fresh-baked bread – all prepared the night before. Fiona had decided she wasn't going to miss any of the spectacular scenery, including "The Cut," a steep-sided rock wall on either side of the canal where the channel was painstakingly hewn out of solid rock, a reported twenty thousand men dying from heat exhaustion, malaria, and yellow fever in the process.

We reached the three "down" locks at about 1400 hours and, rafted up again, *Lorcha* and *Joan D* III proceeded into the lock chamber, this time ahead of a cargo ship. It is something to see a fifty-thousand-tonne vessel bearing down on your little seven-tonne ship in that confined space!

The most likely place for yachts to suffer a mishap is in the last lock. Fresh water from Lake Gatun rushes over the high-saline-content Pacific Ocean water and the two mix together in a roiling turbulence. A big ship coming in behind a smaller vessel will push the smaller one along with the current generated by its bow wave. As soon as the gates close behind the big ship, which has the mules controlling its movements so doesn't have to worry about getting lines ashore, the lock begins to drain at the end where the yachts tie up. This can all combine to build up a 4-knot current which will propel the small boat or boats towards the lock gates. The lines from the

15

yacht must be ashore before the current builds, or it can wash the vessel onto those gates, surely damaging it. This is not an unusual occurrence.

And, when *Lorcha* reached the last lock, something did go wrong. The onshore line handler missed his throw; the monkey's fist headed for *Lorcha* fell short. With about two hundred metres to go, the two yachts, still rafted together, went into forward and reverse, acting like a single vessel with twin screws and trying to stay in place. Once again the line whistled down – and missed! One hundred metres to go . . .

The engines of both yachts were whining at high revolutions now; we were holding back and there was time for a third throw. Suddenly another line handler snatched the monkey's fist from the first one's hands, tossed it, and the line snaked across *Lorcha*'s bow.

Quickly, the lines were hauled ashore, we each strained on our creaking ropes, and, with the engines still engaged, the boats were pulled into position.

Down we went, and at the bottom we watched the lock gates open. Before us lay the Pacific Ocean, a fiery setting sun just above its horizon.

As we neared the end of the channel after the last lock a pilot boat roared up to snatch Gonzales off *Lorcha*. We dropped Wim off at the Balboa Yacht Club jetty so he could return to *Anna* to prepare for her transit the day after next, when I would accompany him through, and Toni and Warrick were relieved to see *Sounion* still safely anchored and unmolested as we came alongside to drop them off.

Lorcha sailed on to Taboga Island, about seven miles from the end of the canal, where we safely anchored in the failing twilight at about 1900 hours.

The following day I took the ferry to the mainland, then again rattled across the now-familiar isthmus on the old train. I spent the night at the yacht club on board a friend's boat to be ready to help Wim through on *Anna*, my fourth transit of the canal.

I was greatly relieved when *Anna* sailed into the same anchorage to let me board *Lorcha* the following night. The Panama Canal hurdle was behind us, and now I could look forward, westward across the Pacific.

PANAMA TO GALAPAGOS

2

"We'll be setting off tomorrow, too," said Bill Townsend, skipper of *Cezanne*. He and his wife, Mona, were on the latter stages of a circumnavigation from their native New Zealand. "What course will you sail from here?"

Lorcha lay at anchor at Taboga Island, a few miles into the Gulf of Panama from the Panama Canal, for four days as I rested up from all the Canal transits, and celebrated my forty-first birthday. Penny and Peter snorkelled over the nearby reef to see the Pacific Ocean fish.

Sailing from Panama to the Galapagos Islands is a tricky passage, and our topic of conversation with crews from other boats in the anchorage always turned to the strategy for making our first long passage across the Pacific Ocean. A look at the pilot charts, those monthly maps showing average wind strength and direction, as well as current strength and set, showed us that the elements would be holding us back, trying to force us away from our destination. You could say that when we set out from Panama, we set out to defeat Mother Nature, pitting our determination and sailing skill, as well as the ability of our boat, not against raging gales, but against frustrating calms and changeable currents.

The skipper of a small sailing vessel at sea is

Strategy . . . tricky passage . . . the indifference of the sea . . .
navigation methods . . . Cezanne and Anna . . .
our middle course . . . masthead navigation lights . . .
the phantom shoal . . . flying fish . . . the doldrums . . .
engine work . . . goose neck barnacles . . . Academy Bay.

---

never free of care, but the cares change. The wind shifts, and you may decide to change direction. When you plot your position you may find a stray current has taken you where you had not wanted to go. A sudden rain squall and a corresponding increase in wind speed and you must reduce the sail area. Then the wind drops, and the sail flops and bangs as the boat rolls in the persistent ocean swell until you raise enough sail to again steady her.

The sea is entirely indifferent whether or not your vessel floats on her. The bow cleaves the surface, parting the water momentarily to let the bulk of your vessel pass. The water closes behind her: a momentary wake and then an indistinguishable vastness. No telltale tracks as there would be on land. No vantage points. No points of reference. Only ever-moving, ever-changing, relentless wave patterns.

Sailboat speeds are archaically slow, and on this passage we averaged only about seventy-five miles per day. Broken down further, that is about three nautical miles or roughly five kilometres per hour – a nice walking pace!

When we decided to enter the Pacific Ocean we also decided to purchase a SatNav (*Sat*ellite *Nav*igation instrument), a navigational computer which would calculate our position about twelve times per day. During our Atlantic Ocean voyaging we had relied upon celestial navigation, the age-old method of position finding. Using a sextant to measure the angle of the sun, moon, planets, or stars above the horizon; a chronometer (an accurate time-piece) to record the moment the angle above the horizon of the celestial body was measured; and a set of tables telling where the above-mentioned are at any given moment, allows you to find your exact position. This method can be used travelling over the trackless wastes of the Arctic, of the Sahara Desert, or of the oceans of the world, or while flying over any of the above. It is a time-consuming calculation, and somewhat limited during periods of cloud, fog, or rain when the celestial body and/or the horizon may not be visible. It can be very accurate, although in a rough sea, taking reliable sextant sights can be difficult.

"Once we round Punta Mala and get out of the Gulf of Panama," said Bill, "we'll steer a direct course for Academy Bay. That's the shortest route, only 850 miles. If the current starts to sweep us off course, we may have to head further south, but I think *Cezanne* can lay the course."

Cezanne is a light-displacement twelve-metre vessel with a generous sail area in her sloop rig. She is a fast boat going upwind and is well-equipped with a reliable diesel engine, SatNav, ham radio, and windvane self-steering gear.

"I'll sail south, along the South American coast until near the Equator," said Wim van Blaricum, our Dutch friend from *Anna*. I hope to find more wind on that route, though the current will be against me until I head west."

At just over seven metres, *Anna* is one of the smaller boats on the round-the-world circuit. She is low-powered with a not very reliable engine and no electronics, but she sails well and has a good windvane self-steering gear.

"I've plotted a middle course," I put in. "We'll round Punta Mala, and then head southwest as the wind allows until about 02° north latitude. Then we'll angle towards Academy Bay at about 01° south latitude."

Our *Lorcha* is a nine-metre, moderate-displacement vessel, but with the Chinese lug sailing rig she is slow going against the wind. We have a small, though reliable diesel engine and carry enough fuel to motor four hundred miles. With our new

20

SatNav we could constantly monitor our course and make corrections as necessary.

At 1000 on the twentieth of April, 1985, we raised our anchor and set off towards Punta Mala and Academy Bay. I say "towards" as sailors are a superstitious lot and one should not tempt fate by stating one's destination with certainty. It is also a much more humble way of describing your voyaging plans. Besides, as any skipper knows, you just might arrive somewhere else. . . .

"We'll catch you up," shouted Bill from his cockpit as we sailed past. He and Mona were enjoying a last cup of coffee before setting off.

Wim was busy lashing his dinghy on *Anna*'s foredeck and gave us a hasty wave.

Hardly an hour later we saw *Cezanne*'s sails coming up behind us. Soon we were snapping pictures of each other as Bill and Mona sailed past. Meanwhile, *Anna*'s sails were disappearing over the horizon to the south.

"Fi, I have to gybe over," I shouted down the companionway at about midnight, warning the slumbering off-watch lest she be tumbled out of her bunk.

Our first night sailing on Pacific waters was rough and blustery with thundery rain squalls. I had seen a dim light ahead of us, but couldn't make out what it was. The colours were indistinct and changed constantly from green to red and then to a blurred mixture.

I suddenly realized that I was looking at the masthead navigation light of another sailboat. She was tacking upwind in the rough seas as we ran downwind. She had right-of-way and I had to act quickly to avoid a collision. Just as I gybed, the other boat tacked, and we quickly separated.

I am sure I elicited a few sailor's oaths from the skipper; they certainly would have issued from me had it been my right-of-way. But the incident made crystal-clear to me the difficulty of judging the direction and distance of a boat from her masthead light. The light is relatively dim – our own, one of the brighter ones, has a twenty-watt bulb. It is a single bulb with a tri-colour lens: red to port (left), green to starboard (right), and white shining aft. The separation of the colours becomes indistinct as the natural roll and pitch of a sailboat sways its mast about. The dim light high off the water (*Lorcha*'s is twelve metres above the water) at first appears to be a light low on the horizon. It is only when a vessel gets quite close and is moving rapidly across your arc of vision that you can make out what the light is.

I had no sooner settled us back on course on this dark night than I got another fright. We were near Punta Mala, an area of converging currents and sandbanks. A white, foamy, phosphorescent line suddenly appeared ahead of us. It looked like waves breaking on a shoal.

I luffed up and dove below to check the SatNav position and the chart. Reassured that we should be miles from any hazard, I again went topside to check. The line of breaking water was still there. I sailed slowly towards it.

Shining our spotlight over the side I could see that the disturbed water was caused by a dense shoal of fish feeding along a current rip. We sailed through one after another of those foaming lines and it was hair-raising to dash headlong through a black night into what appeared to be a wreck-hungry reef.

"Anything on deck, Papa?" are often the first words I hear in the brightening light of the dawn watch. Peter wakes up early and, being keenly interested in fish and marine life in general, he wants to know if any flying fish or squid have come on board during the night.

On many a dawn watch I have guided Peter around the deck, holding his small red bucket and hovering protectively over him as he picks little flying fish, up to ten of them, out of the scuppers. Back in the cockpit he closely examines their diaphanous wings, grey and silver bodies, and bright blue scales.

"Do you know why fish have dark backs and light undersides?" asks our studious and well-read Penny. "Because from the air a predatory bird has a difficult time seeing a dark object at the surface of the sea. But from under the sea a predatory fish has difficulty making out a light-coloured under-body against the bright sky. It's the fish's natural protective colouration, his camouflage."

We try to sail as much as possible, even when moving very slowly, because then our windvane self-steering gear continues to handle the helm. We have to keep watch, but do not have to do the actual steering of the boat, a real drudgery on long passages. But when we turn on the engine in a calm we have to hand-steer, which can get tiring.

Fiona gets upset with the noise of the sail slatting in light winds. "Can't you motor for a while," she shouts crossly on her off-watch. "I can't sleep with all that noise."

In typical doldrums conditions, which can extend from 5° north of the Equator to 5° south of the Equator – a distance of six hundred miles – you sail for a while, and motor for a few hours, then perhaps there's again some wind, followed by rain squalls with strong gusts and drenching downpours. Then the wind again falls away to nothing. With the persistent swell and no wind, a vessel's sails slat and clatter no matter how much you try to tie them down.

With only Fiona or I to stand the night watches, we never get more than two hours and forty-five minutes of sleep at one time while at sea. We stand three-hour watches, allowing ten minutes to get undressed and into our bunk and five minutes for waking up and getting dressed and into the cockpit to relieve the other person.

Fiona is a light sleeper who cannot get any rest when the sail rattles about. With the engine running at a low but steady throb, driving us through the water at an economical four knots, she quickly falls to sleep.

"Don't hit the starter button again!" I shouted to Fiona as I leapt from my bunk, having heard the starter motor groan.

23

On this, the morning of our fifth day at sea, we had been sailing slowly through a rough and confused sea. A wave had broken heavily over our stern, partially filling the cockpit. I hadn't realized it at the time, but it had also forced sea water up our exhaust outlet and into the cylinders of the engine. The wind had fallen light and Fi was going to motor for a while. But if she hit the starter, it could blow a hole in the engine head gasket, something I couldn't fix at sea without a spare gasket. That would mean no more motoring, and no more SatNav or electric lights, as our diesel engine charges the batteries for all our electrical needs.

Opening our engine box I removed the air cleaner and opened the decompression levers on our two-cylinder Yanmar engine. As I hand-cranked the engine, water spewed out the air intake as if out of a drowning person receiving resuscitation. I continued to turn over the engine, knowing diesel fuel would be squirting into the cylinders, lubricating them. A quick check of the crankcase oil showed it was dark, with no trace of the grey milkiness indicating that water had gotten into the lower part of the engine, possibly damaging it.

"Try the starter now," I shouted to Fi as I flipped off the decompression levers and hoped for the best.

With a cough and sputter the engine roared into life – and I returned to my bunk to continue my now-shortened nap.

"Look over the side, Penny and Peter," I said one day as we slowly drifted along on a calm sea. "What's that on the water line?"

"Goose neck barnacles, yuck," said Penny.

"Goose neck barnacles! Can we try some for bait?" said Peter, our ever-eager fisherman.

In the olden days of sailing ships, before modern anti-fouling paints were invented, ships' crews were sent over the side in the doldrums to try to remove as many of these tenacious creatures as possible. They grow at an alarming rate, and can so foul a hull it can hardly be driven through the water.

Listening to a late night BBC (British Broadcasting Corpora-

24

tion) short wave radio broadcast during my watch one night, I had heard that a British company was trying to synthetically reproduce the natural glue a goose neck barnacle secretes to stick to a hull.

The strange thing about these creatures of the open ocean is that when a barnacle-covered hull sails into port where the water is slightly polluted and perhaps warmer and not as aerated as in the open ocean, the barnacles soon shrivel and die.

"There's a seal," shouted an excited Peter as we sailed past steep and rocky Santa Fe Island, one of the uninhabited smaller islands neighbouring Santa Cruz Island where the Darwin Research Station is located at Academy Bay.

"That's a sea lion," corrected our little know-it-all daughter. "A sea lion is larger and has a slightly different colour than the fur seals that live around here. Don't you remember how small the seals were we saw near Newfoundland?" Penny had been reading all about the animals around these islands and was eager to share her knowledge.

Eleven days and one hour out of Taboga Island we entered Academy Bay harbour to moor among the twelve other international yachts in the anchorage. We had travelled, according to our daily positions, 940 miles over the ocean bottom, yet our sum log, the instrument which counts up the distance travelled through the water, indicated we had travelled 880 miles. Early on in the voyage the ocean current had been pushing us back, and we had had to sail more miles through the water to get the same number of miles travelled over the bottom. Now, because of our chosen route, we were travelling with the current sweeping us along, so had a net gain of sixty miles we didn't have to sail through the water. Voyagers always try to sail with the ocean currents to get as many "free" miles as possible.

Where were our two companion yachts who had sailed the same day from Panama? Our friends on *Telstar*, already anchored in Academy Bay, told us that Bill and Mona on

Cezanne had arrived in seven days and had left only that morning. Wim on *Anna* came sailing slowly in just at dusk several days later. He had fallen into some calms off the South American coast. His engine had packed in, and there was so little wind his self-steering gear couldn't maintain a steady course.

"For four days I hand-steered as much as I could," said an exhausted Wim. "I tried to catch every little puff, but only averaged thirty miles per day. I finally got a little wind, but it was slow going all the way.

He arrived eighteen and a half days out from Panama.

Hardly was our anchor down than Peter had a fishing line over the side with a goose neck barnacle for bait.

"Bother," came the exasperated cry a few minutes later. "Dad, can you unhook this puffer fish?"

This is an unusual request from our young son, who prides himself on his self-sufficiency in fishing matters. But the ugly puffer fish is poisonous, inflates itself alarmingly when touched, and can give a nasty bite with its three beak-like teeth.

Doesn't every five-year-old know the flesh of the puffer fish family is toxic and shouldn't be eaten?

THE GALAPAGOS 3

*S*ome books claim the Galapagos Islands were originally discovered in the 1400s by the Inca king,
Tupac Yupanqui. He returned to Guayaquil after a
sea voyage of many months, bringing with him from
some remote islands in the South Pacific black people, gold, a brass chair, and the skin and jawbone of
an animal he claimed was a sea lion, an animal that
abounds in the Galapagos. Mysteriously, his "sea
lion" artifacts were discovered later to be the shin
and jaw bones of a horse, an animal not remotely
similar, even skeletally, to a sea lion. As well, there is
no evidence of an early settlement of black (or any
other) people in the Galapagos.

The islands were most likely first sighted in 1535
by Fray Tomas de Berlanga, Bishop of Panama.
While sailing from Panama to Peru his ship was
caught in a calm and carried five hundred miles off
course by a strong ocean current. Our own passage
attested to the strength of the currents in the vicinity. Berlanga's account of his adventures written to
Emperor Carlos v of Spain included descriptions of
the giant tortoises, the iguanas, and the "remarkable
tameness" of the birds.

The bishop did not name the islands, however.
That was left to various Spanish navigators between
1546 and 1560 who called them *Islas Encantadas*,
the Bewitched or Enchanted Islands. Later names

History of the islands . . . we make new friends . . . cruising
the islands . . . friendly animals . . . geology day . . . sticking to
the rules . . . pelican and penguin . . . the film crew . . .
swimming with the sea lions.

---

included *Las Huerfanas* (the Orphans) and *Insulae de los Galapegos* (Islands of the Tortoise). In 1892, Ecuador named the islands *Archipelago de Colon* (Columbus Islands) in honour of the four-hundredth anniversary of the discovery of America by Christopher Columbus. This is still the official name of the islands. However, the Galapagos is now the name most commonly used.

Today, the famous Galapagos tortoise is a protected species, but from 1780 to 1860 when American and British whalers roamed the South Pacific, thousands of tortoises perished. They were removed from the islands and stacked alive, one on top of another, in the holds of the whaling ships, to be brought out and slaughtered as required for their fresh meat and oil. It is reported that the tortoises could survive in these conditions without food or water for more than one year.

British naturalist Charles Darwin brought world attention to the Galapagos when he visited the islands for five weeks in 1835 aboard the survey vessel, H.M.S. *Beagle*. He realized that the Galapagos flora and fauna must have originated from the continent and become modified by the various environmental conditions on the separate islands. Also, the animal species that had arrived there had adapted themselves to the singular weather that combines the warm South Equatorial Current and the cold Humboldt Current. Undisturbed by man, the various species evolved in complete harmony. Darwin's observations provided the evidence for his *Origin of Species*, in which he established his theory that species are not static

29

entities but are subject to evolutionary change by natural selection.

The examples on the Galapagos are numerous: relatives of the sunflower that have evolved into trees, gulls which forage at night, lizards – iguanas – which feed on seaweed beneath the ocean surface, tortoises which grow to gigantic proportions, finches which use thorns as tools, cormorants which have lost the ability to fly, and penguins and fur seals living on the Equator.

For visiting yachts, there are only two points of entry in the Galapagos: Wreck Bay, the military port at the island of San Cristobal; or Academy Bay at Santa Cruz. Yachts run the risk of heavy fines if they try to stop elsewhere and the thirteen-island group is well patrolled. Yachts are extended a courtesy pass of seventy-two hours, but the time period is flexible depending on the request for an extension, the judgement of the port captain, and the behaviour of yachts in the recent past. It is not permitted to tour the islands with your own boat except in very special, rigidly controlled circumstances.

The dozen boats anchored in Academy Bay harbour were bobbing about, all anchored fore and aft as there was not much searoom to swing about. The water was a turquoise green, with the foreshore a half-moon around us. Volcanic cones were clearly visible everywhere. A straggle of houses indicated the town of Puerta Ayora.

Things went well from the moment we paddled ashore and left the dinghy hauled up above the rocks and the high-water mark. The friendly port captain, ex-Navy pilot Teodoro Ruales, gave us a five-day visa and told us that one of the Santa Cruz tour boats was operated by a Canadian woman and her Ecuadorian husband. That sounded like a good lead, and we wandered through the narrow, dusty streets lined with little stores, houses, and open-air restaurants, till we found the house of Judy (Carvalhal) Angermeyer of Toronto and her Galapagos-born husband, Frederico (Fiddi).

"What brought you to the Galapagos?" we asked Judy, as we sat in her comfortable wood and stone house at the water's edge, with its rough-textured wall-hangings and hand-woven rugs from Ecuador.

"Adventure," answered Judy. "I took a degree in biology at Queen's University in Kingston and did a year of university research. Then I decided I wanted to travel for a year and came down to South America.

"The Galapagos was my last destination," she continued with a smile. "And after I met Fiddi, well, it was definitely my last stop."

The Angermeyers have two charter/tour boats and one, the six-passenger motor vessel *Orca*, was set to take a film crew from England's *Search for Survival* TV series on a tour around the northern islands. The Angermeyers were planning to accompany it part of the way on their other charter boat, the ten-passenger *Cachalote*.

"Would you like to come with us?" they asked.

From Penny and Peter and the three Angermeyer children – six-year-old Jonathan, four-year-old Tatjana, and two-year-old Joshua – by now all firm friends, there was a chorus of "yes!" The adults were no less enthusiastic.

If we had enough money and knew a compatible family that wanted to sail, I think we'd be willing to explore the world on a bigger boat with them. With the right combination of committed, active cruisers who work and play together and are supportive, the pressures would be halved and the plea-sures doubled. Or so we were to find on this four-day trip. From sailing the boat to cleaning fish to cooking meals and washing up, our roles were interchangeable. We did not expect the Angermeyers to wait on us, and they treated us as family, not passengers. The children caught the spirit of the thing and looked after each other. All this would have been pleasure enough, but we were also in an area of intense won-der and interest.

A fast sail to Mosquero Island, where the sea lions were as eager to look at us as we were to see them.

"They're trying to stand on their tails to see us," screamed Penny. "Oh, don't they look funny."

And so they did, propelling themselves upright for a moment and then flopping back in the water with a heavy splash, dignity quite forsaken. Then they'd try it again, so curious were they to get a closer look.

Even when we were in the dinghy, the sea lions pressed around us, short barks commanding other sea lions to come over and join the parade. As the dinghy grounded, Penny and Peter were apprehensive about getting out with the animals so close, but Jonathan quickly showed them the way.

"Just jump out," he said importantly. "They won't hurt you." And he swung his little legs into the shallows and waded ashore, completely ignoring the sea lions pressing around him, still barking and grunting excitedly as they slithered through the shallows, flippers digging into the sand, quite determined to follow Jonathan, and then the others, ashore.

There were lots more sea lions ashore, lying contentedly on the sun-warmed sand. They scarcely moved as we walked within arm's reach. Some of them did throw a withering glance at the excited children who had given up all pretense of trying not to disturb the animals. Their laughing, shouting, and running didn't seem to be alarming the sea lions at all, so why not?

The sea lions did have different personalities, though. One lively youngster decided to chase along after the children. It wasn't as easy for him on land as it was in water, and his dismayed grunts as he failed to keep pace with the fast-moving youngsters had us all laughing. Chagrined, he stopped, his grunts of disappointment going up a note or two in delight when the kids ran back to him. But as children are wont to do, they soon charged off again, leaving the valiant and curious young sea lion alone once more.

Though the hundred or more sea lions lying about seemed a lot to us, Judy, who is an official Galapagos Islands guide, said most of the colony were out fishing.

"The rocks are covered with animals in the evening," she said, pointing out the centuries-old paths the sea lions had worn smooth slithering over the stones.

32

Scuttling between the animals on the rocks were the distinctive scarlet Sally Lightfoot crabs that were, strangely enough, more skittery and fearful of us than their sleek-flippered and seemingly unconcerned companions.

A three-hour visit to Mosquero seemed almost too short, but it was time to sail on to North Seymour, where we would anchor for the night.

Ashore there were no sea lions; it seems as though particular animals have chosen particular islands as their home, so on each of the thirteen separate islands (and on many islets) in the Galapagos, you'll find only one or two species. The flora, fauna, animals, and physical setting of each island are unique. Seymour is the home of blue-footed boobies and great frigate birds.

"This mummy's got an egg," shouted Peter.

"This daddy's got an egg," yelled Jonathan, not to be outdone.

"This egg's cracked," chimed in Penny.

"And here's a baby bird!" topped Tatjana in utter triumph. The five children were beside themselves with excitement as they ran ahead of us in Seymour, exclaiming and wondering at the birds nesting alongside the path. Fearless of predators (there are none), these birds were downright careless about where they nested. Nests, eggs, and babies were strewn haphazardly everywhere.

"Not so close. Not so close," we'd say to the children as they stood about a foot away from a nesting bird. But the birds were not bothered, occasionally uttering a puzzled warning cry when it seemed as though one or other child was actually going to come right into the nest.

In the centre of the island, we watched the mating ritual of the red-throat-pouched great frigate birds. Puffing out their scarlet pouches, the males threw back their heads to make a strange whirring sound as the females circled overhead, lazily debating which mate deserved their attention, while juveniles watched attentively.

"We'll see something a little different today," said Judy the next morning. "Yesterday was the animal and bird day – today we'll learn something about geology."

The Galapagos Islands are volcanic in origin; they arose from lava outpourings on the bottom of the sea, and have never been attached to other land masses. Virtually all material constituting the islands is either basaltic lava or basaltic pyroclastic rock. The islands can be divided into two groups of different origin, the older group being formed by the uplift of lava flows from the ocean floor and the remaining islands formed above sea level by younger volcanos. Geologic activity in the area is intense. Earthquakes are common and volcanic eruptions are said to be more frequent here than anywhere else on Earth.

We climbed to the heady heights of the highest extinct volcano on Bartholomew Island, passing many-layered rock formations in various shades of dark red and the large and small cones of dead volcanos. The climb was so steep that for the last part, steps made out of hand-hewn logs had been fixed to the side of the shale and cinder slope. The children charged on ahead.

Tourists are not permitted to visit any of the islands without a guide and the paths one may walk on are clearly marked. Though this sounds strict, the islands, which were declared a national park in 1959, make up the most cared-for park we have ever seen. The rules are there to protect the animals and the environment – making them all the more interesting to see because the animals remain unthreatened and unafraid. The kids may have made a lot of noise, but they did stick to the paths.

If there were volcanos to climb, there were also beaches to visit. Bartholomew's sandy beach was as long as its volcano was tall. There was not a soul on the white sand except for ourselves – and the large grey pelican who flew by, looked us over, and decided to join us. Lazily he flew back and crash-landed on the beach beside the children, avidly interested in the sandcastle they were building. It was the kids' turn to be nonchalant. Oh, just another friendly pelican.

But when a small Galapagos penguin chose to swim up to us, there was chaos. If there was one thing Penny and Peter had really hoped to see, it was one of these little black-and-white birds. With his wings spread out, the tiny twenty-one-inch-long penguin looked for all the world like a little underwater aeroplane as he zoomed along the shoreline on a fish hunt, the children scampering after him. Up and down the shore they went, cries of excitement indicating the little fellow had stopped, sometimes to swallow a fish in his beak, sometimes to check where he was, and sometimes to keep a watchful eye on his excited followers.

That night we met the film crew when they came over for dinner. *Cachalote*'s saloon table was big enough to take us all. Fiddi produced a large platter of thinly sliced, marinated raw tuna which we had caught earlier in the day. The bonito had been lightly spiced and tasted like smoked salmon. He taught us the secret of slicing it as thinly as the professionals do – freeze it first.

There was no problem in getting the kids to bed during this trip. First of all, they were tired out every night, and secondly, the four older children were sleeping at the stern of the boat in one cabin. They could play and talk as far into the night as they wanted and we couldn't hear them.

Next morning we sailed to Plaza – more sea lions and also iguanas. This island had a little jetty we rowed to, but the sea lions had not been told that it was for people getting off dinghies. They were piled so thick, we couldn't even get one foot between them. Judy clapped her hands.

"Oh all right," barked the sea lions, moving just inches. But even inches pushed some of them into the sea. Judy moved forward and clapped her hands some more and we followed, soon making our way through as the sea lions hurrumphed grumpily out of the way.

On the warm rocks, the sea lions were sunbathing, slipping into the water for a cool-off, or nursing pups, some of them quite small. There were many iguanas under the cactus plants and we took photos of them eating cactus leaves. This is not their normal food, but was indicative of the eight months of drought at the time we visited.

After a pleasant lunch on *Cachalote*, Fiddi provided his greatest surprise.

"Why don't you swim with the sea lions?" he asked.

We hesitated.

"It's perfectly safe," said Judy. "You jump in from the dinghy. Just don't swim to the rocks. That's the bulls' territory. It's fine if you just stay in the channel."

Paul and I jumped in, with Penny and Peter watching.

And did those sea lions ever want to play! The more we dove underwater and splashed about, the more sea lions joined us. They were incredible, coming at us full speed, only to veer off when they seemed just inches away. We could see the peculiar violet colour of their eyes. In an almost sexual gesture, they arched their bodies and swooped up from our feet to our faces. On and on it went, with sleek grey-brown bodies curving above, below, and around us, their skins sometimes actually caressing our arms and legs.

Penny and Peter finally got up enough courage to join us, and we laughed and laughed as we tumbled and played with sea creatures in their own environment.

It was an unbelievable end to an incredible voyage.

GALAPAGOS TO PITCAIRN

4

"**G**o away, garua," chanted Penny and Peter as we made our way from the Galapagos Islands in the drizzly mistiness the locals call "the garua."

Leaving the Galapagos, we sailed out of Academy Bay about midday on a light wind. The cold Humboldt Current flowing from Antarctica passes near the islands, causing the temperature to drop dramatically and visibility to decrease. Everything was damp – drizzly and misty. What a way to start a passage that could take a month!

We were headed for Pitcairn Island. Out of Galapagos, most yachts head for the Marquesas Islands of French Polynesia, an easier route because it is all trade wind sailing. Both Pitcairn and the Marquesas are approximately the same distance, nearly three thousand miles – the longest passage necessary when sailing around the world.

May, the month we set sail from Academy Bay, is autumn in the southern hemisphere, not the best time of year to be sailing towards Pitcairn Island (January to April are best) as the winds become more changeable and blustery as the autumn advances. At 25°04′ south latitude, Pitcairn's location is roughly equivalent to the southern tip of Florida in the northern hemisphere.

We would be sailing away from the doldrums at the Equator to enter the trade wind belt, where the

Autumn weather . . . trade winds . . . Pacific history . . .
our animal companions . . . whale problems . . . sea-going
routine . . . becalmed . . . Henderson Island, land ho!

wind should blow at 11–16 knots (20–28 kph), a nice passage-making breeze. When the trade winds ran out – at about 20° south latitude – we would enter the variables, with changeable winds, often light in strength and variable in direction. When we crossed the Tropic of Capricorn (23°30′ south latitude) we would be technically in the temperate zone, with cooler weather. Winds there can blow from any direction and gales can be expected at any time of year.

The first European ships to sail on the Pacific Ocean were those of Ferdinand Magellan's fleet. Magellan, a Portuguese navigator sailing under the flag of Spain, in 1520 sailed through the southern archipelago of South America, a strait that would later bear his name, and found himself in the "Southern Ocean." So joyful was the explorer to at last find this fabled body of water that it is reported that he broke down and wept. He must have emerged upon it during a tranquil time to have named it as he did – the Pacific Ocean. Magellan's ship then sailed on for fifty-seven more days before next sighting land.

Magellan was killed in the Philippines, but one of his ships, captained by del Cano (Juan Sebastian de Elcano), continued on around the Cape of Good Hope, returning to Spain just short of three years after having left. His was the first ship to circumnavigate the world, a remarkable achievement for the era.

Polynesian seafarers had been making major voyages

across the Pacific Ocean perhaps a thousand years before Magellan. In their double canoes they ranged from Hawaii in the north to New Zealand in the south. The Austronesian language group is spread from Easter Island to Madagascar, an area encompassing more than half the circumference of the globe.

The speed and sea-keeping ability of the Polynesian craft so impressed the early explorers that they ran out of superlatives to describe them. Pigafetta, Magellan's chronicler, marvelled at the canoes he saw in 1521. In 1774, at Tahiti, Captain James Cook, a man who made many major discoveries in the Pacific Ocean, observed the "magnificent scene" of a "grand and noble" naval review at which he was "perfectly lost in admiration." It contained 330 traditional Polynesian vessels with no fewer than 7,760 men.

The early Pacific voyagers used the stars, wind direction, and wave patterns, as well as the daily flight of island-roosting birds to help them find land. They used island groups as stepping stones across the vastness of the Pacific Ocean. The Pacific Ocean is not only the largest ocean of the world; it also has more islands in it than exist in all the other oceans combined.

The light doldrums sailing conditions made working our way through the Galapagos group slow going. We ran the engine when we were becalmed, as the currents are strong and variable near the islands. We saw the remnants of two yachts lying on Galapagos beaches, pounded to pieces by the surf as those currents swept them onto the rocks.

By dusk, under power, we were leaving the last headland behind, with a clear path for night sailing. At 0020 we were again under engine, motoring until daybreak. Our noon position that day was 3°27′ south latitude, near the edge of the doldrums. We felt a light but encouraging east-north-east wind, the start of the trade winds, which steadied to a nice sailing breeze during the next twenty-four hours.

As we got further away from the Galapagos Islands the

boobies and frigate birds – island roosters – disappeared from the skies, replaced by the ocean wanderers such as the tropic birds, skuas, petrels, shearwaters, and the Arctic terns who annually migrate from the Arctic to the Antarctic, a round trip of sixteen thousand miles. Many a night watch was interrupted by the high-pitched nervous giggle call of petrels swooping low over *Lorcha*'s cockpit to see if we were awake. During the day they delicately dip their feet in the water as they hover to snatch a living morsel from the sea. Tropic birds, with their long wispy tails, hover above us, and Arctic terns and skuas bunch together when feeding on schools of shrimp or squid.

We were often surrounded by flying fish. These little creatures shoot themselves off wave tops, launching into the wind, then bearing away to drift downwind. After their initial take off, they skip off another wave top with a few quick flips of their tails and can remain airborne for three hundred metres. During the day, flying fish see *Lorcha* plunging headlong through the waves and easily avoid her. At night, especially if it is a bit rough and moonless, they often land on deck, dying in the scuppers, to be found stiff and dried out when Peter and I clear the decks during the dawn watch.

We began to see many species of whales and dolphins we had not seen before. Penny and Peter would dive below to get Eric Hoyt's *The Whale Watcher's Handbook* to try to identify the dolphins and porpoises as they leapt and cavorted at *Lorcha*'s bow or rolled about in her unchallenging wake.

One unforgettable evening, just as it was getting dark, a whale stuck its head vertically out of the water about a boat length from *Lorcha*'s bow. We had sailed past it before I recovered enough to call for the others to come for a look. It appeared to be a small – perhaps eight or nine metres long – humpback whale.

During the nineteenth century up to six hundred sailing ships were involved in intense whaling activity in this area of the Pacific. The whalers sought humpback whales migrating from the Antarctic feeding grounds to the calving and breeding grounds of the tropics. Sperm whales were also plentiful in tropical waters, often living amongst island groups. In *Narrative of a Whaling Voyage Around the Globe from the Year 1833 to 1836*, Frederick Debell Bennett tells of having seen many "small parties of half grown [sperm whale] males journeying eastwards" south of the Equator at about 112° west longitude – about eleven hundred miles west of the Galapagos. Frank T. Bullen, first mate of the *Cachalot*, recounted his five months among the Vava'u Islands of Tonga hunting sperm whale in 1875, in *The Cruise of the Cachalot*.

In years past there have been some unhappy incidents involving whales and yachts in the equatorial South Pacific. In the seventies, Maurice and Marilyn Bailey aboard their nine-metre wood sloop and the Dougal Robertson family on a fifteen-metre wooden schooner had their vessels attacked and sunk by killer whales. Both crews spent a long time in life-rafts before being rescued by passing ships.

During the season in 1985 that we crossed the South Pacific, our friends Ian and Nauri Carlin of Auckland, New Zealand, on *Challenger*, an eleven-and-a-half-metre ferro-cement sloop they had built themselves, had a humpback whale surface under them as they sailed about eighteen hundred miles west of the Galapagos Islands.

"We were below during the afternoon, when we felt *Challenger* suddenly being lifted and heeled to windward," said Nauri.

"I dashed into the cockpit to see a large – longer than *Challenger* – humpback whale lying alongside," Ian continued. "He dove under the keel but didn't touch the boat again before surfacing on the other side and slowly swimming off."

Their rudder was broken off and the propeller shaft flattened against the hull. The windvane self-steering gear was lifted off its mounts, but remained attached to the boat. Though they could do nothing to repair the rudder or propeller shaft at sea, they managed to get the auxiliary rudder self-steering gear working again and continued sailing the one thousand miles to the Marquesas Islands where they made temporary repairs.

Ian told us they had met a French-registered steel-hulled boat in the Marquesas that had been attacked by a pod of killer whales in about the same area. They showed Ian the dents in the steel hull plating where the boat had been rammed. Luckily the plating held and there was no serious damage.

In Papeete harbour we met people from a Gibraltar-registered boat who also had had a whale surface under them during their Pacific crossing. There was no damage, just the loss of some anti-fouling paint where the whale seemed to be rubbing his back on the bottom of the keel. . . .

The Pacific Ocean lived up to its name; it was calm for most of this voyage. It was one of the few long passages we had when Fiona and Penny were not seasick.

By day five we were fully into our sea-going routine.

Bread was baked every other day. On the day bread was not baked there would be showers in the cockpit – perhaps it would be better to say water play for the children, as there was always much splashing and sputtering. As we were on a long passage, sea water was used for the main washing, with only a cupful or two of fresh water used to rinse the salt off.

We occasionally got a squid on deck, for as we ran through the schools swimming on the surface of the ocean they would shoot out of the water, like grasshoppers out of a meadow when you walk through the grass. The rare one would land on deck and we greatly increased our success with the trolling line when I put a squid on a hook for bait. Not ten minutes later we would be fighting a high-spirited *mahi-mahi*, as the dorado or dolphin fish are known in the Pacific basin.

"How long do you think we've been at sea, Peter?" we asked on our tenth day out from the Galapagos.

"Oh . . . four days?" he replied, uncertain of the time. We thought that was a good indication that he and Penny were not bored or fretful with long passages.

43

Penny was working hard on her school correspondence lessons, trying to complete her Grade Two work before the end of this voyage. Peter often looked on wistfully at Penny's organized time with Fiona. He could read simple books, but was not enough of a reader to be able to occupy himself with longer books.

"What can I do?" he said fretfully, mid-passage. Oh, that phrase every parent knows so well.

In desperation, Fiona got out the box of Grade One materials we had received from the Ontario Ministry of Education while we were in Panama. School wouldn't officially be in session for Peter for a few months, but he was eager to get on with it. However, with the usual sea-going duties keeping her busy, Fiona wasn't eager to take on a new pupil.

"I'm going to teach him, Mummy," said Penny eagerly. With Peter in tow she disappeared below decks, proud of her assumed role as teacher. It probably isn't usual Ministry of Education practice to have an eight-year-old teach a six-year-old, but Penny took on her role with sympathy, enthusiasm, and good sense and left relatively few holes for Fiona to fill in.

Teaching Peter also motivated her to spend more time on her own school work. She finished her Grade Two during this passage, as well as helping Peter do three weeks of his Grade One.

On our sixteenth day at sea I noted in the log book that the barometer had been unusually high, up to 1020 millibars. The light and fickle winds that usually accompany a high barometer were well in evidence, with our noon-to-noon run down to seventy-five miles on the trailing log. The South Pacific high-pressure centre had perhaps moved to the north and west, spreading over our part of the ocean to produce these conditions, unlikely ones for the heart of the trade wind belt.

The following day I recorded a light southwest wind from the direction of Pitcairn, then a light east-north-east wind, then "all sails down, no wind" as we drifted about.

At about 18°15' south we seemed to run out of the trade

winds. I noticed a band of puffy cumulus clouds just to the north of us; these usually accompany the trade winds, so I angled a bit north of west in the light and fitful wind. It worked; we eventually regained the trade winds, and again angled to the southwest.

Being becalmed on a sailboat far out to sea is a real agony. The boat rolls about in any direction, with no wind in her sails to stabilize her on a relatively consistent angle of heel. The sail flops, the battens and gear rattle annoyingly, and it is stiflingly hot.

At dusk on our twenty-fourth day at sea, a light on the horizon promised our first sighting of a ship since leaving the Galapagos Islands. Fiona is always ready to talk with radio operators, and the radio officer of the British-registered *Polybena*, headed for Auckland, New Zealand, with 23,000 tons of bitumen on board, was soon chatting.

"Did you live anywhere near Owen Sound?" he asked when he heard we were from Canada. "I have a brother who teaches at a college there."

"Land ho!"

About noon on our twenty-eighth day at sea I came on deck to scan the horizon. From our position on the SatNav I knew we must be near Henderson Island, one of the Pitcairn Group, which also includes Ducie and Oeno, all three uninhabited islands.

Henderson, though much larger than Pitcairn Island, is lower – only thirty metres high – with little soil, no source of fresh water, and covered in dense scrub. It went undiscovered until 1819, but soon became a graveyard for ships, as several piled on its rocks. There have been skeletons found there, but they are of recent origin, presumably shipwrecked mariners rather than an ancient people.

We passed about one mile from the northern tip of Henderson. We just wanted a look at this barren outcrop. It is rarely visited, except by the Pitcairn Islanders who occasionally come to cut the stunted trees which grow there for wood for their carvings, and is best known as the home of *Nesophylax ater*, a flightless chicken-like bird found nowhere else in the world.

Though Henderson Island is not an inviting place to land, sighting it was a milestone. It is just 106 miles from Pitcairn; this meant our long passage was almost over – we would probably reach our destination the following day.

PITCAIRN ONE

5

"There it is," said Paul triumphantly at dawn. "Just where it should be."

But strain my eyes as I might, I couldn't see the faint blue outline Paul was pointing to. Perhaps my eyes were tired. I know the rest of my body was. Twenty-nine days at sea had taken its toll. I was fatigued and conscious of how pale and drawn I looked. "Ugh," I thought, looking at my long, stringy, grey hair in the small mirror above the sink. I clipped on the galley bum strap and filled our brown enamel teapot with water to make everyone a morning cup of tea.

Lorcha was surging along in the 30-knot wind – great for sailing; not so good for the steaming tea I was carefully passing out mug by mug.

"Come on up," called Penny down the companionway. "You can see Pitcairn clearly now."

Shrugging back into my white foul-weather gear, I clambered out into the cockpit. This time I saw the faint smudge on the horizon that confirmed Paul's original sighting. Legendary Pitcairn, hideout of the mutinous crew of H.M.S. *Bounty*, was now only a few hours away.

The *Bounty*, a British vessel, sailed from England to Tahiti in 1788 under its commander, Lieutenant William Bligh, to collect a hardy species of the breadfruit plant which had been suggested as a

Travel takes its toll . . . mutiny on the Bounty . . . VHF
surprise . . . unable to land . . . ashore by longboat . . .
Pitcairn's Harlequin Romance . . . more history . . . an
overnight invitation.

cheap but nutritious dietary supplement for the growing
black slave population in the West Indies. But, even as yachts
today find they have to stay a few months in French Polynesia
to allow for the cyclone season, so did *Bounty*.

When the ship set sail again, a number of circumstances
brought some of the crew to mutiny. The most pressing reason was the alleged harsh treatment of his crew by Commander Bligh; a secondary reason may have been the desire
of some crew members to return to the paradise they had
found in Tahiti.

With the crew becoming increasingly discontented, the vessel reached Tongan waters. On April 28, 1789, the discontent
culminated in tragedy. Members of *Bounty*'s crew, under the
leadership of second-in-command Fletcher Christian, mutinied against Bligh. They took control of the ship and set the
deposed commander and the eighteen men who remained
loyal to him adrift in an open boat – to face almost certain
death.

Christian and the remaining crew then sailed *Bounty* back
to Tahiti.

Under British law, mutineers are hung if they are tried and
found guilty. Tahiti was too public a place to stay for long, and
in due course, Christian, eight of the mutineers, and a
number of Polynesian men and women with whom they had
formed attachments set sail to find a remote island on which
to hide from pursuit and to build their own colony.

They first attempted a settlement of the island of Tubuai in

49

the Australs, south of the Society Islands, but the natives did not look kindly on these new settlers and violence erupted. The mutineers were forced to sail on.

They eventually found Pitcairn, an island charted only twenty-two years earlier by Philip Carteret on board H.M.S. *Swallow*, and named after the first man to sight it.

It was isolated, uninhabited, fertile, and, being a high island, there was a plentiful supply of fresh water. It could have been paradise.

If the story of the mutineers' settlement on Pitcairn had been written for a Harlequin Romance, it would have had a happy ending – after some initial hardships and trials the mutineers would have settled down into an ideal colony. That, alas, was not what happened. Instead, murder, intrigue, bloodshed, and jealousy were the order of the day.

When the American sealing vessel *Topaz* stopped at Pitcairn in February 1808, eighteen years after the mutineers had landed, they found one man, John Adams (also mysteriously referred to as John Smith, Alexander Smith, or Reckless Jack Adams), nine Polynesian women, and nineteen children. The other eight mutineers and all the Polynesian men were dead.

"I think I'll give them a call on the VHF," I said optimistically. Optimistically because our information was that Pitcairn had no VHF radio facilities.

We all jumped when a voice came booming back.

"Pitcairn Radio to *Lorcha*. Pitcairn Radio to *Lorcha*. Tom Christian speaking. What took you so long? We were expecting you yesterday."

We were talking to a seventh-generation descendant of Fletcher Christian himself. We were later to discover that about 85 per cent of the current islanders are *Bounty* mutineer descendants, with five surnames between them (Christian, Young, Warren, Brown, and McCoy). The accent over the radio was English but with a strong dialect. The islanders had developed a way of talking to each other in what seemed like another language.

50

Speaking excitedly, we sorted out the radio story. The island had had VHF radio facilities for over a year. The freighter we had spoken to a few days previously, the *Polybena*, had radioed the islanders to tell them a Canadian yacht was on its way.

"Unfortunately it's blowing a gale here," continued Christian. "We won't be able to come out and get you. But Brian Young [a descendant of of *Bounty* mutineer, Midshipman Edward Young] is going to take his hand-held radio up to Long Ridge and direct you to the best anchorage. Head round the rocks on the west side of the island. The water's deep right to shore."

Leaving Bounty Bay to port, we gybed around Young's Rock while Brian's voice came over the radio, directing us a little more to port or starboard and urging us to look for a certain light patch of sand. When he radioed that we looked to be in the right spot, we let go *Lorcha*'s anchor, using all sixty-one metres of chain as well as extra rope. We were in about twenty-five metres of water, more or less in the lee of the island and more or less safe, but it was a most uncomfortable anchorage, with swells coming round the island from two directions.

Time passes relatively quickly at sea, as there is always something to do. But here at anchor, we were soon bored.

"When are we going ashore," Peter kept repeating in uncharacteristic exasperation. "Isn't that what we came for?"

The day passed slowly and there was little sleep that night for either Paul or I because of the wicked thud of the waves as they slapped against the hull and the short lurching motion that rolled us around in our bunks.

The wind increased and shifted during the night and at three o'clock in the morning our anchor dragged. We started the engine and reset the anchor, making sure it was well caught.

The next morning, Brian was on the radio again.

"The wind is still shifting," he said. "That's good news and bad. It means we'll be able to pick you up tomorrow – but for

51

today it's still too much out of the north. We can't launch the longboats to come get you when a north wind is blowing. You'll have to raise your anchor again and move to the anchorage off Point Christian."

We had known that Pitcairn's shoreline made it impossible for yachtsmen to go ashore in their own dinghies. Not only is there no harbour on Pitcairn, but there are also no beaches. Steep volcanic cliffs drop to the sea on all sides to meet rocks and foaming breakers, with no mitigating coral shelf to break up the seas before they crash on shore. The spray from the breakers threw itself so fiercely into the air that it seemed to shake the dreary mist which lay heavily over the island. And all the while the breakers roared their disapproval.

We had no choice but to change anchorage and wait it out. We bundled up in our foul-weather gear and spent the morning hauling in our chain and rope and motoring in driving rain a few hundred metres along the island's forbidding coastline to where we estimated the Point Christian anchorage was.

That evening Paul and I discussed our alternatives. Perhaps we should sail away and come back another time.

"I think I can give it one more day," I said. "But two nights without much sleep is all I can manage."

"Good news," boomed Brian early the next morning. "We're coming to get you at noon."

"Come on, kids," I said. "Mix this dough for me. We'll take some fresh bread ashore with us."

Exactly at noon we saw the eleven-and-a-half-metre longboat with four men on board come round the eastern point of the island. It manoeuvred alongside, and Brian, a robust man in his late thirties, chief magistrate of the island as well as the official welcomer of yachts, leapt aboard. Brian's tanned skin and dark hair reflected both his Polynesian and English heritage, though some islanders looked totally English and some very Polynesian.

"Wind's shifting again," he said cheerfully. "Haul up your

anchor and we'll take *Lorcha* to Down Rope anchorage. Then we'll go ashore."

"About time," said our young son darkly, quite fed-up with all the waiting.

With Brian helping haul in the anchor (we made a mental note never to visit Pitcairn again with a broken-down anchor windlass), *Lorcha* was soon moved and safe. The diesel-powered launch gave us a tour of the craggy eastern shoreline before roaring towards Bounty Bay. As we paused at the line of surf at the island's main landing place, we could see why visitors don't come ashore by themselves. A few large rollers lifted us, then Brian gave a nod to the helmsman and the longboat roared through the surf. One of the crewmen had a heavy mooring line with a large loop in it ready to throw over a bollard as the longboat came alongside. Nonetheless, full reverse was called for, as the following surge can dash the longboat onto the rocks, now just underneath her forefoot at the landing stage.

We leaped ashore, and the longboat was immediately hauled up the ramp to safety in the boat shed. A large colourful sign over the shed read "Welcome to Pitcairn."

There was a beehive of activity on the short concrete jetty. Visiting British engineers Basil Williams and Jim Russell were overseeing the installation of a million-dollar repair project. As well as repairing the jetty, the British government had undertaken to instal a six-ton crane on Pitcairn Island, the last Colony of the Empire in the South Pacific Ocean. The new crane would be a welcome accessory for the unloading of goods from the longboats, as everything imported to the island has to be ferried ashore from freighters which heave-to in the lee of the island for off-loading.

We were prepared for a muddy walk up the imposing Hill of Difficulty, a steep track leading up the cliff behind the landing place, but Brian had other plans.

"Hop on," he said, sitting astride a three-wheeled all-terrain vehicle. "Nothing but the best for visiting yachtsmen. We can take two passengers aboard each bike."

In a spray of mud we set off, Penny and Peter enjoying this new adventure immensely. Up on the plateau there was a maze of muddy tracks and we turned right and left and right again before finally stopping at Brian's house where we were welcomed by his Norwegian-born wife, Kari.

"How does someone from Norway get to Pitcairn?" was my first question.

This was the Pitcairn Harlequin Romance story!

Kari had read the story of the *Bounty* mutineers and the Pitcairn settlement as a young girl and had dreamed of visiting the legendary island. She knew there was no regular passenger service, so she trained as a ship's radio operator with the hope of finding work on a freighter which would eventually drop her at Pitcairn. She did and it did, and in 1975 a longboat came out to pick up a visitor from a Norwegian vessel. Kari was granted permission to stay on the island, and she used her radio knowledge to help with the island's communications. Two years later she married Brian.

Now, eight years later, we sat in her Pitcairn kitchen exchanging bread recipes. Our fresh-baked loaf was indeed welcome.

"It's the first loaf of bread I haven't had to bake in eight years," laughed Kari. "And as the island store has just about run out of yeast, I'm going to ask you for some of your yeast supplies before you leave."

It was my turn to laugh. I am paranoid about running low on my yeast supply and always carry at least one extra kilo. That extra kilo was now like gold, and I was glad to let Kari have it.

We were anxious to hear more about the history of Pitcairn. Over lunch, Brian filled us in.

"Christian and his crew were almost desperate when they sighted Pitcairn," said Young. "They had been two months at sea combing the Cook Islands, Tonga, Fiji, and the Australs for a home. Nothing seemed right. Then Christian remembered reading about a remote island called Pitcairn. He had only a vague recollection of where it was located, but they headed in the general direction the island was thought to lie, and chanced upon it.

"*Bounty* reached Pitcairn on January 15, 1790. Fletcher Christian went ashore to reconnoitre and found an island he was later to describe as 'lonely, inaccessible, uninhabited, fertile and warm.' The possibilities exceeded his highest hopes."

"They did find evidence of an earlier civilization," continued Kari. "But being good Christians, they threw what they took to be pagan platforms and statues (said to be similar to those on Easter Island) into the sea. Who those first inhabitants were and where they went remains a mystery, though there are some petroglyphs at Down Rope and we still find the odd axe head."

Coconut palms and breadfruit had been left as a legacy from those earliest settlers, a welcome addition to the yams and sweet potatoes the new inhabitants would plant.

After stripping *Bounty* of everything they could possibly use, including carrying the valuable pigs and chickens ashore, the ship was set on fire so that nothing would remain visible from the sea.

A major site for the building of shelters was chosen – the same ridge where Adamstown (named after John Adams) stands today – on a plateau where the houses are still scarcely visible from the sea.

"But the mutineers were a mixed lot," said Young. "Christian, and my ancestor, Midshipman Young, seemed decent and educated men and Cockney John Adams was described as loyal and helpful. But the other mutineers treated the Tahitian men more as slaves than as fellow human beings and the Polynesians staged a revolt which led to the slaying of some of the mutineers and finally to their own deaths. By 1794 the only men left were Young, Adams, and the rough seamen William McCoy and Matthew Quintal.

With the dwindling numbers, there came a sort of peace, Midshipman Young's journal recorded, ". . . building their houses, fencing in and cultivating their grounds and catching birds and constructing pits for the purpose of entrapping hogs, which had become very numerous and wild, as well as injurious to the yam crops . . . kept the settlers busy."

But disharmony came to the settlers within a few years, when McCoy, who had once worked in a distillery, discovered how to brew a potent spirit from the roots of the ti plant. By 1799, Quintal had been killed by Young and Adams in self-defence, and McCoy had drowned himself. In 1800, Young died of asthma, leaving John Adams as the sole male survivor of the party that had landed only ten years before.

Adams, though no scholar and scarcely able to read and write, was a benevolent patriarch. When the British ships *Briton* and *Tagus* discovered the settlement in 1814, they were so charmed by the simplicity and piety of this little colony of Adams's, they recommended to the British government that Adams not be arrested to stand trial for his part in the mutiny. Thus he was left on Pitcairn to continue as patriarch to his extended family until his death in 1829.

We would read more about the lives of the Pitcairn Islanders and how the community grew and developed in later years, but now there was scarcely time to pick up Brian's children from school – Penny and Peter were dying to meet them – and to get down to the longboat and back to *Lorcha* before sunset.

Brian took one look at Penny and Peter's disappointed faces.

"Why don't you let Penny and Peter stay with us tonight," he said. "I'm sure our kids would be delighted to see some new faces. That way they'll have a good time – and we can get you back to your boat before the wind changes again."

It was a welcome suggestion, but the day was coming when our children would be stranded on the island by the weather, and Brian would have to work out a plan to get them off the island and back to *Lorcha* – or we would face sailing away without them.

Dolphins play in the bow wave as *Lorcha* sails with the trade winds in the South Pacific Ocean.

Cook Island girls teach Penny to weave a pandanus leaf ball.

Lorcha runs downwind in the Trade Winds of the south Atlantic Ocean. On some of the longer passages when we were far from land, with no obstructions nearby, we didn't turn on the SatNav, but reverted to celestial navigation. Paul takes a sextant sight while seated on the raised deck of the aft cabin.

Paul carries a stalk of bananas from the plantations at Aitutaki, Cook Islands. We carried three large stalks as deck cargo from Aitutaki to Palmerston Atoll, where bananas don't grow and are much sought after.

Representatives from a village group on the beach before offering gifts of a
tapa cloth and foodstuffs to the grieving family elders during funeral
ceremonies for Faka Tulola in Falevai, Vava'u, Tonga.

John Marsters holds his hands up over his head after he, Andrew, Tupou,
and three other Palmerston Atoll residents came aboard *Lorcha* as we
approached the Atoll. Their skiff is tied on behind, and the first of the
motus is at the extreme left.

The men of Falevai begin to remove the whole roast pigs from the umu, the underground oven, ready to carry them to the banqueting tables.

Penny holds Sixpack, a young koala, at Lone Pine Koala Sanctuary, near Brisbane, Australia.

Kookaburra birds joined us for breakfast at our campsite at Eungella Park, Queensland, Australia.

Peter opens the water tap for a kangaroo to get a drink. Our station wagon and tents are in the background at Eungella National Park.

At the Incwala festival, a young Swazi warrior wearing an antelope-skin loincloth and cow-tail cape hams it up with Penny and Peter. Penny holds his cow-hide shield.

Looking at the anchorage at James Bay from Ladder Hill on St. Helena. Everything imported to St. Helena must come ashore on the cranes along the wharf at the extreme right. At the end of the wharf are the stone steps, the only landing place on the island.

Paul and Penny hold up a sailfish, the largest fish we boated while on our circumnavigation. We caught this fish in the South Atlantic Ocean, between Brazil and Bermuda.

PITCAIRN TWO

6

The next morning Brian came out to get us in the "rubber duck," a big rigid-bottomed inflatable boat which could be used when the seas calmed and the wind was more southerly. Its advantage was that it could be manoeuvred by one man – the longboat needed four. We changed *Lorcha's* anchorage again before going in. The surf had calmed a trifle, but it is never safe to leave the island boats in the water. We hauled the rubber duck into the boat shed.

There were sixty-one inhabitants on Pitcairn in the year we visited the island, and Penny and Peter seemed to have met them all.

"Wut a way you?" ("How are you?") we'd be greeted in the local dialect as we met people on the muddy paths. "You must be Penny and Peter's parents."

Twenty-one of the inhabitants were children under the age of fifteen and Penny and Peter lost no time in joining their peers at the local school. With its comprehensive library, cassettes, film projector, sewing machine, record player, and typewriters, it was much more extensively equipped than the one-cabin schoolhouse on board *Lorcha*. Quietly I put away the five hundred sheets of written-on-one-side paper that I'd brought to this remote institution. Isolated it was – poorly equipped it obviously wasn't.

Rubber duck . . . Pitcairn's people . . . school . . . how they
make a living . . . Pitcairn Miscellany . . . the islanders'
camping trips . . . Pitcairn rescue . . . a hasty farewell.

While the children were at school in the morning, Paul and I leisurely strolled around talking with islanders, visiting homes, and learning about the island way of life. It was good to put our shaky leg muscles to use again.

The colony of Pitcairn is administered through New Zealand. Every person on the island has some sort of paid job, though few of the jobs are full-time. Wages are paid from a balanced island budget, with income from British grants and the sale of postage stamps. Skilled and unskilled workers are equally regarded, with the average wage in 1985 being approximately $1 per hour. The highest paid job – just over $1,000 per year – is that of island magistrate.

The private economy depends almost exclusively on subsistence farming, trading, and the sale of handicrafts – "curios," as they are called on Pitcairn.

As well as paid work, everyone is expected to contribute a set number of hours to "public work," which mostly has to do with the maintenance of the jetty (except for major new projects like the erection of the crane) and the maintenance of the island boats, co-operatively owned by all the islanders.

On average, an islander will spend about a day a week working in his garden, one day fishing, a day at public work, two days of carving or making other curios, a day of trading in one way or another, and a day of rest. As the islanders are Seventh Day Adventists, the day of rest is Saturday. And thereby hangs an unusual religious conversion story.

From the days of John Adams, the islanders had been

staunch adherents of the Church of England, with the Bible their only reading material. In 1876, however, Seventh Day Adventists in the United States sent a box of their literature to Pitcairn. On an island with a paucity of reading material, it was eagerly seized. When a Seventh Day Adventist missionary arrived in 1887, he was made welcome and, as Mary McCoy's diary of that year records, "The forms and prayers of the Church of England [were] laid aside."

And though the islanders now have their own library with books from all over the world, they have all remained Seventh Day Adventists.

The island curios are sold in an unusual and demanding way. A passing freighter or passenger ship radios to say it will stop in the island's vicinity for a few hours. Would the islanders like to visit and trade?

The bell in the main square is rung, and all those wanting to trade (nearly everybody) gathers at the jetty, all incongruously sporting briefcases filled with stamps, specially franked envelopes, carvings, pressed and decorated leaves, weaving, and T-shirts. Tightly fastened woven baskets contain bananas, oranges, lemons, and grapefruit.

The longboats shoot out from the landing stage and across open seas to where the ship drifts with her engine running, but not making way.

Now the longboat manoeuvres alongside, and, holding their precious trade items, the islanders scale the Jacob's Ladder up the ship's side. Trading is about to begin! Those in the longboats wait patiently for their turn. Sometimes there is enough time for the visiting ship to serve a meal, but rarely can the shipboard people leave their vessel to visit the island.

The ship sounds its horn to signal its departure and the islanders descend to their longboats again, grouping together to sing a song of farewell as the vessel engages its engine to resume its journey.

Many freighters pass without stopping. Later we read in the "Shipping News" section of the four-page island newspaper *Pitcairn Miscellany* (put out monthly by the school) that nine vessels, including *Lorcha*, had been in the vicinity of Pitcairn in the month we were there. Five freighters had radioed but had steamed past, while two vessels had stopped to trade. We, of course, had anchored; a French yacht, our friends on *l'Alose*, had come within radio distance of the island but deemed it imprudent to head inshore because of the heavy winds and seas and had reluctantly sailed on.

Of the two vessels that did stop, one was the *Vibeke Clipper*, which had sailed from Britain via Ecuador. Her intended destination was Pitcairn as she had the aforementioned British engineers Basil Williams (with his wife Jeanne) and Jim Russell aboard. Included in Williams' supplies and equipment for the new jetty were 300 kilograms of explosives. As Williams waited to board the *Vibeke Clipper* in Panama, he was worried about whether the ship would take his dangerous cargo. His fears proved groundless, though his worries were not exactly allayed. The vessel was already carrying 250 tonnes of explosives and armaments, destined for parts unkown.

The other freighter to stop was the Dutch vessel *Antwerpen*, carrying mail and supplies from New Zealand, the third Dutch ship to do so in three months. Islanders were treated to a barbecue lunch on board the ship, which hove to for four hours.

"For us on Pitcairn," writes Leon Salt, the editor of *Miscellany*, "These ships are looked upon as the 'Robin Hoods' of the sea. Their visits are deeply appreciated."

It was a particularly busy time for work when we were at Pitcairn, with most of the island men busy opening up and establishing a quarry at Adam's Ground, and a second gang working all day at the jetty, but we still managed to meet and talk with many islanders. We'd mostly come upon them in their gardens, at the radio station (which was a steep walk on weary sea legs to Pitcairn's summit), or sitting on the verandas of their houses carving.

And it's a yachtsman the islanders have to thank for their carving skills.

Early in this century a German yachtsman who was a

professional carver visited the island. He remained for a few months and saw possibilities in the island's handsomely grained miro wood. He was so successful in passing on his trade that today not only does everyone on the island carve, but they have created an international market for their distinctive shark, bird, and animal pieces. The demand has, in fact, been so great that the islanders have depleted Pitcairn's supplies of miro wood to the extent that they now have to journey to Henderson Island once a year to replenish supplies.

In addition to visiting Henderson for wood-cutting expeditions, the islanders make the eighty-mile passage to nearby Oeno Atoll for a yearly camping holiday.

The stories of the islanders' annual "trip" in the open longboats to Oeno range from descriptions of one-week holiday idylls to the near-tragedy of 1931. Returning merrily after their week-long sojourn, the islanders ran into such heavy weather that they were forced to turn back to Oeno when breaking waves threatened to swamp their open craft. Having brought enough food from Pitcairn for seven to ten days, they now had to forage for survival during a three-week nightmare as abnormally bad weather kept them virtual prisoners on Oeno. The frantic islanders on Pitcairn had just about given their relatives up for lost when that familiar longboat appeared on the horizon with twenty-nine well, but very hungry, islanders on board.

We had been watching the weather anxiously ourselves and were relieved when the wind went due south and we were able to anchor in Bounty Bay on our fifth day at Pitcairn, for though Brian still had to come out to pick us up it was a much shorter trip than when we were anchored on the other side of the island. We seized the opportunity to thank the islanders for their hospitality and welcome by doing an evening slide show of our travels (courtesy of the school slide projector). This was one of our most appreciative audiences; every man, woman, and child on the island turned out.

Our pleasant (comparatively speaking) anchorage in Bounty

Bay was short-lived as the wind continued inexorably round the clock. We moved to our original anchorage at Tedside on the west side the next day, having now been in every anchorage of the island.

Early the next morning, Brian was on the radio.

"The wind is now at thirty knots out of the north and we're in for a blow," he said. "We can't get the longboats out. I suggest you and Paul sail away for a couple of days and then come back to pick up Penny and Peter."

There was a very long pause.

There was no fear on our part that the kids would not be well looked after, and we knew the school was well equipped. But leaving the kids on a remote Pacific island and sailing off in bad weather not knowing when we might be able to return didn't appeal to either of us.

"What's the alternative, Brian?" asked Paul quietly.

"Well, you see the cliff just to the northeast of where you're anchored off Tedside?" asked Brian slowly. "There is a small landing point there. We've used it in emergencies before. What we'd have to do is bring the kids down the cliff and you'd have to row to that line of surf and come through a break in the rocks which you won't see till you're close. The surge is about six feet, but there should be no problem lowering the kids down to you. But if we're going to do it, we'd better do it now, because the wind is going to keep rising. Soon you'll have no choice but to leave. What do you think?"

We thought we didn't have a choice. We definitely didn't want to leave Penny and Peter, no matter how well they'd be looked after.

The dinghy was still on *Lorcha's* coachroof so we hurriedly set it loose and lowered it into the water. Then we started *Lorcha's* engine and pulled in the anchor. As soon as we saw Brian and the kids clambering down the cliff-face, Paul dropped into the dinghy and made his way towards shore, hoping to find that gap in the surf. I kept *Lorcha* moving in a tight circle, ready for any emergency.

I knew Paul well enough that if he thought the odds were

against his either making it through the gap or picking up the children, he wouldn't do it. From my point of view the worst scenario would be if he, too, got stranded ashore and I was left to sail away (and come back) on *Lorcha* on my own.

I anxiously watched Paul head for shore and saw the dinghy rise and fall, rise and fall – and then disappear through the breakers. . . .

Meanwhile Brian and Tom Christian with Penny and Peter were making their way down the cliff. The children were soon jumping from rock to rock along the bottom of the cliff to the rocky cleft where they would rendezvous with Paul. The going was slow because Peter kept finding octopi and squid which the rough seas had thrown up on the rocks. He wanted to collect as many of these as he could so that he could enjoy a day's fishing with great bait when he got back to the boat. While I was fighting wind and spray on *Lorcha* and Paul was making his risky passage through the breakers, our six-year-old was stuffing squid in his pockets and saying "Patience, patience," as Brian Young tried to hurry him along.

Once Peter saw Paul in the dinghy, however, he was persuaded to get moving. The dinghy surged as near to the rocky ledge as Paul dared let it, and Brian lowered first Penny and then Peter into it. Amidst shouts of good-byes and thank-yous, Paul fought his way out again.

It was with much relief that I saw the dinghy appear – with three figures in it. I put the engine in neutral and let Paul row up to the lee side, leaving the helm – after an appraising look at our distance from shore – to help Penny and Peter on board before running back to the cockpit, engaging the motor, and making sure we were headed seawards. We fought to get the dinghy on board and safely lashed down in those large seas.

"But I don't want to leave," shouted Penny, stamping her foot, her eyes flashing and bright with tears.

"Penny, go below if you're going to be a nuisance," I said sharply, brushing away my own tears as I revved up the engine.

Paul hauled up three panels of *Lorcha's* sail, all we needed in the rising wind.

"I don't want to leave either," sobbed Peter. "Mummy, it was a beautiful island and they have such lovely stamps."

With the boat heading west under shortened sail and everything under control, I called Penny back into the cockpit and the four of us silently said our private good-byes as we watched the "island of children" disappear in the rain squalls.

Our sadness was tempered with slightly hysterical laughter when Peter began emptying his pockets of unlucky but still very much alive and wriggling octopi.

PITCAIRN TO GAMBIER
AND ON TO TAHITI 7

As we sailed from Pitcairn Island the wind went to full gale. With nothing in our way for more than three hundred miles, we didn't worry about making any particular course, concentrating only on riding out the storm. After a wild and wet night, the wind came down to just over 20 knots and we could get back to the serious business of covering those miles to our next destination. But plain sailing it was not destined to be. The wind shifted around to come from the northwest, the direction we wanted to go. We sailed as close to north as we could, hoping the trade winds would be nearby, giving us those easy-sailing easterly winds.

This became one of our most frustrating passages. After the wind headed us (shifted around to come from the direction of our destination), it died. The log entry on our fourth day at sea reads: "Flat calm . . . 11 miles in last 24 hours."

The wind shifted back and forth in fitful puffs and gusts. I was fed up and wanted to get into harbour as soon as possible. I was exhausted; the previous long sail and having had only a short stay on Pitcairn Island were taking their toll.

As well, I was urged on towards the Gambier Islands by a short description in Earl R. Hinz's *Landfalls of Paradise: The Guide to the Pacific Islands*: "Rikitea is the principal village. . . . It once was one

From full gale to flat calm . . . motoring to Gambier . . .
pamplemousse . . . *a suspicious* gendarme . . . *atomic testing*
. . . she sells sea shells . . . the outriggers . . . happy ending.

---

of the most popular ports in the South Seas for whaling vessels who put in there for rest and recreation with their ships secure in the well-protected lagoon."

At dawn of our fifth day at sea, with a brisk wind blowing right from the direction the islands lay, I started the engine and gave it full revolutions. It was a rough splashy ride, with spray leaping over the bow to douse the person steering, but I was determined to make harbour before nightfall – I was going to get a good night's sleep.

Ten hours later, just before dusk, we lay at anchor. What a relief! And we had friends already in harbour! Of the two yachts lying at anchor, one was *l'Alose*, a French-registered boat we had first met in Cayenne, French Guiana, and the yacht that had sailed past Pitcairn while we were there. Gérard, Brigitte, and Marie-Hélène were on board.

"Anchor just here beside us," shouted Gérard as we neared him. "Would you like a *pamplemousse?*"

After a long sea passage, one craves fresh fruit. Our onions had run out, we were down to our last few wrinkled potatoes, and the closest thing to fresh greens we had on board were the bean sprouts we occasionally grew. Nearing this high volcanic group of islands, we had been savouring the fragrance of fertile land and abundant vegetation. Yes, we would like a *pamplemousse* – very much.

As soon as the anchor was down, our understanding sailing friends rowed over to introduce us to the new fruit. The Polynesian *pamplemousse* bears only a slight resemblance to

67

a grapefruit. It is slightly pear-shaped, larger than a canta-loupe. It is so juicy that a large one in full, yellow ripeness yields nearly a litre of juice. It is so sweet that even Penny and Peter slurp it down with never a thought of adding sugar. To our lips, cracked from salt spray, and our fresh-fruit-hungry bodies, it was a welcome gift.

"You can't buy fruit in the stores here," warned Gérard, but he was smiling. "When you see a garden with lots of fruit trees, though, you can ask the owner to sell you some. Only about fifteen yachts a year stop here, so you're very welcome in the community, especially if you speak French."

Gambier was one of the places we had thought we'd get some supplies, which only goes to show how little we under-stood about remote Polynesian islands! There are four small stores, but they are totally dependent on the monthly supply ship, and it had been held up a few days, so the stores were out of nearly everthing we craved. There was no meat, fresh or frozen; there were no fresh eggs, no potatoes, no green vegeta-bles. The local baker had run out of flour, so not even a fresh baguette or croissant was available.

Here we were in paradise, and Fiona was opening a can of corned beef for supper!

Next morning Penny and Peter were like eager puppies, noses pointed to the beach, as they waited to go ashore. I also noted that a *gendarme* had driven up to the landing stage in a jeep, and was sitting there, looking expectantly in our direc-tion. With boat registry papers and passports in our bag, we rowed the dinghy ashore.

We had been aware that, as Canadians, we might not be welcomed here by officials. We were in Mangareva anchorage, the nearest harbour to Mururoa Atoll that foreign vessels are allowed to enter. Greenpeace, a Vancouver-based organiza-tion, had sponsored fleets of boats to come here to protest the nuclear weapons testing which the French government car-ries on at Mururoa.

Currently in the news was an incident involving Green-peace. *Rainbow Warrior*, a Greenpeace vessel outfitting for a

68

voyage to protest the nuclear testing, had been blown up and sunk in a New Zealand harbour by a team of French government agents. We heard daily reports about the affair in the short-wave news broadcasts. David Lange, New Zealand's prime minister, decried this act of aggression on a ship registered to a nation allied to France while it was in a country which is also allied to France.

Our policy when travelling outside our own country is that we are apolitical. Regardless of how strongly we might feel about some local issue, we try to act impartially. If we are going to protest something, it is best done in our own country where we understand our legal rights.

I greeted the *gendarme* and answered his questions while Penny and Peter did their usual tumbling about on the shoreline, searching for whatever new shells or rocks might lie here. He asked me to accompany him to the *gendarmerie*, while allowing Fiona and the children to freely wander about.

At the office, the man in charge was clearly trying to size me up, trying to judge our intentions. Were we potential protesters, wanting to focus world attention on what was presently already getting too much attention in the eyes of the French officials? Or were we just another family out to see the world in their own boat?

The uniformed officer and one plain-clothes man conferred briefly, then I was told: "Under international law we must grant you permission to stay in harbour for three days. But in view of your long time at sea to get here, we will grant you five days. After that time you must head directly to Tahiti to report to the officials in Papeete."

Knowing full well that five days in harbour would be all too short, especially since we had hoped to spend perhaps a month here, I pleaded for extra time.

"Come back on the fifth day, and we will talk again," he said. "Meanwhile I will radio my superiors." Our names and passport numbers would be checked by computer to see if we had made trouble in any other countries or had committed any border violations.

69

After completing the inevitable forms, I set off down the main street, a dirt track more for pedestrians than for vehicles. My enthusiasm for being here was somewhat lessened: I felt under a dark pall and definitely on trial. But I felt cheered by the sight of my family wandering down the fragrant, frangipani- and hibiscus-lined walkway. Young Polynesian women wearing bright cloth wraps called *pareos*, with babies slung on their hips, chattered noisily and good-naturedly with each passer-by. Young children, with their natural curiosity about strangers, began to follow along behind us, delighted to find that Penny could converse with them in the same halting French that they spoke.

Rikitea is a meandering village of about five hundred inhabitants, with most of the houses strung along the main street. As we walked towards the edge of town, we saw a well-tended garden with many vegetables, flowers, and fruit trees, including two *pamplemousse* trees so heavily laden that their branches bowed towards the ground. Fiona and I looked at each other and shrugged. Wordlessly, we both decided that if we were to ask about getting some fruit, we may as well start here and now.

We opened the gate and walked to the open door of the main house of the family compound. Following the Polynesian tradition of announcing our presence at an open door, we clapped our hands. No reply. We moved to a small house at the side, and called a greeting.

"*Entrez. Entrez,*" said a voice from somewhere inside. We stepped over the threshold out of the bright tropical sun and waited for our eyes to become accustomed to the shadows of the interior.

The first room was empty, but we soon heard another "*Entrez*" coming from the room beyond. We crossed to a doorway in which an elderly Polynesian woman was framed. She sat on the floor, surrounded by piles of different sea shells, stringing a few first from one pile and then from another to make an intricate pattern of colours and textures. We squatted down beside her as, without the least hesitation,

70

she explained to these visitors from Canada who had unexpectedly entered her house what it was she was doing.

She was making necklaces, most of which would be sent to a relative in Tahiti for the tourist trade there. The shells are collected from a certain beach on the other side of the lagoon, where the wave action is gentle and the shells are in good condition when they wash ashore. Her nephew took her there, handling the outrigger canoe needed for the journey of several miles.

"Some species are hard to find, but necessary for some traditional patterns," she explained. "What I make depends on what I find on the beach."

Eventually there was a pause in the conversation. "Could we pick some *pamplemousse* from the tree in the front yard?" I asked. "We will pay you whatever you think they are worth."

"Take what you like," said our new friend, Ann. "Only small children eat them. They are too sweet for adults. We've got too many."

By now Fiona and the children were enthralled, so I left them chatting to Ann while I went out to try to pick some of the heavy fruit, nearly the size of basketballs, without letting them fall to the ground where they would smash to a juicy pulp. I soon collected fifteen by climbing the tree and stuffing them, five at a time, into the knapsack we always carry on shore excursions, and then carrying them to the ground and starting over.

Meanwhile, in the house, Ann, a typical Polynesian woman and therefore very fond of children, had given Penny and Peter a few of her necklaces, and Fiona had bought a few more to send as gifts to people at home. Loaded down, each of us carrying some fruit, we returned to *Lorcha*.

The following day the long-awaited supply boat arrived, so people from all over the island group came into town. We met John David, a man in his early thirties who lived on a neighbouring island. His father, as a young man, had travelled to Tahiti from California and had married an island girl. John David had been born there, spending most of his early years

71

in a small village, but had been sent to high school and university in California. He had returned to French Polynesia to work with his father, who had unfortunately died of a tropical disease soon after his return. Through his mother's family he had inherited an island in the Gambier lagoon, and had come out here to try to establish a small resort.

As we strolled around Rikitea with John and his two small children, he told us a bit about the history of these islands, and about how fed up the local residents were of the French nuclear testing going on at the nearby atoll.

"You see that big shed over there?" he said, indicating what would pass for a large farm equipment shed built of corrugated iron. "It was built to house the island population should an emergency occur during a nuclear test. One time when a test was in progress the wind shifted to blow the fallout towards us. The French officials rounded up everyone on the island and put them in the shed. There are big irrigation-type sprinklers mounted on the roof, and they pumped sea water through those sprinklers over the roof for several days to try to protect the population.

"After they let the people out, they went around to all the gardens and collected all the fruit and vegetables. Even now they continue to test some plants and animals, but they never give us any information, only continuously telling us that everything is safe."

One of the local shopkeepers complained to us that he could no longer sell fish caught in the lagoon. Much of the fish has a toxin called *ciguaterra*, which occurs naturally in some fish in some parts of the world. The Gambier group residents find that no fish caught in the lagoon is safe to eat. Even the pelagic fish caught outside of the lagoon sometimes have the poisoning, something unkown in the rest of the world.

"The French keep telling us the poisoning of the fish isn't caused by the test explosions," one shopkeeper told us. "They say they are looking after the islands and its people and not to

72

worry. If the nuclear testing is so safe, why don't they do it in the Mediterranean?"

The Gambier Island's European discoverer was Captain James Wilson of the London Missionary Society's ship, *Duff*, which entered the lagoon in 1797. In ensuing years they were a hotbed of missionary activity, eventually becoming the domain of a fanatical Belgian Roman Catholic priest, Père Laval, who with his own hands toppled the great dreaded stone effigy of the god Tu on the island's sacred stone altar, called a *marae*. Laval made virtual slaves of the locals and imposed a rigid moral code. However, the magnificent twin-towered church he built, with its intricate mother-of-pearl inlaid walls, still stands and is well maintained and attended.

The story of Père Laval's tyrannical hold over the Polynesian people and the destruction of their culture was the inspiration for a story in James Michener's book, *Return to Paradise*.

When we were at Rikitea, two religious brothers from Montreal were running a technical school to teach the local youngsters such trades as carpentry, metal-working, and mechanics.

Once, pearl-diving was a lucrative trade here because of the dark pearls unique to this lagoon. The natural pearl oysters have long been fished out, but pearl culture, with oysters raised in beds, is an important local industry. The oyster farms are controlled by the Japanese who bring in their technicians to implant a small plastic bead into the lips of the living oyster in a secret process they will not allow the local people to observe. The Polynesians look after the oyster beds and collect the pearl oysters for harvesting three years after the implantation. Japanese technicians grade the pearls and take the best back to Japan. The remainder are sold in the tourist trade at Papeete.

Because this was our first exposure to an indigenous South Pacific culture, it was our first look at the outrigger canoe in use. The traditional dugout log canoe is no longer found here, but the boxier, easier-to-build plywood model was everywhere. With small outboard engines, perhaps five- to eight-horsepower, they travelled across the lagoon at high speeds carrying heavy loads.

Many are built by the locals at their houses, using plywood and fir or spruce timber imported from Canada. While it is a shame that local materials are no longer used, it is understandable: with the increasing population there is not enough wood on these small islands to meet all needs.

It also seems a pity, at least to my romantic mind, that the canoes are no longer sailed. But it seems even people on far-flung South Pacific atolls are affected by international monetary exchange rates and the intricacies of world trade. They too are dependent upon Japanese outboard engines and motorbikes.

"We are going over to Aukera Island," said Gérard as he motored past *Lorcha*. "There are some abandoned fruit plantations over there, and we were told by some local people that we could pick whatever we want. See you in a day or two."

Aukera Island was only a few miles across the lagoon, and we could see *l'Alose* and *Atesoue*, the other yacht we had met here, close together at anchor at the island opposite us.

The crew of *Atesoue* is the sort of mixture one sometimes meets on the cruising circuit. Gilles and his brother had outfitted the eight-metre engineless boat in France, and set sail on an open schedule. During the year they spent in Brazil, Gilles met Fatima, a beautiful and charming young woman. When it came time to leave Brazil, Gilles couldn't leave without her. Gilles's brother took passage on another yacht, leaving the boat to Gilles and Fatima. Now, with Egore, just turned four years old, they are still sailing.

During that night a strong and gusty thunderstorm came through the area. Though we were perfectly protected in the main anchorage, the other two boats were open to the strong wind as it changed direction. *Atesoue* got into trouble.

During the storm *Atesoue's* anchor cable fouled a coral head and snapped under the strain. Before Gilles could do anything they were in the surf, being washed up on the beach, with *Atesoue* pounding her bilge on the bottom. The rudder was broken, and there was some other damage, though it wasn't serious. If he could get her afloat, Gilles felt, he could make the necessary repairs.

The wind had now eased, but manpower and a powerful boat were needed to drag *Atesoue* to deeper water. Gérard motored *l'Alose* back to the main anchorage at dawn to try to get help from the *gendarmes*. Luckily the supply ship was still in harbour, and the captain agreed to allow his crew of seventeen burly Polynesian stevedores to take one of the ship's tenders. The *gendarmes* sent over their fast and powerful launch to see if they could help pull *Atesoue* off.

Eventually, with all their belongings loaded into the ship's tender, and with it and the other launch pulling, and with the stevedores in the water heaving at her sides, *Atesoue* was again afloat. She was towed back to the main anchorage and at high tide Gilles leaned her against the jetty with her keel resting on the bottom so at low tide her underwater area was exposed. Her rudder stock was removed and taken to the technical school where the brothers set their students to work on a practical exercise.

Atesoue was soon judged seaworthy, and her thankful crew prepared for the passage to Tahiti, where permanent repairs could be made on the slipway.

These islands were a pleasant introduction to the South Pacific for us. We met Polynesian people in an isolated area and found them to be as gentle and friendly as we had always heard. We hiked the volcanic hills of the main island to strengthen our leg muscles, weakened by the inactivity of long passages. Penny and Peter swam over most of the coral heads near the anchorage, and enjoyed seeing many new fish species.

The gendarmes had allowed us another seven days, and thus we were a total of twelve days in the Gambier group. We wanted to stay longer, but there was no question of another visa extension, and we had to move on.

SAIL TO TAHITI – THE HEART OF POLYNESIA 8

"There's Vanavana abeam," I shouted to the children as they played below decks. Tussling with each other, they raced up the companionway, each eager to be the first to stand on the cockpit seats straining to see the tops of the coconut palms as *Lorcha* rose and fell in the swells.

We were sailing through an area of widely strewn coral atolls known as the *Tuamotu* or Dangerous Archipelago. The atolls are low-lying, some with the highest point of land only a sandspit perhaps three metres above the high-tide line. Luckily for mariners, most *motus* that ring lagoons have coconut palms on them growing to a height of eighteen to twenty-one metres. But the tops of these tall trees are only visible for a distance of about seven or eight miles, less in a big sea or in conditions of poor visibility. Many atolls are uninhabited and have no navigational lights. The lights on those which have some villages are usually dim kerosene lamps. Sailing at night, the unwary mariner can be suddenly caught in the surf pounding on the outer reef of an atoll; the vessel will likely be lost.

We had met a Frenchman who had taught school for fifteen months on one of the outlying atolls. During that time, he said, he knew of eleven yachts which were wrecked and unsalvageable. In the season we sailed through this area, we knew of two

Dangerous Archipelago . . . many wrecked yachts . . . high tech
fails us . . . a minor medical emergency . . . Papeete at last . . .
Mainstay *is missing . . . anchored in pollution . . .*
friends arrive.

---

yachts which had run onto these reefs. One was dragged off
and saved; the other lies on her bilge with the sea washing
through her hull, a dismal warning to all who sail these reef-
strewn waters.

The use of modern navigational aids is a help, but no insur-
ance. Many of the reefs are poorly charted; some are even
charted in the wrong position. The surveys of this area were
done in the last century and many have not been updated.
Even as your SatNav shows you to be at a position which,
according to a current chart, is a safe distance from any
obstruction, you many be fighting to keep clear of the surf.
Our informative French acquaintance told us that of the
eleven wrecks he knew of, nine had had SatNav. The vessels
were likely lost because of poor watch-keeping and/or failure
when plotting a position or planning a passage to take into
account the variable and powerful currents flowing around
these islands.

I was glad that we were passing Vanavana Atoll in daylight.
If our course had taken us past it far enough away that we
hadn't seen it, I would have been worried about whether or
not we had really passed it by the time it got dark.

Peace of mind and confidence that the action taken was the
right one are important to the small-boat skipper. Arriving
safely is always more important than the speed with which
the passage is made.

"Dad," said Penny as she looked up from her school work at

the dinette table, "the SatNav is making some strange noises, and the numbers are flashing."

A SatNav is a computer which calculates a boat's position accurately to within a few hundred yards by receiving very high frequency radio signals from satellites circling the Earth. The position is calculated using the Doppler Effect, a phenomenon which in high-school science books is usually illustrated by a picture of a person receiving sound waves from a car as it rushes past. The sound of the car increases until the car reaches the person and then decreases as the car recedes into the distance. The signal received by the SatNav from the satellite changes as the satellite rushes past the boat, thus allowing the position to be given with great accuracy. It now seemed, however, that in our case, the Laws of Physics might be giving way to Murphy's Law – if something can go wrong, it will.

It was about 1000 on our sixth day out from the Gambier Islands. A changeable and light wind was heading us and we had not been able to maintain our planned course. I quickly recorded the last position the SatNav had registered, and then switched it off. After crossing my fingers, I turned it on again, to see if the start-up program would be accepted. No luck. We would be without our high-tech instrument for the rest of the passage. That was another four hundred and twenty miles in a straight line – much more if we couldn't maintain our course in this contrary wind.

We tacked back and forth for the next three days. I was very uneasy, as the cloud cover was now also uncooperative, and for those three days we were unable to get any celestial sights. The sun, moon, planets, and stars remained obscured, and the sextant stayed in its box. Rain or drizzle further decreased visibility.

With the SatNav and sextant unable to give us a position fix, I began to use our next back-up – our radio direction finder (RDF). This piece of equipment receives the signals of radio beacons, usually those at airports. We were near the Mururoa Atoll, where the French have airports on Hao, to the northeast,

78

and Anaa, to the northwest. Thus I was able to use the RDF to get a fairly good position fix. However, we were near the limit of the range of the RDF for the beacon at Hao, and, although we were getting closer to Anaa, two beacons are needed to get a reasonable fix, three to get a proper one. I hoped the sun would shine soon.

Four days after the SatNav stopped working, the skies began to clear. I took a series of sextant sights and was happy to find that our position differed little from the dead-reckoning position based on our RDF bearings.

My anxiety was further relieved because we were back in the trade winds. We were again laying our course to Tahiti.

"Peter," I tried to say calmly to our six-year-old, "always make your cuts away from your hand."

On several long passages we had gotten out wood scraps and carving knives to spend some time during the day whittling. I like to whittle and had been teaching the children to make small animals. Peter was at work on a turtle.

I had barely got the sentence out of my mouth when the knife slipped. Peter had slashed across the back of his thumb about midway between the knuckles.

The cut bled profusely. It was a deep one; so deep that I feared he might have cut the tendon. I forced him to wiggle the thumb, and was relieved to see that he could.

Binding the thumb up tightly with some paper towel, I left Fiona to keep pressure on it to slow the bleeding, and dove below to get the first aid box. As I was coming back up the companionway, I noticed a French military vessel on the horizon. We were near the limit of the restricted zone around the nuclear testing site and had seen low-flying planes on patrol. I had expected to see military vessels, and now I wondered – should we radio this ship to ask for help? I knew that had we been in Toronto we would have taken Peter to a doctor's office to have the wound stitched up. We were three days from the nearest harbour – Papeete – where we could get medical attention. Perhaps the French ship would have medical personnel on board who could advise us? But suppose they suggested that we transfer Peter over to them for treatment? That would likely be dangerous. Perhaps we should just bind the thumb up as best we could, start Peter on a course of antibiotics to safeguard against an infection setting in, and carry on to Tahiti?

In the end, that's what we did. We got the bleeding stopped, and I put a butterfly plaster over the wound to hold the two edges together. It looked okay so we decided to carry on.

Early in the morning on our twelfth day at sea we sighted Mehetia, a high rocky islet only sixty miles from the southeastern tip of Tahiti.

In that evening's sunset, Tahiti's 2,165-metre-high jagged peaks were silhouetted against a colourful sky. We sailed along the shore, gliding past coastal villages and watching their twinkling lights. We rounded Point Venus with its powerful lighthouse, visible for forty-four kilometres, flashing every five seconds. Point Venus, the northwestern tip of Tahiti, was named by Captain James Cook, who observed the transit of the planet Venus here on June 3, 1769. Past the point, the intense harbour lights and the city lights of Papeete lit the sky. We soon sighted the red and green navigation aids marking the harbour entrance. Carefully consulting our chart while trying to keep an eye out for the many small fishing craft along the shore, we made our way to the yacht anchorage. By 0400 we were secure at anchor at this fabled place – Papeete – the heart of Polynesia.

Though we had been given temporary clearance for French Polynesia in the Gambier Islands, we knew we would have to obtain official clearance and visas here. We had also been told that we would have to post a bond. Loaded with our cameras, registry papers, clearance papers, passports, crew lists, travellers cheques, and credit cards we went ashore to visit the port captain's office.

"Welcome to Tahiti," said the genial official, whose features clearly showed his mixed Polynesian and European back-ground. "I hope you had a nice voyage getting here?"

As I filled in the papers he explained about the bond. If any crew member is tossed off his ship, or if people should be ship-wrecked among the islands, or if someone simply runs out of money, the local government wants to be sure that they won't have to pay the air-fare to get them home. Thus, they demand a bond usually equivalent to the cost of a one-way ticket out of Tahiti to the traveller's country of origin. At the discretion of the local officials, this could be a flat rate of $500 (U.S.) per person. This is low; airfare from Tahiti to Europe would be much more.

"You have such lovely children," said the official after chat-ting in both French and English to Penny and Peter, "I think that in your case a total bond of $1,500 is sufficient."

He advised us to go to the bank with the most branches among the islands. We should show the bank the "demand bond" paper from the officials, and deposit that amount at the bank. No interest is received on the money for the time it is on deposit (usually ninety days, the length of a visa) and the bank also requires a fee – in our case about $60. The local bank branch at our last port of call in French Polynesia would give us back our money in whatever currency they had on hand.

As we were about to leave the port captain's office, Fiona saw a notice on the bulletin board near the door. "Posted Miss-ing." it read, "The yacht *Mainstay* with Larry and Fleur Rayner on board. Please report any information on the whereabouts of this yacht." Included in the notice was the date and place the yacht was last seen: the Galapagos Islands about four months previously, and their destination: the Marquesas Islands.

"But that's *Mainstay*," Fiona said in disbelief. "She can't be missing."

We had met Larry and Fleur several months earlier at the

San Blas Islands of Panama. They were a cheerful and enthusiastic couple, and we had shared dinner. Larry had completed a circumnavigation of the world before he met Fleur. After their marriage they build *Mainstay* in their native New Zealand, as Larry said he wanted to show Fleur all the magical places he had visited around the world. In the San Blas Islands they had been celebrating their first pregnancy.

Our boats had lain near each other at the Cristobal Yacht Club in Panama for four days. I had gone through the canal as a line handler on *Mainstay*. She was beautifully built, and sailed well. I knew she was completely outfitted with life-raft, amateur (ham) radio, and VHF for two-way communications, as well as all the other equipment a proper sea-going yacht would have.

We were stunned. We couldn't imagine a yacht and a crew less likely to have had a mishap.

As we left the office, we bumped into Peter, the skipper of *Emerald City*, whom we had met about a year earlier. He and Larry and Fleur had been good friends.

"All I can think of is that they are dead," said Peter bluntly. "We both sailed out from Academy Bay along with three other yachts. The rest of us arrived within a few days of each other at Taiohae Bay, Nuku Hiva. None of us had encountered any bad weather.

"When *Mainstay* didn't arrive," he continued, "we began to call on the ham radio, but got no response. We alerted other yachts making that crossing to keep a lookout for them."

When they were three weeks overdue their friends called the authorities, who notified all ships and planes crossing that area to look for a yacht in distress or a life-raft.

"It's been about three months now since they were reported missing," said Peter mournfully. "That's about the maximum time anyone has been known to live in a life-raft."

We talked for a while, taking comfort from each other's company and speculating on what might have happened. We assumed that Larry and Fleur must not have made it into their life-raft and that for some reason *Mainstay* sank very quickly. There must have been no time for a Mayday call. If they were still alive and still afloat, the ocean currents would have swept them to the Marquesas by now.

Perhaps they had had an explosion and fire on board. Perhaps they had run into a floating ship's container or had had a whale surface under them. Perhaps they had been run down by a cargo or fishing vessel in the night.

Petalyn, another New Zealand-registered boat, was one of those which had sailed out from Academy Bay in company with *Mainstay*. Their crew were presently in Papeete, and they had notified Larry and Fleur's relatives in New Zealand that they were missing. The relatives had enlisted the aid of a clairvoyant. She said they were still alive and were on an uninhabited island somewhere far to the south of the Marquesas.

Carl, from *Petalyn*, asked if we had seen anything near Henderson Island? What about Oeno or Ducie? Could Larry and Fleur have been washed ashore at one of the uninhabited islands of the Gambier group? He was pressuring the French authorities to mount a sea-and-air search-and-rescue operation in that area, as well as in the far southeastern Tuamotus.

Much as we wanted to help and wished Larry and Fleur could be found, I felt that their friends and relatives were grasping at straws. *Mainstay* had not been headed anywhere near that direction. A life-raft would not have been swept to that area, as the currents do not run that way. Also much of that area is within the nuclear-testing restricted zone and is heavily patrolled by the French military. Had they been in that area, they would have been sighted.

To this day, nothing has ever been heard or found of *Mainstay* or her crew.

Much subdued, we visited the bank to pay our bond, and then headed for the market area for a first-day-in-port lunch in town.

There didn't seem to be any inexpensive restaurants, so we settled for a small place, busy and noisy with local people. We ordered *poisson cru*, raw fish marinated in lime juice and served with chopped vegetables in coconut milk. It is a local speciality, and one we like.

Upon our return to *Lorcha*, we found a note from the harbourmaster saying we were restricting navigation in the harbour because of where we were anchored. We were to shift anchorage immediately, or be towed away. It was time to join the yachts lined up ten metres from the quay along Boulevard Pomare, but finding a place where the traffic noise wouldn't be too bothersome was tricky.

We settled on a space next to Place de Gaulle, where there were at least some bushes and trees between the shore and the busy roadway. The disadvantages were that there was a sewage drain about fifty feet away and the water was shallow, with only inches under *Lorcha*'s keel at low tide.

Two days later our friends the Capers on *Shedar*, Frank, Ginny, and five-year-old Cari Ann, sailed into harbour. The yacht next to us had sailed away that morning, so Frank squeezed *Shedar* into the line-up, lying hard against our fenders.

"Ah, pollution," said Frank, sniffing the mixed odours of diesel fuel floating on the harbour water, exhaust fumes from the busy streets, and run-outs from the nearby drain. "The sign of civilization."

SAILING AMONG THE SOCIETY ISLANDS 9

Captain James Wallis from England was the first European to visit Tahiti; he anchored there in 1767. Wallis found his frigate surrounded by hundreds of canoes filled with strong, laughing men and lovely young *vahine* who performed, as one of Wallis's officers wrote in his journal, "a great many droll and wanton tricks."

Thus was born the fantasy of a free and easy life in a tropical land where food fell from the trees, the climate was unceasingly benign, and caring and intimate companionship began as soon as one arrived.

The Society Islands were so named by Captain Cook as he felt that "they lay contiguous to one another. . . ." This group of fourteen islands, along with the Marquesas group, the Tuamotus, the Gambiers, and the Australs make up French Polynesia. The Society Islands group contains the best-known islands of the South Pacific. Mention Tahiti, Moorea, or Bora Bora to most people in northern climes and watch their eyes glaze over and a distant, dreaming look come over them.

We, too, had fallen under that spell, planning to spend the cyclone season here, a period of several months, before sailing on, perhaps north to the Hawaiian Islands before heading for the west coast of Canada. We soon changed our minds.

The tropical fantasy . . . Tahiti, a tourist mecca . . . effects on
the natives . . . Gai Charisma *. . . shipboard pets . . .*
Huahine Island . . . Dorothy Ann *and the Jones family . . .*
Bora Bora . . . goodbye to Polynesia.

Until the early 1960s these islands were largely self-sufficient. The inhabitants grew much of their own food, harvested copra – dried coconut meat – and mined phosphates.
Then, in 1962, the *Centre d'Experimentation du Pacifique* (CEP)
was set up; fifteen thousand French soldiers, technicians, and
bureaucrats arrived over the next few years to establish the
test site for nuclear weapons on Mururoa Atoll. Tahiti remains
the main staging area for that test site, with international
flights landing there. The island is also a major naval base for
the French and an important tourist destination. "Prices
aren't so high here," the many Californian yachtsmen say as
they guzzle half-litre bottles of locally brewed Hinana beer.
"About the same as in L.A."

The men of French Polynesia left their traditional way of life
to work for the French. Today, with the newfound prosperity
of a wage economy, the population is rapidly increasing. It
was estimated in 1980 that a full 60 per cent of the population
was under sixteen years of age. The phosphates have largely
been mined out, and little copra is now harvested. Approximately 95 per cent of all goods used in these islands is
imported. About 65 per cent of the island's food is also
imported.

"What if the French should leave?" I asked a local man.

"Oh," he said with a typical Gallic shrug, "there is some talk
of separating from the French as well as trying to end the
nuclear testing, but nothing will ever come of it. If the French
should leave," he stated with certainty, "the local people

would have to give up their cars, motorbikes, and refrigerators. We couldn't go back to a traditional way of life now. We have forgotten how to survive on our own."

As we walked down the busy streets of Papeete we could see that there were no people of pure Polynesian background here. They were a tawny mixture of European and Oriental blood with a dominant Polynesian cast. The girls in their colourful cloth pareo wraps are still beautiful as, with red hibiscus blossoms in their hair, they speed through the traffic on noisy motorbikes. The young men are still strong and laughing but their laughter seems to centre on the sidewalk cafes along Boulevard Pomare, where they ogle and comment upon the passing tourist women with boisterous good cheer.

All this may have been fun and interesting, but it wasn't the Polynesia we had hoped to visit.

"Have you seen *Gai Charisma* yet?" asked Frank Capers from *Shedar*'s cockpit. "We last saw them in Ahe, in the Tuamotus, and they said they would meet us here."

Frank, Ginny, and Cari Ann were going to leave *Shedar* in the care of fifteen-year-old Chris, one of the four children aboard *Gai Charisma*, while they flew to Hawaii and then to Connecticut to visit relatives. They would be gone for about two weeks. Chris would also be looking after Spinnaker, the Capers' pet dog. Left alone on board, especially at night, Spinnaker was apt to whine and bark, and worse – to tear up the cushion covers and bite and scratch at *Shedar*'s finely varnished interior.

Pets can be a problem on internationally travelling yachts. Fearful of introducing potentially deadly diseases like rabies, some island nations, such as Samoa, will not allow yachts with pets to enter their harbours. Others, such as New Zealand, will only allow yachts with pets on board into certain anchorages, never to lie alongside a dock. The owners must post a bond of $1,000 guaranteeing that they will not violate the regulations. The pet must be shown to a quarantine officer on demand, and if it is ever known to have gone ashore, it is immediately destroyed, and its owners forfeit their bond. French Polynesia is more relaxed about yachts with pets. If the animal has the necessary shots, it is allowed in harbour, although not on shore.

The day before the Capers were scheduled to leave, *Gai Charisma* with Richard Harvey at the helm finally sailed in, and moored on the far side of *Shedar* from us. Penny and Peter were ecstatic when they realized that the fifteen-and-a-half-metre Australian-registered ketch had four children aboard: Stacy, aged ten, Andrew, aged twelve, Mark, aged fourteen, and Chris. They were most happy to have some "big brother and sister" children to pal around with for a few weeks while we waited for our SatNav, which had been sent to England for repairs, to be returned to us.

The return of the SatNav and of the Capers meant that it was once again time to begin sailing. We planned on heading down the chain of islands, and we would have company – Richard, his wife, Gail, and the four children in *Gai Charisma* would sail with us.

But though the company was great, our sail through this fabled chain of islands was less than perfect. We first anchored among Moorea's outer reefs to enjoy the clear clean water, well-aerated by the crashing waves, and where the coral was most colourful. No sooner had we lowered the anchor than an irate expatriate landowner, with all the authority of a barking dog in a manger, told us to move away from his property. A couple of days later we shifted to Cook's Bay. The most recent film of *Mutiny on the Bounty* was shot among these shark-toothed volcanic ridges. The water was cloudy and most of the coral was dead. After swimming we itched at welts caused by biting sea lice infesting the bay. The lice crawl under the waistbands and straps of swimsuits to feed.

With hundreds of yachts sailing through this island group every year, there are some strange accidents. Two years previously, the weather had been clear with good visibility the day a local fishing boat rammed into fifty-year-old British solo sailor Margaret Hill's six-and-a-half-metre yacht at the entrance to Cook's Bay. The bow had been sheared off and the boat sank in sixty seconds. Though Margaret's dreams of a solo sail around the world have come to an abrupt halt and a nasty battle for compensation has ensued against the non-Polynesian fishing boat fleet owner (she was not insured), she recounts with great good humour how one minute she was sitting in her cockpit and the next she was floating on the ocean, her large and floppy sunhat still tied becomingly under her chin, her boat settling, clearly visible, on the outer reef edge twenty metres beneath her.

Huahine Island was an island I had been looking forward to visiting. It is quiet, with a low population and few tourists, but lush and scenic and rich in sacred sites with stone altars and monuments, called *maraes*, built by ancient Polynesians.

As we entered the lagoon we could see about a dozen yachts moored in a clump over the only coral-clear patch of bottom. As we slowly motored around the anchorage, looking for a suitable space, I suddenly realized from our sounding lead that the water here was twenty-five-metres deep! (We generally like to anchor in less than nine metres of water as the necessary swinging room, as well as the amount of anchor chain required to moor safely, is less.)

Penny and Peter saw something important to them – another boat with children on board. Soon Hillary, Diana, and Kate Jones, ten, twelve, and thirteen years old, were swimming around *Lorcha* making conversation. "Come aboard for some lemonade and cookies," invited Fiona, always ready to entertain companions for our two children.

The five children played and swam around *Lorcha* all afternoon. The Jones family had left England three years previously, and had just arrived from New Zealand the day before, after a passage of about three weeks. We told the girls that we would be going to visit the maraes at the end of the island the following afternoon, and asked them to come with us.

"We usually do school lessons in the morning," said Kate, who was obviously the organizer. "Come over tomorrow morning to visit my parents and I am sure they will let us go with you."

Consequently, the next morning, Fiona and I rowed over to *Dorothy Ann*, a fifty-year-old wooden gaff ketch. "Vicki," called Josh Jones to his wife down the companionway, "make some tea for our guests."

"I'll just carry on with this as we talk," said Josh, hewing at a tree trunk twenty centimetres in diameter. "We were still a few days out from here when a sudden wind squall came up. It carried away the bowsprit before I could get the jib off her.

"Sorry the cockpit is in a bit of a shambles," he rushed on. "The exhaust pipe broke when the engine jumped off its beds as we motored into the lagoon, and I had to take up some of the cockpit to get to it.

"I'll be busy for the next few days," he continued. "I hope to get some caulking in the foredeck before we leave here. *Dorothy Ann* dips her bow in anything of a sea, and the water pours right through the deck planking so the girls can't sleep in their bunks in the forecabin.

"Nice thing about old wooden boats is that they are so easy to repair," said Josh cheerfully as he accepted the mug of tea from his wife and sat down, probably for the first time that day.

"Sure, take the girls for a bit of sight-seeing," he said when we asked, "I'll be glad to get them out from underfoot. Vicki," he never even paused, "you go along, too. It would be good for you to have some time off the boat.

"I'll stay here and continue my work," continued Josh. "We'll be leaving here in a couple of days, stopping briefly in Tahiti for a few supplies before heading towards Hawaii to get there before the cyclone season."

I bit my tongue to keep from blurting out that we were virtually at the beginning of the cyclone season for the area between French Polynesia and Hawaii.

"Then we'll head right up to Alaska," said the skipper. "I've got a friend who says he can get me a job there. We're getting a bit low on funds."

We all had an enjoyable time that afternoon taking "le Truck," the local transportation, to Maeva village, and looking at the twenty-eight maraes overlooking Lake Fauna. In ancient times all the district chiefs of Huahine Nui lived side by side and worshipped their ancestors at their respective maraes. Sixteen of the twenty-eight maraes have been restored. Replicas of some meeting houses have been constructed of local materials on their original sites, and some ancient fish traps have been rebuilt. Nonetheless, the site is undeveloped in a western tourism sense. Only the lonely coral slabs erected to represent the gods stand sentinel over the lagoon. A few children and dogs wander along the pathways. On the day we visited, we were the only tourists there.

The following day *Gai Charisma* arrived. We soon introduced the three girls from *Dorothy Ann* to the four young crew members on *Gai Charisma*. Fiona, in a flash of insight, invited all seven children to join us for dinner that night on *Lorcha*. Nine children ranging in age from six to fifteen makes quite a boatful.

Fiona and I were the cooks and servers. We took great pleasure in watching these youngsters competing with each other for the best jokes and stories, as well as trying to establish who was the fastest talker and vying to get the floor amongst all the competing voices. Peter and Penny, being the youngest, could hardly participate at all. Their mouths were agape at all this "teen talk." They were certainly paying attention, however, because they retold the stories and jokes over and over in the following months.

"But we don't want to go. Why do we have to leave? We've only known Peter and Penny for three days, and the others for only a day. We could all have dinner together again tonight, and none of us want to go." With that, Kate Jones burst into tears, leapt into *Dorothy Ann*'s dinghy, and rowed ashore, to sit in sobbing disappointment on the beach beside the anchorage.

Josh let her be for a few minutes, before rowing ashore in *Dorothy Ann*'s second dinghy. He sat beside Kate on the beach speaking quietly to her. A short while later they were all on board, waving good-bye as they motored out the pass.

We heard later, through the yachting grapevine, that they made good their passage to Alaska. They worked there for about one year, then travelled down the west coast of Canada and the United States. Off the coast of Mexico, heading for the Panama Canal, *Dorothy Ann* sank during a gale. The family made it safely into their life-raft and less than twenty-four hours later were picked up by the passenger liner, *Canberra*, which happened to be in the area. They are now back in England.

"What's that over there, that black fin at the surface of the water?" I called to the rest of the family as we motored through the pass into the lagoon at Bora Bora.

"Whales! It's whales," shouted Penny as one of them surfaced and spouted with its exhaling breath.

We slowly motored over towards them, seeing a few small fishing boats doing the same. It was a family of humpback whales, a bull, a cow, and a calf, slowly swimming about the entrance. As we motored slowly near them they dove under us, and we could clearly see the calf swimming under the mother's protective fin. We drifted about, watching the whale family, for about twenty minutes before they moved off towards the end of the lagoon opposite the anchorage off the Oa Oa Hotel.

James Michener wrote that Bora Bora was "the most beautiful island in the world." It was home to five thousand American servicemen during the Second World War. There are still some crumbling remnants of the military presence, including a few rusting artillery guns overlooking the reef pass.

Bora Bora has a well-developed, if low-key, tourism industry, with several hotels and a few restaurants and souvenir shops. The main town is a bit ticky-tacky and rambling, but quite pleasant in overall effect.

"Look, Mummy," said Penny, scanning a notice board, "here's a list of excursions. One of them is to go on a shark-feeding boat ride."

Later we met some tourists who had gone on that boat tour. We were aghast to hear that the boat operator thumped the side of the boat, then threw in raw meat for the sharks to feed on. This in a lagoon where both tourists and locals swim and snorkel, scuba dive, and go board sailing! Granted they fed the sharks near the reef pass and not off the tourist beaches, but would that mean that sharks might follow boats looking for a handout? What if someone fell overboard?

"You want your $1,500 bond back in U.S. cash?" said the dubious bank manager as he scanned our documents for checking out of French Polynesia. "Well, we'll see what we've got."

Slowly he counted out a huge pile of mostly ten-, five-, and one-dollar bills, then pushed it across his desk.

I could just imagine the trickle of these small bills coming into his bank. No doubt the money came from tips from American tourists to the many islanders who now depend on tourism to support themselves in a lifestyle increasingly different from that of their ancestors.

AITUTAKI AND PALMERSTON

10

We sailed out of the pass at Bora Bora for the Cook Islands on October 4. The course was 238°, with the wind east-south-east at 10 knots.

It was an exciting leave-taking, not because of wind or weather, but because by heading west we were, for the first time, committing ourselves to a circumnavigation.

True, we could sail back from New Zealand to French Polynesia via the Pacific Ocean's Roaring Forties (40° south) and thence to Hawaii and western Canada, but once we were in Australia, there would be no reason to try to turn back. It would be simpler, easier, and shorter to head west across the Indian Ocean.

That was quite a thought – a circumnavigation would be the easiest route home.

Before we had left Toronto, sailing round the world had seemed a daunting and challenging prospect. Now, in mid-Pacific, we no longer thought of a circumnavigation as a strength- and soul-testing endurance sail of over twenty-eight thousand storm-filled and dangerous miles, but rather as a leisurely and ordered trip on an ocean whose wilful ways could be forecast and tempered to our wishes.

Our well-ordered family life on board a small vessel with predictable trade winds pushing it along would be more concerned with cooking, reading,

Circumnavigation . . . the Cook Islands . . . Canadian flags . . .
wreck rescue . . . on to Palmerston . . . grinding over a reef . . .
church of old boats . . . Polynesian welcome . . . Refuge Hill
for cyclones . . . island politics . . . why yachtsmen are
welcome on Palmerston.

doing lessons, fishing, and day-to-day coping than with hurricanes and life-threatening equipment failures.

Perhaps, we thought, the ocean was also wishing us well; on our first day out from Bora Bora we covered 126 miles over the bottom. But as if the Pacific were wagging her finger at us not to get too confident, we managed to cover only 102 miles the second day and 97 miles the third day. Finally, just to make the point, the wind fell off completely on day four and we made good only 34 miles.

So we had the ocean under our control, did we? That night, the wind roared up to 40 knots, and *Lorcha* surged along under only two panels of sail. I sat in the cockpit marvelling again at my perception that the faster the boat goes, the faster time goes. There's nothing boring about doing a three-hour watch in a fast-moving boat with spray flying overhead, waves to look out for, and the wind roaring behind. But sit on a boat that is doing only 20 miles a day, with the sails sullenly slatting from side to side and it's the most boring drawn-out passage imaginable. Those are the days Penny and Peter ask, "What can we do?"

"Bit brisk, isn't it?" asked Paul when he came up for his dawn watch.

The waves started breaking later on his watch and Paul decided to heave to. He turned the boat into the wind, lashed the tiller to one side, and we stopped moving forward.

I eyed the seas, the chart, and the distance we had to go. It was more comfortable sitting as we were, but we still had forty miles to cover and if we wanted to make harbour that night, we'd have to start moving soon.

"What do you think, Penny?" I asked after we had finished our breakfast. "Do you want to help me raise the sail and we'll start moving again?"

"Sure thing, Mum," said Penny, and together we fussed with the sail, tiller, and self-steering gear until *Lorcha* was surging forward. In truth, the wind had eased off a bit and the waves were no longer breaking.

"Land ho!" yelled Peter in the early afternoon.

The Cook Islands were discovered by Captain Cook in the 1770s. He charted five of the fifteen islands, but the whole group was named after him. The island we were headed for, Aitutaki, was discovered in 1789 by Captain Bligh, shortly before the *Bounty* mutineers set him adrift.

Aitutaki is a tricky landfall. The island is completely surrounded by a reef with one passage not much more than seven metres wide and two metres deep, and it has a dog-leg part-way along as well as an outflowing current that can reach 6 knots. Only shallow-draught boats and lighters make it inside the lagoon.

We made our way slowly along the surrounding reef in the late afternoon. The port side of *Lorcha* was perhaps twelve metres away from the shallow reef, the coral quite visible in the clear turquoise water. The reef dropped away quickly to starboard where the depth was perhaps thirty metres and the water a deep, dark blue. Ahead of us a freighter lay at anchor, with a lighter alongside. As we drew near, the crew of the loaded lighter waved to us and pointed to the pass. They would lead us through.

The tide was slack, and we were soon in the shallow, triangular lagoon which has a three-metre-deep anchoring pool near the small town jetty. There were two boats at anchor, both sporting Canadian flags.

Luana was from Victoria, British Columbia, with Ron and

Terry Longbottom and their four children – Debbie, sixteen, Greg, fourteen, Steven, twelve, and nine-year-old Tammy – on board. The boat name is a Hawaiian word meaning leisurely. The Longbottoms had sailed from Victoria to California and Mexico and we had been more or less following them across the South Pacific from French Polynesia.

The second boat was John Hunkin's *Zephyr v,* a twelve-metre Brandlymar ketch. John was also from Canada's west coast, but had lived in New Zealand for the last nine years, and did he have a story to tell!

"I'm here to try to take a sixteen-metre teak sailboat off the reef," he said. "She ran on the reef almost two years ago and a friend of mine bought the salvage rights. He sold off some of the equipment, but still has the masts, rigging, and sails. The boat's survived one hurricane season and is badly holed, but I think she is still salvageable."

The boat lay on its side in shallow water. John's idea was to get it upright and supported. He would then repair the two holes and attempt to roll the boat forward on lengths of coconut palm tree trunks up and over the edge of the reef.

It looked a formidable and dangerous task, but we heard from friends a year later that John and his partner, though unable to launch the boat over the lip of the reef, had managed to roll the hull ashore and make the necessary repairs. They had then trucked her to the harbour, launched her, and sailed her engineless to New Zealand, where she is presumably undergoing a splendid refit.

Some sailors will try anything.

Aitutaki was an extremely pleasant stop, especially the interesting reef-walking just a few yards from the boat. When the tide was out, the coral reef just had pools of water or was only shallowly covered. We would walk for miles over the rocky reefs, examining the marine life trapped in the pools and under rocks – including giant blue starfish and wonderfully coloured clams of all sizes – as well as finding an astounding variety of our favourite cowrie shells.

The outdoor Polynesian dancing by groups from all over the island every Friday night at the modest Rekai Hotel was the most abandoned, joyous, and vigorous dancing we had seen anywhere. We appreciated the entrenchment of island ways every time we heard the baker blow his trumpet triton shell when the new bread for the day was ready to sell.

Our stay was all too short, but we had to keep moving west. There was another island in the Cook Island group that we didn't want to miss – Palmerston.

Only about twelve to fifteen yachts stop each year at Palmerston, usually between May and November. Though Palmerston is just a few miles from the main yachting highway from French Polynesia to Tonga, the surrounding reef is difficult and shallow. If your vessel draws no more than 1.2 metres, you can get into the lagoon. If not, you have to anchor outside the reef in the open ocean, possible in good weather, but both uncomfortable and potentially dangerous.

The islanders like having visitors. When a yacht is sighted on the horizon, the young men leap into their outboard-powered skiffs, roaring out to her to plead with the surprised crew to stop, even if only for a few hours.

The palm trees of this low-lying atoll were scarcely in sight when I saw something on the horizon. It was moving so fast and throwing up such an amount of water that at first I thought it was a whale. But no, it was Tupou and Andrew Marsters, the grandson and adopted son ("feeding parents, not true parents," explained Andrew) of Joseph and Meheu Marsters of the First Family.

It seems that in 1835, a fourteen-year-old from Birmingham, William Marsters, ran away to sea on board a whaling ship. Eventually he found himself among the South Pacific atolls, where, in 1850, he married the daughter of the chief of Penryn (another island in the Cook Island group). In Polynesian fashion, he collected two other wives before he settled on the then-uninhabited Palmerston Atoll in 1860.

He had seventeen children and fifty-four grandchildren and today's sixty-one Palmerston inhabitants include Mars-

100

ters' sixth-generation descendants. Before he died, Marsters divided the main island and thirty-five motus equally among his three families, also setting up rules for intermarriage and government. The families were named the First, Second, and Third families, as they are still known today.

Tupou and Andrew tied their skiff to *Lorcha*'s stern and clambered aboard, relieved that they did not have to talk us into visiting the island. About ten minutes later, another skiff roared alongside and burly seventeen-year-old John Marsters of the Second Family came alongside.

"Just over a metre draft?" asked John cheerfully. "We should be able to take you right into the lagoon at high tide."

Never has *Lorcha* had such a trip. The two skiffs led us in, and it was not long before we started grinding over coral heads, stopping completely several times. The skiffs ahead tried to find an inch or two more water and we rocked the boat to get her through one spot, only to grind to a halt on another coral head. Two things kept us going – we knew we were going to sandblast and completely repaint the boat in New Zealand – and we kept expecting the water to deepen. It did, but only after an excruciating half-mile of scraping and dragging.

John kept shaking his head and saying (with a straight face): "There should be more water than that!"

"You are coming to my house," whispered Andrew. "John will ask you, too. But Tupou and I saw you first."

It is considered prestigious to act as host to a passing yacht, so there is lively competition to be the first to "capture" a vessel.

The island and its main village were among the prettiest we had seen, with pristine and neatly swept sparkling white coral sand pathways, a general meeting house for each of the three families, and an interesting church.

The church was built of the planks and timbers of wooden sailing ships that had foundered on Palmerston reefs. Its walls were fashioned from ships' planking, the rafters from deck beams, the shutters were ships' panelled doors, and a complete teak companionway formed the steps to the pulpit. A ship's bell signalled Sunday service.

Joseph and Meheu Marsters, a couple in their sixties, welcomed us to their house for lunch. We were astonished at what Meheu served out of her small kitchen – fish, turtle meat, pork, chicken, pumpkin boiled in coconut cream, boiled papaya, yam, greens, boiled coconut sprouts, rice, sweet bread rolls, and pastries. And the special dish? Corned beef and cabbage! This was a real delicacy to the islanders as they had so few opportunities to buy canned goods. I am sure not one of the Marsters' yachtie guests – and there had been a few – ever had the nerve to tell her that her pride-of-place dish was one that we, well, ate a lot of, to put it mildly!

The table was set for four. In Polynesia, guests are expected to eat first. Though we urged the family to share the table with us, they gently declined, and we feasted with the family waiting on us, pouring cold coconut milk into our glasses, gently waving away the flies, and all the while urging us to help ourselves.

"Do they have more in the kitchen or can we eat everything?" asked Peter in a loud whisper.

We spent that afternoon with the Marsters, talking about island life.

"And of course you must have lunch with us tomorrow, too" said Meheu, as we got ready to leave and row back to *Lorcha* in the late afternoon.

Andrew and Tupou were visiting the boat early the next morning when Paul said casually, "There's another yacht on the horizon."

The boys grabbed the binoculars, checked the yacht's position, and were off like a flash. Two sets of visitors were obviously more prestigious than one.

The yacht was New Zealand-registered *Chianti*, with a three-generation crew – John and Susan Allen with baby Jennifer, Susan's sister Wendy, and her mother, Bridget. Our hosts now had nine people for lunch and they seemed genuinely pleased. They just added more food and more chairs.

102

Everywhere we went on the island, we were asked to sit down and made welcome, whether we were watching someone build a house, fashion a canoe, feed the pigs, or women weaving pandanus leaves into mats.

On our third day, we decided to spend the morning swimming around *Lorcha* and not go ashore until afternoon. It was noon and I had just made everyone a sandwich for lunch when Tupou appeared in his skiff.

"Aren't you coming ashore?" he asked anxiously.

"I thought we'd come in this afternoon," I said. "Penny and Peter have some schoolwork to do."

"But lunch is ready," blurted out Tupou. "The family is expecting you. As long as you are on the island, you must have lunch with us *every* day. That is the custom."

We rowed ashore to our third right royal lunch with these incredibly friendly and hospitable people. It was hard to believe we were on an island where everything had to be caught, imported, or grown and where the supply ship came at irregular and infrequent intervals. Perhaps that was the point.

While we were eating, Andrew and Tupou suffered a severe disappointment. Another yacht had been sighted, and they had neither sighted it nor nabbed the crew. It was a boat that had sailed into Aitutaki just as we were about to leave, *Clypheus* with Peter and Shirley Billings on board.

This was the first time there had ever been three yachts at Palmerston – another indication of the explosion of the travelling yacht population. There are not only more yachts on the round-the-world circuit, but that circuit is broadening as more information filters into the peripatetic community about the attractions and possibilities of islands once considered remote and off the beaten track.

At lunch the subject was cyclones. One thing had been puzzling us greatly. How did people on Palmerston survive during cyclones, when the tops of coconut trees were the highest point?

"We go to Refuge Hill," explained Joseph.

We looked around in puzzlement and Joseph laughed gently.

"It is true that Refuge Hill is only six metres above the high-water mark," he said, greatly enjoying our consternation, "but the waves are sucked down by the taro swamp which stands between the beach and the hill. We can watch the whole thing from up there. If the wind and waves get too bad, we tie ourselves to the coconut trees."

"Sometimes we lose everything," said Meheu. "But we have only once ever lost a life – and that was a woman who ran back to her house to get some jewellery she had left there."

Apart from the cyclone threat, we had arrived at a tiny self-sufficient island which seemed as close to Utopia as a human community perhaps ever will get. But it is always a mistake to try to lay the cloak of perfection on anything. The islanders were currently involved in a bitter political struggle about their leadership.

William Marsters had died in 1899, and was succeeded by his eldest son, also William, who had died in 1946. The next William was a wanderer who had left the island and been away for forty years. His brother Ned had assumed the mantle of leadership until 1982. Now William Marsters (known as Reverend Bill) was back on the island once more, and the community was bitterly divided – should someone who had not lived on the island for decades become leader when he came back?

Notwithstanding the disputed leadership, Reverend Bill held the official Cook Island government titles of Chief Administrative Officer, Customs Officer, Postmaster, and Chief of Police, and was as well one of the church elders. He preached the sermon from the pulpit every Sunday, and feelings were running so high that some islanders were staying away from the services.

We talked with the eloquent Reverend Bill, but the subject was yachties, not politics. He explained why yachtsmen were made so welcome on Palmerston.

"In 1935, the island was devastated by a cyclone, and we

lost everything," he said. "Only the church and one other building, also built of heavy ships' planking, withstood the battering of the waves. The coconut palms were ruined and we produced no copra for thirty months. Ships didn't stop to bring supplies because we had nothing to sell.

"Three yachts, two American and one German, were the only boats to visit us during that time. They saw our plight and gave us virtually everything they had on board. We have never forgotten it."

Yachtsmen still try to do their bit for the islanders today, as well they might in return for the warm welcome they receive. Knowing there were no bananas on this coral atoll, we had brought three giant stalks of bananas with us as deck cargo from Aitutaki, which has many banana plantations. Paul lent his mechanical expertise to some local engine problems, and I found some fabric and some tins of the precious corned beef to give to Meheu. Joseph had an eye problem, and his eyes were very sensitive to the bright sunlight. We left him a pair of dark sunglasses. And of course we had the family out to *Lorcha* for dinner – but not every night and with only one main dish! John Allen of *Chianti* was a medical doctor and he gave his attention to some minor medical problems. Peter Billings repaired some generators and freezers. We also promised to publicize the island's school problem, which was a serious one. Although there were twenty children on the island (one-third of the population), Palmerston had had no school teacher for three years. We lined the children up for a photo and wrote an article about their plight for the *Cook Island News*, a newspaper published in Rarotonga, the capital city.

We were happy to do these small things. If yachtsmen want to maintain a warm welcome amongst remote island communities, they must find some way of reciprocating the generous hospitality that make those visits so special.

TONGA

11

The eight-hundred-mile, seven-day sail from Palmerston Atoll to the Vava'u group of Tonga was memorable because of the coconuts. Andrew, Tupou, and John had brought about forty big green ones to the boat as we were leaving and, two days out, Paul, fed-up of stepping on the hard green husks in the cockpit, gave his sailing orders:

"Everyone has to eat two coconúts a day."

Coconut milk, coconut jelly – the soft flesh of the undeveloped coconut meat – coconut chips, coconut cake, fried coconut pieces, and grated coconut sprinkled on everything: we tried them all.

Peter said that all *Clypheus*, leaving Palmerston the day after us, would have to do to find Tonga would be to follow the ocean trail of green coconut husks, as it would take several days for those empty husks to become waterlogged and sink. Penny hoped that Tonga grew a lot of other produce besides coconuts. . . .

On day six of our passage, *Lorcha* began to roll and pitch in a manner uncharacteristic for the weight of wind.

"Have a look at the chart for the depth of water," I told Penny when she complained of the motion.

"Yikes! It's 9 kilometres deep," she shouted up.

We had passed over the Capricorn Seamount, a

Trail of coconut husks . . . Friendly Islands . . .
yachting paradise . . . island feasts . . .
ceremonial funeral . . . tapa cloth . . . Tongan voices . . .
the underground oven.

---

mere 227 metres underwater, to the Tonga Trench, where the ocean floor drops steeply and dramatically to a depth of 10.6 kilometres. What maelstroms were churning up beneath us we could only imagine.

Archaeologists claim that Tonga has been inhabited since the fifth century B.C. It is the only remaining kingdom in Polynesia and the present monarchy can trace its origins from the Tu'i Tonga who ruled the kingdom more than a thousand years ago. At the height of its influence in the thirteenth century, the power of the Tongan monarchy extended as far as Hawaii.

There are 169 islands in the group, 45 of them inhabited. The islands are grouped in three clusters, with two-thirds of the population living in the northern Vava'u group, usually the first destination of westward-bound yachts. Tongatapu in the south is where the capital and government is based, and the least visited group, the Ha'apai with its low-lying atolls and active volcanoes, is in the middle. It was near this middle group in 1789 that the mutiny took place on the *Bounty*.

The first Europeans to sight the Tongan archipelago were the Dutch navigators, Shouten and Lemaire, in 1616, while the main island, Tongatapu, was first visited by the Dutch explorer, Abel Tasman (after whom Tasmania was named), in 1643. Continual contact with Europeans did not begin until more than a century later when Captain Cook explored the islands, bestowing upon them the name that is still used today (accompanied by a smile of remembrance from anyone who has been there) – the "Friendly Islands."

We approached the western corner of Vava'u at midnight, glad of the bright full moon and clear skies. We made our way slowly and carefully through the deeper channels, conscious that we were in coral-strewn waters. Our charts showed an anchorage called Port Refuge, but we either missed it or misjudged it; though we approached the indent where Port Refuge should have been several times, the water shoaled too quickly for our liking and we headed into the safety of the channel again. We sailed slowly on, turning into the channel for Neiafu, the capital and main anchorage for Vava'u. By now it was one o'clock in the morning and there was not a glimmer of light to be seen anywhere. The channel was deep, but, with high hills on three sides of us and unable to see what lay directly ahead, we did the sensible thing: we simply made our way to where we judged the edge of the channel lay and put out an anchor. We tumbled into our separate bunks (Penny and Peter were already sound asleep in theirs) for our first full night's sleep in a week, although Paul remained nervous enough to slip up on deck for a quick look around and check on the anchor at four o'clock in the morning.

As soon as the sun came over the horizon, we upped anchor to continue into the main anchorage, which looked more like a pleasant inland lake with hills rolling down softly to the water's edge on all sides, the contours of the hills behind us masking the wide channel entrance. It was as safe and protected a harbour as we have ever been in.

Lorcha's distinctive rectangular red sail made her instantly recognizable, and, as we headed for the Customs and Immigration Dock (the sign was large), there was a call on the VHF.

"*Lorcha, Lorcha, Lorcha*, this is *Challenger*, do you copy?"

Penny charged down the companionway to grab the microphone.

"This is *Lorcha*. Change to channel 70, please."

"Glad to see you made it safely," said Ian Carlin. We had

first met Ian, his wife Nauri, and their infant son Roger in Papeete. "Tell your mum and dad that the customs office is closed on weekends. Why don't you just make your way over and raft alongside? We've just put the kettle on."

"Sounds good to me," Paul said, looking down the harbour at the dozen yachts at anchor about half a mile away. "Penny, tell Ian we're on our way."

Ten minutes later, Ian was taking our bow line, and Penny had hopped onto *Challenger*'s deck to tie our stern line to *Challenger*'s stern. There was no need these days to check any knots that either Penny or Peter had tied. Such activity had become second nature to them; they were more likely to hear a howl of criticism from each other than from their parents if ever a rope was tied incorrectly.

Soon the adults were sitting in *Challenger*'s cockpit, exchanging voyaging stories and eager to learn about this new country, while Penny and Peter, after a quick hello to Roger, now eighteen months old, slipped over the side into crystal-clear, turquoise water.

"Tonga probably comes closest to anybody's idea of a yachting paradise," said Nauri, cutting up a fresh papaya and pouring tea. "There's this safe anchorage, fresh food and water within easy reach, the Polynesian culture here is interesting and intact and the islanders are friendly and outgoing. As soon as you anchor properly, you'll have visitors. And there's lots of anchorages close by. A few of us are going for a barbecue lunch on a sandspit just an hour-and-a-half's sail from here. Why don't you join us?"

"Sounds great, except that we haven't got anything to barbecue," I said. "We've just about forgotten what fresh meat tastes like."

"Share ours," said Nauri. "Do sausages sound good to you?"

An hour later we got Penny and Peter out of the water, both of them exclaiming about how much marine life they could see, and our two boats were setting sail for the tiny uninhabited island that the yachties had claimed for weekly barbecues. I baked some corn bread on the way and, after anchoring, we spent a pleasant few hours on the beach, the adults lazily cooking and chatting, the children once again in the water. We may not have had any fresh meat, but when we produced potatoes wrapped in foil for the barbecue, it was almost as good.

"Where did you bring those from?" asked Nauri, in astonishment. "Potatoes cost a fortune here – if you can find them."

"From Panama," I said. "But we're running low."

As we came alongside the customs building the next morning, Isaah (very few of the islanders ever gave us their last names, so first names will have to suffice) took our lines.

"I have an invitation for you," called this dark-skinned man who never stopped smiling. "Would you like to come to my island feast on Saturday?"

Ian and Nauri had given us a lot of information about Tonga, but somehow they had omitted to mention the feasts.

"That sounds great," I said. "Come on board and tell us more."

"No, I'll row out to your boat later," said Isaah. "I know you would like some fruit, so I'll get that first."

The wily Isaah was mixing island tradition (Tongan feasts) with the ways of the west (commercial marketing). His "invitation" was not quite what we'd understand as an invitation: the feast would be a paying affair. In the two hours we were at the customs dock, we received no less than three "invitations" to feasts, all for the following Saturday.

But Isaah knew how to clinch a deal. That afternoon he paddled out to *Lorcha* in a canoe, the gunwales of which were scarcely above the water, loaded with twenty large papayas. Then he produced a logbook dating back to 1984, full of comments from other yachties about his feasts, comments such as: "Great food," "Terrific dancing," and "Best feast on the island." We recognized the names of some yachts we knew.

"My feast is on the beach in a very nice setting with the cliffs behind," explained Isaah. "It will take you about an hour to sail there.

"It is $10 each," he continued, adding quickly, "but even though Peter will probably eat a lot, I will make no charge for him."

Now, all this might sound pushy and commercial, but Isaah was trying so hard to please and was so cheerful and friendly that it didn't seem that way. We admired his spirit and enterprise, for Tongans are not rich people.

Then he added the capper.

"If you anchor overnight in the bay," he said, "I will pick you up in the morning and we can all go to Sunday church services. Afterwards my wife would be happy to welcome you to our house for lunch."

We waited for the addendum of, "and that will be another $10," but it never came. In the west, we would perhaps think of this as good marketing, but in Tonga, it was the island way of combining commerce with genuine hospitality.

The crews of about seven yachts had elected to go to Isaah's feast, held, appropriately enough, on Isaah's Beach (was there no end to this man's marketing skills?) and you might think we would be happy to go ashore in shorts and shirts in the tropical heat. But the Tongans are modest people – though shoulders can be bare, thighs must always be covered – to the extent that when Tongan women go bathing, they do so fully dressed.

We arrived at the anchorage off the beach at about five o'clock, and, dressed in long skirts and pants, we rowed to shore where we could see some thatched roofs. A long length of plaited pandanus-leaf mats on the sand under the roofs served as table and chairs. Isaah's extended family outnumbered the thirty or so guests (which included some tourists other than yachties). The backdrop to the food and cold fruit juices – to the utter delight of Penny and Peter – was Tongan handicrafts and the craftsmen, who were working on and displaying carvings, shells, woven mats, and jewellery. Apart from their presence, however, there was no "sell."

The entire feast had been cooked in the *umu*, the traditional Polynesian underground oven. A hole is dug into which firewood is thrown and set alight. On top of the wood are laid coral stones. These are heated and the various foods, wrapped in protective banana leaves, are placed on top of the hot stones. Finally the oven is sealed with earth. It does not take long for the food to cook, and it is delicious, retaining full flavour, rather like the food baked in a clay oven. Isaah's menu included taro, yams and other root crops, and specialty dishes like small clams, lobster, pork, and fish wrapped in coconut pulp, and papaya cooked in coconut juice. We ate with our fingers, enjoying each new taste, guitars and drums playing in the background and the sky taking on its night hues as the sun set behind our anchored boats.

Now it was time for Isaah's nieces to dance for us. No hotel floor-show this, but rather appealing as four young girls in home-made long grass skirts, arms glistening with coconut oil, performed traditional dances under the light of the moon.

We rowed back to *Lorcha* at about midnight to discuss the only real commercial issue at hand. In examining the crafts and picking out some woven bracelets (Penny) and unusual cowrie shells (Peter), the kids had come to the conclusion that they needed to start managing their own money. We settled on a figure. From now on, they would get a dollar a week each as pocket money.

A couple of days later, we were anchored at one of our favourite spots, Port Maurelle at the island of Kapa. Fishing was good everywhere in Tonga, but at this particular spot, Peter discovered that when we threw the dishwater overboard he didn't need to bait his hook to catch a meal. So many fish were vying for the food particles, they grabbed his bare hook – enough for a luncheon panful if he was quick!

That particular morning, we also noticed that an unusual number of people were walking in the direction of the village of Falevai. The people were dressed in black with their *ta'ovalas* (a mat worn around the waist) extra long, sweeping the ground.

Our curiosity aroused, we rowed ashore to see what was

112

happening. A group of islanders told us that the island chief, Faka Tulola, had died the day before and that funeral ceremonies were in progress.

"People from all the islands will be going," said our informant. "Faka Tulola was of royal blood so the ceremonies will last at least a week. You may like to come, too," he added hesitantly.

In North America, it would be an imposition to go to the funeral of an unknown person, but the Tongan tradition is different. Though the death of anyone is an emotional event, the funeral is also a celebration, and the more people that attend the more honoured that person becomes in the eyes of the community. It is also an occasion for traditional ceremonies performed only at funerals for important people. "Are you *sure* it will be all right if we come today?" we double-checked.

Everyone in the group nodded vigorously. "The family would be honoured," said the spokesperson positively. The four of us hurried back to *Lorcha* to change into more subdued and modest clothing before making our way along the two-kilometre path through pine, papaya, and banana trees to Falevai.

The little village, usually of about 160, was bursting at the seams. There were already about 300 visitors from other villages and more people were arriving by the boatload. Much as we would have liked to blend into the background and watch inconspicuously, this was not possible: we were the only *papalangi* (white people) there.

We walked down to the beach where a huge open-air kitchen had been set up. Women were stirring big cauldrons on open fires and men were cleaning fish. All along the beach there were scenes of bustling activity as food, people, and gifts were carried ashore from boats. We were accepted and treated as all the other visitors, people coming over to ask where we were from, to give a hot deep-fried goodie to Penny or Peter, and working naturally to include us in the activities as far as this was possible.

113

"Would you like to sit down and help me make a basket for the food?" said one friendly lady to Penny, who was watching intently as she magically wove pandanus leaves into a sturdy green basket. "I have to make a few dozen to help serve the food at the feast tomorrow." It was the friendly invitation of any mother who sees a curious child nearby. I left Penny absorbed in the intricacies of basket-weaving, knowing that she was genuinely eager to learn and that she understood this was a solemn day and would conduct herself with propriety – not bad for a nine-year-old.

Paul and Peter had wandered off to talk to some of the men by the boats along the beach, and I walked a few steps to the open-air kitchen to talk to a lady named Vivian as she stirred a cauldron of boiling fat.

"The big feast will be tomorrow," she said, in the sing-song English of a Polynesian uncomfortable not speaking her mother tongue. "But we must cook every day as it is our custom to offer a meal to all visitors who come to pay their respects. We are happy you are here with us and we hope you will return tomorrow."

Our welcome was officially ensured when one of the village headmen, Hermani, came over.

"I know that many people have spoken with you," he said. "I would like to add my welcome and to offer you my house if you want to rest" – he pointed to a big house in the distance – "and also to ask you to remain with us as long as you want."

Men seated cross-legged on straw mats under the shade of tarpaulins strung between trees were drinking *kava*, the Tongan national drink. Kava, a mild narcotic, is made in a large hand-hewn wooden bowl by soaking and then straining out the pounded roots of the pepper bush. It takes on ceremonial importance on occasions such as this, when it is always made by a woman but drunk only by men. The kava drinkers on this occasion were village elders who had gathered to accept gifts brought by visiting villagers for the dead man's family. The spokesman presented his gifts – ranging from whole pigs to

114

fifty-kilo sacks of root vegetables to cloth and cigarettes – to the circle of elders. An important part of the proceedings was a dialogue between the presenter and the elders describing the gifts and their relevance to the dead man and telling stories of the dead man's life. Though we could not understand the words, it was interesting to see how the solemn occasion was tempered by fond memories and humorous tales. There were some shaky voices, but the feeling was one of the joy of story-telling and remembrance. After each family, represented by the man doing the talking, had made its presentation, the elders would thank them for their participation and kava in a coconut half-shell would be distributed around the circle.

Paul sat among the men outside the main circle, where he could feel he was among the close observers. Noting that the only woman there was the kava-maker, I observed from the shade of a nearby tree, and Penny and Peter wandered about with other children.

The gift presented with the most ceremony was the tapa cloth made from the bark of the paper mulberry tree, layered and pounded until a sort of felt is formed. It is painted with natural dyes obtained from boiling the roots of the mangrove tree, in striking patterns of brown and black. The colour of the dyes depends on how long the roots were boiled. Tapa cloth is a mainstay of Tongan life and is featured at weddings and funerals, with different designs applied for the appropriate occasion. Tapas are often used as blankets or room dividers, but here we were seeing special tapas, made with patterns used only for royalty. The large panels, suspended from bamboo poles so they could be admired by all when presented to the elders, eventually would be hung alongside the grave during the interment ceremonies, then divided among the closest female relatives of the dead man.

About mid-afternoon, Hermani singled us out again, pressing upon us that visitors must eat with their hosts and leading us to one of the many long temporary tables set up under thatch shades. Those already seated simply moved along to make room and we were served bowls of curried goat and large chunks of cooked taro and yam.

"You must come back tomorrow," said Hermani earnestly. "We have ceremonies for many days, but tomorrow is the most important because we must bury our Chief."

Though we didn't know the dead man or his family and the death meant little to us personally, we had been drawn into the spirit of the ceremony at this village. We had been planning on visiting another island the following day, but we felt now that it would be rude if we didn't return. And we were glad we did, because it was a day of memorable images.

The first was of the thousand or so mourners, seated along the beach under the trees, the ocean at their backs as they faced the raised burial ground. Around the newly dug grave stood Faka Tulola's immediate family, the women with their long hair hanging loose and uncombed to signify grief. The band, a children's choir, and important mourners sat at the front. Noble and important government officials were in attendance and thirteen Protestant church ministers were lined up facing the huge crowd. It was as dignified and royal a spectacle as we had ever witnessed. And when those thousand voices were raised in song, they created a sound that the best-known choirs in the world would like to emulate. During the entire four-hour ceremony, we sat engrossed, as did Penny and Peter, carefully watching the people around us to know when to stand, our bodies swaying to the music like everyone else's.

At one point I saw Hermani edging towards us from the front of the crowd. I was fearful we had done something wrong, but it was nothing like that.

"Please help us," he whispered passionately. "We have run out of film and I must have photographs so everyone will always remember this day. Will you take some pictures for us?"

I was glad to do so – especially of the feast preparations that followed.

116

"It will be a long time before there will be another feast as big as this one," said Hermani as he led us to a nearby field after the interment ceremonies. We were astonished. This umu was about three metres wide and at least fifteen metres long. About a thousand kilograms of root crops had been laid on banana leaves on the hot coral rocks. Next came the meat from eight horses and eleven cows and twenty-four whole pigs. More banana leaves and palm fronds had been laid on the food to protect it and then sheets of corrugated iron. Finally, earth sealed the umu.

We arrived in time to witness the Dantéesque scene of the villagers opening the immense oven. Barefooted men hopped about as they shovelled off the hot earth and tried to avoid the steam which rose in clouds around them, in what almost seemed like a ceremonial dance. Everyone was chattering and cheering as each new layer of food was made visible. Penny and Peter were soon hopping around with everyone else; we had to hold them back as they gave little thought about how hot that oven area really was. And through it all I was taking photographs.

Palm fronds had been laid on the ground to lay the steaming food on. The cut-up beef and horse meat, the whole pigs, and the vegetables were placed in the newly made pandanus baskets (including the one Penny had helped with) and carried by hand about two hundred metres to the waiting tables.

It was very late in the day; time to return to our little floating home, leaving the friendly villagers to their feasting. They would be celebrating long into the night, but Penny and Peter were ready for bed, their minds filled with the images of a very different day on a remote South Pacific island.

REEF WALKING AND COLLECTING SHELLS 12

"Oh, Daddy, look," said an excited Penny. "*Cypraea punctata!*"

It seems that when our curious children become interested in a subject, even one so broad as sea-shell collecting, half measures won't do. They want to become experts. Penny and Peter weren't content to have a few pretty shells decorating the boat; they wanted a full collection of several of each species.

We had first begun picking up nice-looking shells when we landed on islands in the Atlantic. It wasn't until we were well into the lower Caribbean, however, that the full possibilities of shell-collecting were spread before us. As well as the well-known large edible conch of these islands, there were many, many other glossy collectible shells. By the time we were sailing among the Pacific islands, our library of sea-shell reference books had grown, as had our knowledge of the relative rarity of various species and where to find them.

The animal kingdom is divided into a number of major groups called *phyla*. The phylum Mollusca, one of the oldest and largest groups, comprises soft-bodied animals which have, in most cases, a hard external skeletal covering known as a shell. Over a hundred thousand species of mollusks are known, ranging from scarcely visible sea snails to giant

Shell collecting . . . kinds of shells . . . preparations for
reef walking . . . collecting dangers . . . tidal pool of life . . .
olive shells . . . Peter's pets . . . trading . . .
encyclopedia Penny . . . giant clam shells.

---

squid over fifteen metres long. Of the seven different classes of Mollusca, the shells from the animals of the class Gastropoda are most sought after by amateur collectors. These include the most colourful and showy of the mollusk shells. They range in colour from the pure porcelain white of the Ovulidae through shades of rose, tan, lavender, gold, blue, and green to the dark, almost black of the olividae. In size they range from small cowries and mitres of hardly twelve millimetres long to the *Syrinx aruanus*, of which specimens are often found measuring up to sixty centimetres. They are classified in shape as spirally coiled and snail-like, but in some families, such as the Ovulidae and the Cypraeidae – the ovulas and cowries – the spiral has all but disappeared, the shells having evolved into an elegantly rounded shape.

"Can we go walking on the reef today?" was a plea often heard, especially when Fiona announced that schoolwork would begin right after breakfast.

Walking on the reefs, especially early in the morning and at low tide, is the best way to see mollusks in their natural setting, but unless you are in a fairly isolated anchorage, the local people will have taken most of the specimens.

The schoolwork would be tackled with eagerness when the carrot of a few hours of reef-walking was dangled before our active children, especially when there was some new reef to explore. "We'll set off from *Lorcha* about an hour before low tide," I'd say, and then I'd begin the formidable task of gathering our equipment. Even such a seemingly safe outing requires preparation and some caution in the tropics.

We would be out in the tropical sun for several hours, so sun block cream, hats, and long-sleeved cotton shirts were necessary. Plastic sandals or rubber-soled canvas shoes had to be worn to protect feet from coral cuts and abrasions which can cause painful swellings and infections. People from cooler climes are, for some inexplicable reason, more susceptible to the minor irritant poisons of echinoderms (spiny sea urchins), some soft and semi-soft corals, sea anemones, and some of the other marine life abundant in these waters. Anyone who is going to turn over coral rubble (likely the stronger people on the excursion) should have gloves to protect their hands. They should also return the rubble to its original position, as many egg sacs may be clinging to the underside. We each carry kitchen tongs. These are for lifting interesting specimens from crevices to see what they are and to check whether they are alive or an abandoned shell. Many mollusks are poisonous, with venomous barbs able to inflict a deadly sting. Thus, unless a reef-walker is experienced enough to be sure of the species, shells should never be picked up with bare hands. Deaths have been caused by members of the family Conidae (cone shells), a common species throughout the Pacific and Indian ocean regions.

The children knew that they must not grab at a colourful specimen tumbling down a crevice. Many varieties of sea snakes live in sandy-bottomed reef areas. They are near relatives of the cobra, and all of them are venomous, though not aggressive; given half a chance they will flee and hide in another crevice. Many sea snakes lay their eggs in the sand at the edge of inter-tidal zones, so the youngsters of these snakes are often seen. Deaths have been reported from sea snake bites, but the venom is slow acting and rarely fatal.

Another danger is the many small eels which can inflict a painful bite. They live under coral rubble and in small holes in the coral, but they are not aggressive as long as hands are not suddenly thrust into their holes.

Next I'd find a couple of buckets to hold any interesting findings, before digging up the snorkeling gear in case the reef-walking was not up to expectations and a wider-ranging expedition was needed . . . the dinghy would be nearly full before the crew was even aboard.

We all decided early on in our shell-collecting that we would not collect any live specimens. This is the opposite of what a serious collector would do. Specimens from which the animal has been removed after being boiled have the glossiest shells, but we did not want to teach Penny and Peter to have this sort of disregard for life. Anyway, from a purely practical point of view, cleaning live specimens is a smelly and time-consuming task.

We look for empty shells in good condition, and we are not above evacuating a hermit crab if he has chosen a nice home. (Hermit crabs are small crabs common world-wide. They inhabit empty shells as protection. As the crab grows he abandons one tight-fitting shell and looks for another that fits him better.) We whistle at the opening of the shell, the hermit crab peeks out, and we grasp his pincers and pull gently. He can easily move on to another shell.

But what fun it is to walk the reef! Tide pools are full of a colourful array of darting fishes and small crabs slowly backing away, pincers raised ready to ward off an attack. Sea anemones with all the colours of a flower bed sway in time to the wash of waves rather than to the wind. An overturned coral rock might have the children skipping about as an eel snakes between their legs, escaping fluidly to the sanctuary of another rock. We have seen spiny crayfish (a type of lobster) only five centimetres long ogle us in the startling sunlight before backing away. We have found octopus so small that they squirm on a finger tip, changing colour from grey to pink to mottled brown as they try to work their way to a hideout.

The profusion of life between the high-tide line and the

121

low-tide line in tropical waters, especially in areas hardly disturbed by man, has to be seen to be believed. Mollusks are everywhere, but it takes a trained eye to find many of them. For some, their colour is their camouflage in a world of waving shapes and textures. Others are covered with sea growth, rendering them indistinguishable from the pebble beside them.

Many mollusks are voracious carnivores who hunt at night. They drill neat holes through the shells of their prey, usually smaller snails or clams, to rasp out the meat, though some gastropods, such as the cones, prey on marine worms and small fish. In the early morning a track on the sandy bottom might end suddenly. Dig a few inches into the sand with your tongs and you'll find a gleaming, glossy olive shell, or the long spike of an auger shell decorated in orange and cream.

We became particularly fond of the live olives. They have a high-gloss shell because when they move they spread their shine-producing mantle over their shell. Dug from its sandy daylight refuge, the little creature will quickly emerge from its shell to spread its mantle and crawl on your hand. Olives seem friendly, though their crawling about may simply indicate a need to retreat to find a new dark and wet place.

Many times we took live mollusks back to the boat in our buckets to be observed – not only by Penny and Peter, but by Fiona and I as well. A good mixture of snails, some hermit crabs in various shells, some cowries sporting interesting mantles, an olive or two, and perhaps a few empty shells and coral bits makes for a fascinating aquarium. We put them in our wide-bottomed plastic baby bath, which also did duty as a laundry tub. With about ten centimetres of fresh sea water in it (changed often to keep it cool with a high level of oxygen), and kept in the shade of the cockpit awning, it became a sea in microcosm. We watched hermit crabs try on different shells, looking for a good fit as if shopping for a new pair of shoes. The cowries and olives spread their mantles for us in displays rarely seen in the wild.

What amazed us most was Peter's uncanny affinity with

these animals. He'd call them, caress them, and speak to them for hours, and then show us how they responded to his bidding, climbing on his fingers and shyly extending their heads or spreading their mantles over their shells as he cooed and clucked to them.

We usually kept the animals on board for a few hours before returning them to the same area of reef we had found them in. If we kept them overnight we had to be sure to put a porous cover over the baby bath to prevent fatal wanderings into the recesses of the boat.

Much of our shell collection was bought or traded from islanders. Often as *Lorcha* settled into a new anchorage, a dugout canoe manned by a few small children would be paddled out to her. Courtesies would be exchanged, our questions would elicit some shy responses, and a basket or bag of shells would be produced and dumped on the side deck. Picking through, we might find a new species, or discover a particularly nice gem-condition shell to upgrade our collection, and the trading would begin.

We were always surprised when isolated islanders far from tourist markets knew the relative rarity of shells and had a good grasp of their value. Could they have the same reference books as we did?

By the time we reached the Vava'u island group of northern Tonga, we were eager reef walkers and shell collectors. Studious Penny became our expert, quoting at the drop of a shell the Latin names for family and species. She meticulously sorted and labelled our collection with the common and scientific names, the dates and places the shells were found or purchased, and whether they were rare, uncommon, or common shells. She seemed to have a computerized list in her head. When presented with any shell she would accurately state if we already had it, how many we had, and their condition relative to the one in front of her. This encyclopedic knowledge of mollusks ensured that Penny was always in demand to look over the shell collections of other yachtsmen.

Our food locker was being filled with shells. As we removed

tins, shells took their place. What would happen when it was time to restock?

One day we dinghied over to the fishing co-operative at Neiafu, the main village of the Vava'u group, to buy some fresh fish. There at the landing stage lay some shells of the giant clam, a delicacy in these islands. The shells of these clams can grow to more than a metre across. I saw Fiona and the children eyeing the largest, appraising its size and beauty. Horrified, I gasped, "No!"

The pleading and wingeing began.

"Daddy, I'll empty some of my book locker," said Penny.

"One-half can stay under the foot of my bunk, down by my toys," said Peter.

"Oh, come on," said an impatient Fiona. "We'll never have such a good chance for such a nice specimen so close to *Lorcha*. Peter," she continued decisively, "pick up that one and put it in the dinghy."

A happy Peter darted to the shell and grasped its rim. It wouldn't budge. He grunted and groaned, but couldn't lift it. Fiona thought he was just pretending and marched over to claim our prize. No luck, but the astonished look on her face was my reward. I got out of the dinghy to hoist this great lump of white calcified material into our small vessel. It was like lifting water-logged concrete blocks!

After allowing the two halves to drain and dry on deck for a few days, I stored the clam shells under the kids' bunks, down low where ballast belongs.

All I could think of was *Lorcha's* disappearing waterline as she settled ever lower in the water, loaded with these non-essential (but, I must admit, delightfully interesting) items.

TONGATAPU TO NEW ZEALAND

13

*L*orcha with crew on board for an ocean voyage? Wouldn't our four-berth, nine-metre boat be a little crowded? But it was Toni Woodman, not overcrowding, that was our main consideration.

We had met fifty-three-year old Toni in Panama, where she was crewing aboard an Australian boat, *Sounion*. She had acted as a line handler on *Lorcha* through the Panama Canal. We had met up with her again on various occasions while crossing the South Pacific, usually on a different boat from the one we had last seen her on.

This remarkably independent American grandmother had, in fact, boat-hiked more than half-way around the world for her ultimate destination, Australia.

Now she was in Nuka Alofa, again looking for passage on a yacht, this time headed for New Zealand.

But on this particular morning, she happened to be in Nuka Alofa's police station where we were checking out with immigration officials. The previous evening she had been threatened by a knife-wielding man. To get away she had thrown her handbag at the man and then, as she put it, "I ran for my life."

The Tongan officials were almost as shaken as she was. The Friendly Islanders are a gentle people, and this was the first time such an incident had

Toni Woodman . . . we take on crew . . . good-bye Tonga . . .
the big wahoo . . . dried fish . . . our calmest crossing . . .
Toni's tale . . . we pick up a buoy . . . a magical
New Zealand arrival . . . eyes in the sky.

---

ever been reported. That didn't make it any easier for Toni.
She hated to make a fuss.

To cap it all, she was dubious about the boat on which a
father and son combo had tentatively offered her passage to
New Zealand.

"I'm not altogether comfortable about going with this
boat," she told us. "The skipper has twice joked to someone
else when I've been around about needing to get laid. I'm
interested in crewing, not coupling, but it's the only boat with
space available going to New Zealand this week. After yesterday's incident I want to leave here, as I'm really upset, but I
don't want to have to contend with an unpleasant situation on
the way to New Zealand, either."

We were just completing our official clearance out of
Tonga, headed for New Zealand that afternoon, and though
we hadn't planned on taking crew, impulsively I said: "Toni,
put us on your alternate list. If you'd like to sail with us, I'm
sure we could work it out. There are only four berths, but as
someone's on watch all the time, it just means we rotate the
sleeping spaces. And I'd like to try an ocean passage where I
get to sleep for six hours at a stretch. Penny and Peter would
probably get a lot more attention, too. But make up your mind
soon – we're sailing this afternoon."

It didn't take Toni long. Two hours later, she tossed her bags
into the cockpit.

"I'd never have asked you if I could come," she said. "You
can obviously cope, and I like to crew on boats where I'm

needed. But if I can do watches and help with the kids, that sounds great."

Time was when Tongan officials were relaxed about when yachts sailed out of harbour after official clearance. This very much suited the yachties because we could do our checking out, shop for fresh fruit, vegetables, and bread, have a good night's sleep, and then go on our way the next day. But some yachts are regrettably short-sighted in their compliance with official regulations. A Californian vessel had stayed in Tongan waters an unwarranted three weeks after she had obtained official clearance. Unfortunately she had gone aground on a reef about a hundred miles south of Tonga and had radioed Nuka Alofa for assistance. It was not hard for the Tongan officials to realize that a yacht that has travelled a hundred miles in three weeks has had to be anchored somewhere in their territory. Now there was no leeway for any yacht. You had to leave within a few hours of clearing, and certainly on the same day.

We stowed Toni's gifts of papaya and pineapple and found a place for her two small kitbags – her total possessions. We checked that she had gone through the formalities of obtaining a visa for New Zealand and that she still had a valid passport. Taking her with us meant adding her name to the number of people on board *Lorcha* and amending our crew list with the Tongan authorities. We didn't want there to be any surprises when we arrived with five people on board in New Zealand, a country known to have rigid entry formalities.

Had we been taking on a stranger as crew, we would have checked personal references, asked for a deposit to cover that person's air fare from our next port of call to the person's country of origin, and we would also have held the new crew member's passport until we had cleared both ship and ship's personnel into the next country. It behooves both ship master and crew to check carefully. Though things usually work out, there are strange tales on the international circuit of short-handed vessels disappearing after they have taken on crew. (Is this a new form of piracy?) Or on reaching his destination the

128

skipper finds his new crew member can't support himself and has to be deported home – at the captain's expense. There are no statistics, but even a few strange stories show that the unwary – crew or captain – can get into trouble.

We left harbour at 1400 for the twelve-hundred-mile passage to New Zealand. Penny and Peter, always a gregarious twosome, were especially pleased about having another adult on board. They know only too well how preoccupied and fatigued Paul and I get on long passages, so having another person to play card games or Chinese checkers seemed heaven to them.

The passage down to New Zealand is usually a mixed weather passage, with those in the know predicting "a gale there and a gale back." ("Back" meaning when you sail north again after having spent the cyclone season in New Zealand.) But rather than heavy weather, we were to find this a slow, light-wind passage.

There was so little wind we motored and hand-steered for the first twenty-five hours. But with an extra hand to take a three-hour watch, and a six-hour sleep period at night, Paul and I felt good. The seas were so calm, neither Penny nor I were seasick, and we even put out the trolling line with our favourite plastic red squid lure on the second day, hooking a 1.3-metre wahoo, our biggest catch to date. Paul filleted the fish as usual, but there was so much meat on it we decided to try drying it. Toni had a great idea. Instead of hanging the flesh up in strips to dry, she suggested we lay it out on sheets of aluminum foil, turning the strips every few hours. At night when we brought it inside, all we had to do was roll up the aluminum foil, and in the morning it was a simple matter to roll the sheets out again. Two days of bright sunshine and our dried fish was ready to store. It became Penny and Peter's favourite snack food.

We were moving slowly, sails slatting unremittingly, but Toni's presence was a catalyst for all of us. She never sat back and did nothing; on her off-watch she spent hours with Penny and Peter. She loved to paint and soon had the kids sketching

129

and handling paints in a way they had never learned before. Painting each day now became something they enjoyed. Penny and Peter were as interested in Toni's previous exploits as we were and conversation was never lacking or dull.

One night I sat with Toni for a while after she relieved me from my watch. I was curious about the reactions of the men Toni had sailed with in her two-and-a-half years of boat-hiking. Was she looking for romance?

Toni laughed. "First of all," she said, "you have to understand I'm a very self-sufficient person. My goal for a long time has been to travel and experience different cultures. I'm not looking for romance or affairs. I know what I want from life and people and I have good judgement. It's no accident I'm sailing on *Lorcha* with you people, not on that other boat."

"But how about all those male single-handers you've crewed for?" I countered. Of the seven boats she had sailed on, four had been single-handers, men from Australia, Norway, and Sweden. "How did you cope with that – and why those boats?"

"Well," said Toni, settling down into the corner of the cockpit. "You'd have to know about the single-handers I didn't go with. The ones I chose were people I felt wanted crew, not a sexual relationship. Also if there is only one other person on the boat, you have to do your share of work. I learned a lot and only once felt uncomfortable about my choice. That skipper took the attitude mid-ocean that as we were the only man and woman for miles around, we might as well have a kiss and a cuddle. He didn't force the issue when I said no – though he did say he didn't know what I was, but I certainly wasn't a woman!"

Sitting under the stars that night, Toni told me the rest of her story. At age eighteen, she had gone to Alaska where she had met her first husband. He was a fisherman and Toni was one of the first women in Alaska to work on a partnership basis with her husband, going out fishing with him in all conditions. The couple had had two children, but separated after twelve years.

"That left me with the kids to bring up on my own," said Toni. "I worked pretty hard at that, but promised myself one day I'd be free to travel around the world."

That commitment was almost broken when she married for a second time.

"My second husband was a great guy," said Toni. "And I was deeply in love with him – but I also knew I would begin travelling when my youngest reached eighteen. This was a real dilemma as he'd be that age in three years, but my second husband's two kids were much younger."

It would take a very strong woman to do what Toni did.

"I'll marry you for three years, I told him. After that, we'll get a divorce. I have to travel, and I know you have to stay with your kids."

All Toni's friends said she wouldn't do it, but four years later she was on her own, divorced and travelling.

"It was hard," she said quietly. "Very hard. We were both upset when we parted, but I had to follow my life. I'll never forget Ray. He's a very special person, but I was glad when he remarried two years ago. He deserved that."

It was an exceptional night, with an exceptional person, sitting there in *Lorcha*'s cockpit, miles out on the ocean with only the two of us to hear the intimacies exchanged. What was it that had brought us together to share our lives like this? It was strange to look back and to think that twenty years previously neither of us would have known a sloop from a junk, and we would never have had a vision of ourselves some day being ocean sailors.

Well, I wouldn't get my precious six hours' sleep chatting in the cockpit with Toni. Knowing there were many days of voyaging yet to come, I went below, leaving Toni on watch.

This passage seemed to have a kind of magic around it. We continued to drift along in light winds, often sailing slowly during the day, but motoring at night, as it was easier to sleep to the sound of the engine than to the slatting of the sail. We weren't fretting about the days when we only made good fifty to sixty-five miles because we weren't as tired as we normally were. With the additional crew there was more time to bake goodies like banana bread and chocolate cake, too.

We were in fish-rich waters and the slow-moving boat attracted all kinds of marine life to its shadow. One day, we watched six brightly coloured dorado fish playing around the hull. Quite near them were a school of small striped fish. We kept waiting for the dorado to attack them, but they must have fed recently because they ignored the meal swimming so close. Pelagic fish seemed to be there for the taking, and by the fifth day, when we had eaten our reserves of wahoo, we put the fishing line out again and caught a fat skipjack tuna using the same red plastic squid lure. The fish put up a tremendous fight, running the length of the sixty-metre line three times before Paul was able to haul it in. When we took the hook out of its mouth in the cockpit, we found a still-struggling live squid which Peter immediately freed, throwing the little creature back into the ocean. "There you are, little squid," he shouted. "Live to tell of another day."

Little good it did the squid. A dorado raced out from under the hull and seized the hapless squid as it hit the water, leaving it no time to celebrate what it must have thought was an amazing second chance.

"Bother," said Peter crossly, screwing up his nose in a gesture of helplessness.

It wasn't till day seven that we had a sustained wind; the sails were filled all day for two days. With every mile we were making southwards, it was getting cooler, and we soon began to need sweaters and jackets during night watches.

On day ten we had a different bit of excitement – something pink was bobbing in the ocean ahead of us. Paul reefed the sail, Toni and the kids stood at the bow with the boathook, and I rushed down the companionway for the camera. The object was a round inflated pink plastic fishnet buoy about one metre in diameter. It must have been drifting with the

132

ocean currents for a couple of years, and when we hauled it on deck the disgusting-looking goose neck barnacles were about twenty centimetres long – the longest we had ever seen. We scraped the barnacles off and tied our prize on deck. It was worth perhaps only $100, but the excitement for us was in spotting it and then hauling it on board. It's unusual to see anything man-made and worth retrieving when far at sea. In New Zealand, we gave our float to our friends on the fifteen-metre *Gai Charisma* to use as a fender. We celebrated our find that evening with home-baked (what else?) pizza and fresh tomatoes and cucumber, followed by peaches and cream.

Our last few days alternated between high winds and rain during the day, and flat calm at night, which would set us motoring again. We had never before done so much motoring on a passage.

On the evening of our fourteenth day we sighted the North Island of New Zealand. As we were headed for the estuarine harbour of Whangarei, we still had some distance to go and we sailed all night with New Zealand to starboard. Wonderfully lucky timing brought us to the estuary mouth at dawn, just as the tide was turning. We motored in, watching the sun rise over the lush green hills.

It was a magical entrance. We could smell the pine forests and see the rounded, green hills and fields of the temperate zones. We also had fun counting the sheep – the hills were white with them. Later we learned that for every person in New Zealand, there are twenty-five sheep.

Our radio suddenly crackled into life. It was the customs officer calling us from Whangarei, still a good six kilometres upstream.

"Yacht *Lorcha*. Yacht *Lorcha*. We've just had a call saying you'll go aground if you continue sailing close to the right bank. Please go mid-channel."

There was no one around that we could see – not even a house! For a boat that had been fourteen days on the ocean and had only just arrived in a new land this was a very strange call to receive. But that's New Zealand for you. It's a

133

lush, small, wonderfully scenic country, with a seemingly endless supply of milk, yoghurt, cheese, ice cream, and legs of lamb. But the community is small (population about 3 million), and everybody knows what everybody else is doing. The arrival of a small boat from Canada had already been duly noted.

MODIFICATIONS TO *LORCHA*

14

"We'll cut *Lorcha* in half and add a few feet in the middle," I told Fiona one day while we were sailing towards New Zealand.

Lorcha is a good boat and had served us well for thousands of sea miles, but our children were growing. When we had left Toronto, they had been four and six years old. Now two-and-one-half years later, about the maximum time we had originally thought we would be travelling for, we were half-a-world away from our home port and Penny and Peter were outgrowing their bunks. If only *Lorcha* could have grown along with the children, our problems would never have existed. As it was, the children needed more room for their books and games, and, when we were in port for a few weeks and they met other children, they needed a place where they could play with their friends out of the main salon. The quarter berths, their sleeping area, were overflowing with their books, toys, shells, and assorted flotsam and jetsam, and besides, there wasn't really enough air circulation for comfortable sleeping in the tropics.

We didn't want to trade *Lorcha* in on a new boat. That is difficult enough away from one's home land, what with tariffs and taxes on foreign-built boats, without even taking into account the difficulty of finding a buyer for a boat custom designed and

136

We need more space . . . we find Ian Connors . . .
add a back bedroom . . . finding a temporary abode . . .
labour on Lorcha *. . . our three-month slog . . . car tour of*
North Island . . . fleeing from winter.

built for our requirements. Anyway, we neither wanted nor needed a new boat, only more space.

Soon after we had arrived in Whangarei, New Zealand, we met Ian Connors, a steel-boat builder, and we were quick to ask his advice about our ideas for expansion.

"Sure thing, we can add a bit in the middle." Ian had a brusque and hurried manner, but we had great confidence in his knowledge and ability. "It's done all the time around here. Just let me know what you want and I'll give you a quote." And he dashed off, always in a hurry to get on with his next project.

Fiona and I sat down to draw up a final list of our needs and objectives. Basically, we needed to add another interior "room" without drastically changing the exterior of the boat. The boat's usable space had to be increased without adding in any major way to its length or weight. We wanted to be ready to sail to the tropics at the end of the cyclone season. This gave us three to four months to have *Lorcha* ready for sea.

In the end we didn't cut *Lorcha* in half, though I was sorely tempted – picturing about two metres more boat. But I feared that all the necessary rebuilding, including adding a second mast to increase sail area, would take too much time. We finally decided to do as many growing families do on shore – add a back bedroom!

With a tape measure and a few sticks to simulate the possible shapes, Fiona and I began in earnest to plan our addition.

137

We would make *Lorcha* a centre cockpit boat without moving the cockpit. (See Appendix for drawings explaining how *Lorcha* looked before and after renovations.)

We would cut out the back of the boat, including the cockpit lockers and part of the bench seats, enclose that area with a raised deck to give sitting headroom over the proposed bunks beneath it, and we would have our new room – an aft cabin separate from the main salon so Fiona and I could work late at night or play the radio without disturbing the children. Additional benefits would be a desk for Fiona in the space at the head of what was now Penny's bunk, and increased food stowage at Peter's side.

Modifications such as we were planning are easy on a steel-hulled boat. Parts can be cut out and pieces welded on without sacrificing structural integrity.

With our decision made as to what the modifications would be, we arranged for Ian Connors to do the steel work.

We explored the possibility of renting a house for the few months the boat was hauled out of the water, but we found that there was a general housing shortage in the area and every available dwelling was rented – at considerable cost. We asked Ian about accommodation.

"We've got a five-metre caravan next to the workshop," he said. "We use it as a tea room and a place for the kids to play when Caroline brings them to the boatyard. Toilet facilities are a bit primitive, but you can move in for as long as *Lorcha* is in the yard."

"A bit primitive" meant a chemical toilet in an adjoining tent. Sleeping arrangements were built-in bunks for each of the kids, and a convertible sofa for Fiona and I. There was a lot more floor space in the caravan than on *Lorcha*, and a lot more enclosed space around us, but it was very inconveniently arranged. We always seemed to be in each other's way.

With *Lorcha* "on the hard" (hauled ashore) we were soon busy emptying all the lockers, for not only was she getting an aft cabin, she was going to be painted inside and out.

What a job! Unless you see the amount of stuff you can

cram into a nine-metre boat and still have room to live on board, you would not believe it. We put as much stuff as possible in the caravan, and then stacked large cartons on pallets beside it until we had a pile of boxes three metres square and two metres high, which we covered with a tarpaulin.

"Where did it all come from?" we asked each other, eyeing the stack, wondering if we would get it all back on board again when it came time to leave. We had discovered some tins and packages of food in the lockers which had been on board for two years. They were brands we didn't like, so we chucked them out. There were other items, such as a hand meat-grinder and a vegetable puréeing machine which had been recommended in several cruising books we had read; we had never used them, so they also got tossed out. Old books and games which had sunk to the bottom of the children's lockers through lack of use were picked over by Penny and Peter, who hated to part with any of the few possessions they had. We bundled up several parcels of souvenirs to send sea parcel post to my mother to increase the availability of our limited locker space.

I began my part of the work by stripping out the hull lining and the bunks and lockers from the galley right through to the transom. I removed all the wood trim around the cockpit and transom, and within a couple of days I was ready to help Ian cut out the transom and part of the cockpit. It only took a few hours before we had a gaping hole at *Lorcha's* stern open to wind and weather.

I worked with Ian, helping to hold and measure and figuring out design details as we worked. He cut and fit the steel sheets, then sweated over the welding in the height of the hot southern hemisphere summer.

Fiona and the kids could not help with the steel work, so Fiona enrolled Penny and Peter in swimming classes in the local outdoor swimming pool to help them improve their strokes and stamina. She decided to take lessons herself, as she had never learned the crawl stroke. The stamina of all three was also improved by the four-kilometre walk to and from the pool three days a week. They would return late in the afternoon, having visited the local lending library or done some shopping. Schoolwork also took up part of each day.

After the men of the boatyard downed their tools for the day the grounds were our own. We began to play running and ball games with the children in the evening and found, to our dismay, that the skills required by such games were low down on their list of accomplishments.

"Can't you catch the ball?" I asked Penny, as she always seemed to fumble it.

"Kick the ball right to me," I would tell Peter over and over again as the ball went everywhere except where he aimed it.

We had lived so long on the boat, where any thrown or kicked object would probably be lost forever, that the kids had not had the opportunity to practise these skills. They lacked that hand-eye co-ordination so important for any ball sport. Fiona and I decided to try to improve their co-ordination by playing some ball sport, or badminton, or by throwing a frisby every evening.

As the sun dropped low in the sky we showered, each using a few buckets of water. Then we would listen to the calls of the many birds along the tidal estuary as some roosted for the night and others began their feeding. Opossum, numerous to the point of being nuisances, began their nocturnal perambulations, and it was time for Penny and Peter to go to bed.

After Ian had finished the steel work, I prepared *Lorcha* for the sandblasting of all of her exterior steel to strip the old paint and rust scale off. I sealed the hatches, portholes, and ventilators as best as I could, knowing that the sand and dust from the high-pressure air hose would penetrate even the tiniest crack.

The sandblaster did his job in two days, and Fiona and I spent the next two weeks applying up to twelve coats of paint on *Lorcha's* exterior. I installed ports and hatches in the new aft cabin, and it was now watertight. With several sheets of plywood I insulated, then lined the aft cabin, and I built in new bunks and lockers. Next, I painted all of the new interior while Fiona painted the interior of the main salon, which had also had some small modifications.

We had had a hard three-month slog but it was worth every minute of the work involved. With her sail patched and seams resewn, new paint, new cockpit dodger, raised aft deck, and sporty new scoop overhang running out from her new vertical transom, *Lorcha* looked like a new boat.

"The paint is dry in the lockers of your cabin," I told Penny and Peter as we began to move some of our belongings back on board. "Everyone is responsible for their own stowage, and everything has to fit in your own lockers, so you can begin putting your toys and clothes away."

Always ready to rise to a challenge, Penny and Peter sorted through the pile of boxes to reclaim their belongings and decide where best to store them. There was much moaning and groaning as familiar toys or games wouldn't fit. Though the living area around their new bunks was larger, the stowage under the bunks was less than the area under their old ones. They had more lockers, but most of the cubbyholes were smaller.

"I'll make some netting hammocks to hang alongside your bunks to hold some of your clothes," I told them when the frustration of trying to fit everything in got to be too much for them. "For now, put the leftovers in a duffel bag and push it to the foot of your bunks."

The aft cabin was arranged so that the children would lie with their pillows at the extreme aft end of the hull. With sitting headroom over 1.2 metres of length, the bunks extended under the cockpit seats, making a sort of tunnel to the main cabin. At the sides of the hull, forming a back rest for anyone seated on the bunks, were some shelves and cubbyholes. The bunks were separated from each other by a partition at the heads. There was a small cabin sole (floor) area between the bunks. A small table slid out from under the cockpit floor which could either be used as a step when entering the cabin or a table for games. With the companionway hatch open and Penny standing on the cabin sole, her head stuck out above the raised deck.

We thanked Ian for a job well done, moved back on board and motored to the mid-town mooring facilities which make Whangarei such a pleasure to stay at.

"*Lorcha* looks great," our cruising acquaintances would say when they saw us, now established at a finger pier along the estuary. "But isn't there something different about her stern?"

Penny and Peter loved their new space, and so did we. "Off to bed you go," Fiona or I would tell them, glad to have them out of the main cabin and out from underfoot.

Most surprising of all was their ability to cram their friends into that small space, playing games, reading, or just talking. We might find up to eight children in that cabin, all happily chattering away, secure in the knowledge that no adult would come in to disturb them.

We rented a car for a ten-day tour around the North Island of New Zealand as a celebratory trip before we had to leave this lush green country.

We sought out places of history and Maori culture, driving to Auckland to visit the War Memorial Museum with its complete range of Maori artifacts, including ancient war canoes, and to Rotorua where master carver Clive Fughill took us on a tour of the work area at the Maori Arts and Crafts Institute. Here young Maoris were being taught to carve traditional designs and the lore surrounding the prestigious position wood carvers held in this ancient Polynesian society.

We visited the Bay of Islands area, where the Maori people first settled in about 900 A.D. There is an interesting display of a huge Maori war canoe at Paihai, plus the preserved house where, in 1840, the treaty was signed bringing New Zealand under the protection of the British Empire.

But what really took Penny's attention in Paihai was a notice from the communications department of the nearby

Waitangi State Forest saying that they organized "kiwi hunts." The strange-looking flightless bird with nostrils at the end of its long beak is the national symbol of New Zealand, though few people have ever seen one in the wild. The kiwi population has been diminishing for many years. In any case, they are difficult to spot as they are nocturnal, coming out under cover of darkness to feed on cicada grubs on the floor of the pine forests. The "hunt" was a sight-seeing one; simply a way of introducing more people to the bird in its natural habitat and of publicizing the fact that the kiwi population in Waitangi was on the increase because of a massive reforestation program.

At nine o'clock at night, instead of being tucked in bed, Penny and Peter were standing at the edge of a mass of dark trees, about to head down a scary forest trail. They both knew that there are no venomous snakes or dangerous large predators in New Zealand, but a dark forest on a moonless night can get the adrenaline going. Sorel Olson, the head ranger of the Waitangi State Forest and our guide, explained what we'd do: "We'll walk about half a kilometre into the forest and then we'll stop, and I'll play a recording of some kiwi calls," he whispered. "Stay absolutely still for a least two minutes while we listen for an answer. If we're lucky, we'll hear another kiwi, and we'll head for him."

Holding hands and not talking, we walked quietly among the towering trees, the darkness closing in on us. For once, Penny and Peter were not skipping ahead. They jumped at every owl hoot or at the noisy creak of a tree stirred by the wind. Sorel stopped and we stood close as he played his recording: long, raucous, and other-worldly. It took a long sixty seconds till we heard them, but there were two similar calls, both some distance away. Sorel chose one and we started walking towards it. We walked for about an hour, slowly and quietly, around trees, over ditches and up hills, stopping several times to catch our breath and to play our recording, an enthralling but very different game of hide-and-seek. Eventually, we could hear that we were getting close.

143

"Paul, you and Peter go stand by the large pine tree about ten metres to your right," whispered Olson when he thought we were near enough, "and Fiona and Penny, you stand near those bushes off to the left. I'm going to circle uphill behind him and try to flush the bird out toward you."

I stood still, Peter clasping my hand tightly. He jumped and nearly ran away from me as we heard snapping branches and a whoop from Sorel. The kiwi dashed straight for us. I switched on our torch when it was only about one metre from my feet. The kiwi leapt into the air and scooted off.

Then we heard a shout of surprise from Penny. Another kiwi had been quietly watching the proceedings from under the very bush she and Fiona were standing beside. It suddenly broke cover and practically ran over Penny's feet, both Penny and the bird squawking loudly.

"They're so small," said Penny when she had recovered her equilibrium. "They're only the size of a rooster. I thought they would be like an ostrich."

Olson was laughing as he rejoined us. "I enjoy these kiwi hunts as much as anyone," he told us. "And it's a good way for me to keep track of the population."

It was now half past ten, and we had seen our kiwis, so in great spirits we headed back to Sorel's car, an hour's walk away. From two little kids apprehensive of the dark, Penny and Peter had metamorphosed into explorers striding masterfully down the path a little ahead of us, scaring up opossums and hedgehogs and feeling good about having added a kiwi sighting to their list of adventures.

Fiona, having been brought up in Scotland, decided she wanted Penny and Peter to know all about sheep. She chose an internationally rated indoor stage show with sheep as the main attraction as our next stop. We set off for the Agrodome, just north of Rotorua, to see their sixty-minute educational show featuring nineteen different species of top New Zealand rams. To this day, Penny and Peter have not figured out how the rams were intelligent enough to answer to their names and come up on stage when called, but they did! On stage, each ram was chained to a platform on a different level as a commentary described the different breeds and their attributes. To the delight of the audience, the sheep interacted with each other like naughty children, stealing each other's food, having a playful tussle, or sometimes, thoroughly bored with the whole effort of being on display, simply falling asleep on the job. The Old Vic it wasn't, but Penny and Peter loved it.

Later, promoter Warren Hartford had some more sheep information for us. He told us it took two days to train each ram for his stage appearance. They had found that the various breeds each behaved quite differently; some – the Suffolks – were enthusiastic about their stage roles, and others – the Merinos – tended to sulk. Each sheep was trained according to its own personality. After several weeks of performance, some of the sheep became stressed and had to be replaced by new faces. Others, however, became so playful and adept that instead of ending their days as chops and crown roasts, they spent the rest of their lives as respected actors. The show ended with a sheep-shearing demonstration, expert shearer Mike Boyd pulling the sheep's wool over its eyes to persuade the animal to lie still as he clipped. Like everything, practice makes perfect, and we learned that the world sheep-shearing record stood at 354 sheep sheared in a nine-hour period.

We had one more day of exploration before we had to make our way back to the boat, and we spent it on another boat, inland and underground in the eerie Waitomo caves. Shivering out of the sun, we were silently rowed into underground chambers formed one-and-a-half million years ago. The fourteen-metre-high cathedral chamber is lit only by the lights on the tails of millions of tiny glow worms on its ceiling. Drifting silently we watched the pin-pricks of light high above us. Peter was fascinated by this strange creature's predatory habits. It lets down sticky lines from its body – as many as thirty or forty – like fishing lines. Insects fly into these lines, which are hauled up by the worm. Penny and Peter listened in fascination to the strange story of the glow worm's life cycle. The worm becomes a fly, but it has no mouth; as a fly, its purpose is purely to mate and lay eggs. After it has done this, it dies because it cannot eat, and its nine-month life-cycle is completed.

It was autumn in the southern hemisphere now. The cyclone season was at its end. The nights were getting colder, and some mornings we woke to a rime of frost on the decks. It was time for us to flee north to the tropics to cruise island groups under the brisk winter-time trade winds.

We loaded *Lorcha* with cases of tinned meats, fruits, and marmalade, stacked away brick-like foil containers of fruit juices, plus powdered and condensed milk and cream in tins. Fifty kilos of potatoes and twenty kilos of onions had to be sorted through to find any bruised ones, which were set aside for immediate use. We packed twenty dozen of the freshest un-refrigerated eggs we could find into the bilge, down low where they would be coldest. An unusual item we collected was twenty kilos of kiwi fruit. It was picking time for the fruit. All first-class kiwi fruit are reserved for export, and the smaller or misshapen fruit, every bit as good and still green, were given away at the supermarket. Also purchased were various treats such as chocolate bars, peanuts, cookies, canned steamed puddings, olives, and dried fruit. Bundles of toilet paper and paper towels were located in the driest stow-age areas at the extreme ends of the boat where light-weight items should be stored. We bought several tubes of toothpaste and extra tooth brushes, sun-block cream and insect repel-lent, first-aid supplies and fresh antibiotic tablets, anti-malar-ial pills – everything needed for a minimum of six months of independent cruising. With our fuel and water tanks at capac-ity, our boat was heavily laden, but, we noted happily, she sat

146

on the water at the same line as she had before the addition of the aft cabin.

Now all we needed was a favourable wind to clear New Zealand's North Island, and we'd be in the trade winds before we knew it.

NEW ZEALAND TO VANUATU 15

We looked carefully at our most-used reference book, *Ocean Passages for the World*, in preparation for the thirteen-hundred-mile sea passage north to Port Vila, capital of Vanuatu (formerly the New Hebrides). It's not advisable to sail until the end of the cyclone season, which runs from December through March. The weather turns cold and blustery by May, with the onslaught of winter gales in June.

On April 30, the day we were finally ready to leave, Paul was felled by a five-day virus. It then did the rounds of the family, with Penny next and then Peter. We grimaced as the southerlies which blew hard (as predicted) for the first week of May turned to northerlies by the time the family was again fit to travel. We waited impatiently for the next low-pressure cell which would bring the desired southerly winds. It had turned noticeably cooler.

Then, in mid May, Malcolm Craddock of the British-registered *Thursday's Child*, headed for Fiji, called us on the VHF: "Don't get too impatient about leaving in the next few days," he said. "There's a cyclone brewing up north."

This was an astonishing phenomenon: a cyclone in May occurred less than once every twenty years in these waters. It had been so long since the last one that though there was a vague possibility of a

Felled by a virus . . . cyclone brewing . . . seasick . . . we hit head winds . . . calamity! . . . sail-sewing . . . dilemma: south or north? . . . Vanuatu at last.

---

cyclone occurring in April, we had all assumed that May was safe.

We huddled around Malcolm's ham radio every morning for the next few days, plotting the course of Cyclone Namu, anxiously listening for news of yachts which had sailed north at the beginning of the month. Yachts sailing from New Caledonia to Vanuatu did cross tracks with the tropical cyclone, and several turned back, but none were lost. The worst shoreside damage was sustained in the Solomon Islands.

The cyclone was hundreds of miles from us, but no one goes looking for that kind of trouble; together with the other international cruising yachts in New Zealand, we sat tight. It was not until May 27, a cold, drizzly morning, but with strong south winds, that we threw off our lines and motored out into the channel of the Whangarei boat basin.

Though we were optimistic and glad to be on our way, it was not to be a fortuitous passage. Winds of 30 knots and confused seas faced us as we exited the estuary mouth, and things did not improve out on the ocean, with the temperature falling rapidly and the wind blowing white crests off the wave tops.

We had been thinking about trying six-hour watches on this passage, but it was too cold to stay in the cockpit for that length of time. We did change our watch system so that my first watch went from 2000 to 2300 instead of the usual 2000 to 2200. A small change, but it worked well for both of us. I am usually awake for this period and Paul feels better having three hours of sleep early in the night. We kept to this watch pattern until the end of the trip.

"Please may I have some raisins?" said a white-faced Penny the next morning.

"Penny, you were sick yesterday, sick three times last night . . . no. Just take it easy today. Have a dry cracker if you want to eat something."

It's hard to deny your child, especially when she's pale and upset, but I knew from past experience that Penny's tummy wouldn't tolerate anything but a spoonful of the blandest food. I was surprised she even asked for anything.

Day two was as cold and uncomfortable as the previous day, though the rain had ceased. I donned my foul-weather gear just to keep warm, but could do nothing to prevent the seasickness.

Two down, two to go. By evening Paul succumbed. He is rarely affected by seasickness, so it hits him badly. He was groggy when he took his 2300 watch, but I was in no condition to do anything but feel sympathy and head below for some much-needed sleep myself. It felt good to crawl into Paul's still-warm bunk.

We ran out of the southwesterlies on our third day and the wind first decreased, then headed us. The seas were more confused than ever, with swells running in three directions.

A meagre spoonful of macaroni was all we three sick ones could manage for supper, though Peter enjoyed a couple of sausages, with Penny looking on enviously.

"Maybe tomorrow, Penny," I said. "But only if you're not sick tonight."

There were a few minor mishaps that night during Paul's watch. The first was signalled by a crash as the compass inexplicably fell off its mount. Only the light was damaged, and for the rest of the night we flashed a torch on the compass to check that we were still on course.

The next mishap came when a basket of kiwi fruit and

apples slid off a forward shelf and crashed to the floor. We had stored it too high, but it, too, was a victim of the confused and steep seas.

Lastly, Paul found that the windvane could get caught in the sheets (the lines that control the set of the sail) when the boat lurched in a steep wave and would then be slow in getting back to its upright position. He stretched shockcord (we carry miles of it) over the sheets to hold them down. Now, when the vane came forward, the shockcord prevented the sheets from entangling the vane.

And to think some boats don't keep night watches!

The trip was beginning to feel like a challenging marathon and there was no end in sight. The headwinds strengthened to 25 knots and we tacked every three hours. When the seas went to three metres and the wind to 30 knots that evening, I had had enough; we hove-to. We were still rolling because of the cross swells, but the motion was much more comfortable. My body began to recover and feel a little better.

Lorcha lay hove-to all through Paul's 2300 to 0200 watch. During my 0200 to 0500 watch she began to swing around to point south.

"Ah ha, wind change," I thought, untying the lines that held the tiller and easing the sail to head her north again.

I hate wind changes because they're never clean, and as I have to think through the movements, it takes a lot of energy and concentration to do the right thing at the right time.

Lorcha surged forward, but she wouldn't come about with the heavy seas knocking her head off as she rounded up to them. I set her off the wind again, pulled the sheet, and gybed the sail. Crash! Over went the boom.

Paul appeared at the companionway hatch. "What's happening?"he asked. "Need any help?"

"Wind shift," I said. "Think I've got it."

But as Paul turned to go below, there was a gust which gybed the sail back again, followed by a terrible tearing sound.

"Paul," I yelled. "The sail's split! The sail's split!"

151

I was looking up in horror at the sail. The upper yard (the batten at the top edge of the sail) was hanging nearly vertically, taking part of the torn sail with it. I had never seen the sail look like that. A major repair at the very least.

Paul scrambled into his foul-weather gear and safety harness and crawled forward.

"Stay in the cockpit, Fi," he yelled over the wind. "I'm going to try to haul the sail down. Ease the halyard when I tell you." (The halyard is the line that raises or lowers the sail.)

"It's tearing more," I shouted back, uselessly trying to stop the boat from lurching in the heaving seas and spooked by the fact that Paul's silhouette and the upper yard looked like the setting for a hanging against the threatening black sky.

"Pay out the halyard and haul in the sheets," shouted Paul.

Slowly he gathered the sail and the crippled upper yard and managed to lower everything into the lazy jacks (the lines that hold the sail in position when it is partially or completely lowered).

The boat was really rolling now as there was not a scrap of steadying sail and Paul staggered back to the cockpit, lurching from side to side on the deck. He sat down heavily, pushing his woollen hat up on his forehead.

"Well, that's a calamity," he said.

"Is it repairable?" I asked.

"I suppose so," said Paul. "But we can't really see until the morning."

"It's 0400 now," I said looking at my watch. "Why don't you go back to bed? I won't be able to sleep with the boat rolling like this. I'll wake you at dawn – or before if I need you."

Paul gave a sigh and went below. I knew how he was feeling. His sleep had been interrupted three times already and now he had an emergency to cope with. The crew was willing, but the captain had to shoulder the responsibility.

"What's happening, Mum?" called a sleepy voice from the aft cabin. "Open our hatch."

I opened just the top board of the aft companionway to see Penny's face peering anxiously out into the dark.

152

Lorcha is rafted-up with *Joan D III* as we enter the first lock of the Panama Canal from the Caribbean side. We will go through the lock in the same chamber with the cargo vessel ahead of us. Peter is at right, one of *Joan D*'s crew at left.

Paul and Peter, with their backs to the camera, in the longboat on our first trip ashore at Pitcairn Island. Brian Young is readying the mooring line just outside the surf line at Bounty Bay.

Penny's eighth birthday aboard *l'Alose*, with Gérard, Brigitte, and Marie-Hélène. In front are the two plum tarts Brigitte made for Penny. At Mangareva, Gambier Islands, French Polynesia.

Reef walking at low tide at the Hunga Lagoon, Vava'u Group, Tonga. Peter, Paul, and Penny have their plastic sandals on to protect their feet from the sharp coral, their sun hats to protect them from the intense tropical rays, and each carries kitchen tongs or a stick to poke at any interesting looking specimen to see what it is before touching it with their bare hands.

Peter and Penny doing their school work at the dinette table in *Lorcha*'s salon, in the South Pacific Ocean.

Women hold up a tapa cloth, made from the pounded bark of the paper mulberry tree, dyed with dyes made from the boiled roots of the mangrove tree. The tapa cloths are made for various ceremonies, as banners for weddings or funerals, and they are used as blankets. Pangai-motu Island, Vava'u Group, Tonga.

The men of Nurca village on Santa Catalina Island allowed us to photograph them dressed in their ceremonial costumes and displaying some of their carvings as payment for fixing their fibreglass water tank. They explained that they couldn't dance for us as the village was in mourning because of the death of a child.

In the new aft cabin, Peter and Penny sit on their bunks holding some of their stuffed animals. They sleep with their heads against the bulkhead in the background. The checked pattern is neoprene foam glued to the primered steel for insulation and painted with latex paint. The red post is the rudder post, and a divider behind it holds some cloth pouches for added stowage.

Mike Otis Wagore, in the red shirt and shorts, teaches Peter and Adrian from *Moonraker* to shoot their new bows and arrows. The boys were given the weapons as gifts on Santa Catalina Island, and the bow remains one of Peter's favourite souvenirs of our trip.

On Santa Ana Island, Peter examines a fine specimen of a turtle cowrie (*Cypraea testudinaria*) as Penny holds another shell and Paul looks on. The children in the background are hoping for a good trade.

Penny and Peter look at a coral slab cairn with skulls and ornaments from the head-hunting days on Simbo Island, in the Solomon Islands.

Penny and Fiona doing the laundry at a stream on Telina Island in the western Solomon Islands. The streams are strictly regulated, with the men's bathing place upstream, then the women's bathing place below that, and the laundry place further downstream. There is always a special clean pool for drinking water upstream from any washing. Before using any stream one should ask for the rules lest the stream be used improperly.

The whole family was photographed by Clarke Stede as we walked on the beach at Green Island, near Cairns, Queensland, Australia.

Penny has a close look at a lemur, a primitive primate predating monkeys, at a nature reserve on Nosy Komba, Madagascar.

Between Bermuda and Atlantic City, New Jersey, Peter fought this dorado (also called a dolphin fish or mahi mahi), without any help for more than twenty minutes. He eventually brought it up to the side of the boat for Paul to gaff. It was the last of the large pelagic fish we were to catch on our circumnavigation.

"We have a problem with a torn sail, Penny," I said. "The boat is going to roll around and bump and crash like this for the rest of the night. Try to go back to sleep."

"Is it torn very badly?" asked a second anxious voice.

"Well, it looks pretty bad, Peter," I said. "But we can't be sure 'til morning. Now, I'm going to shut the companionway again. Try to sleep. I'll be right here. Good night."

Soon the boat was quiet again – of human sounds, that is. The wind and waves were as loud as ever. The sky hung blackly over us, with no light from moon or stars. We were three hundred miles from New Zealand and a thousand miles from Vanuatu. What were we going to do?

Dawn was grey and overcast, with a faint pink blush of sunrise under glowering clouds. The seas were breaking, the sibilant hiss of waves foaming and noisily venting their spleen at the world, the other elements, and us.

"I hope it's not going to get worse," said Paul, struggling into his foul-weather gear and safety harness, getting ready to crawl forward. He made his way carefully, hooking his safety harness onto the coach-roof eye bolt. He waited for the right wave to lurch him forward, using the motion of the boat to pitch him in the direction he wanted to go.

"Shall I come up with you?" I yelled.

"No, wait in the cockpit until I get everything untangled," replied Paul. "The yard has twisted and is lying on the wrong side of the mast. I'll need you to raise it enough so I can get it round to the other side."

I pulled and slackened lines till Paul was able to get the upper yard positioned where he wanted it.

"Get the sewing kit and come forward," yelled Paul. "It's very rolly. Keep your lifeline clipped on."

At this point the kids woke up.

"Penny and Peter," I said. "Papa and I are going forward. You are not to open this hatch and neither of you is to come into the cockpit. You can crawl into the main cabin through the tunnel. Help yourselves to bread and jam in the galley."

153

"How long will you be?" asked Peter.

"Maybe an hour," I said. "But, Peter, on no account are you to go into the cockpit. Got it?"

"Got it," said Peter.

I clawed my way along the lurching deck, clutching at hand holds all the way, sometimes dropping to my knees to keep my balance. We both clung to the mast, surveying the damage.

"I know it was my fault," I said miserably. "I didn't haul in the sheet enough when I gybed."

"That wasn't what started the tear," said Paul. "The out-haul line chafed through, and there was nothing left to hold the outer end of the sail to the upper yard. The pull was so strong that even though there are four layers of cloth at the corner, the fabric ripped. And when it got to the single layer it just tore right across until it got to the reinforcing at the other end. It's a major repair, but I think we can do it."

"I thought you replaced that line in Whangarei?"

"That's the strange thing. The original tie held all the way from Toronto – and the new tie has chafed through on our first passage.

"Here's the second reason it gave," Paul added grimly, a moment later. "This taping material is absolutely rotten."

We had had the sail restitched in Whangarei. The sailmaker had added several reinforcements and a number of small patches to the sail, drawing our attention to small areas of strain that he had also worked on. He had replaced all the taping on both vertical edges of the sail. It was strange that after such a thorough going-over, he had not also replaced the taping along the top and bottom of the sail.

Paul forced the thick needle and strong thread through the fabric to begin the repair, taking about ten minutes to make three overlapping holding stitches.

"Okay, Fi," he said at last. "That's going to hold this end for a while. Let me stretch the top of the sail out straight and we'll start on the main sewing."

We pulled the sail taut along the upper yard and Paul explained what he wanted to do. We would take deep stitches

154

into each edge of the torn material, pushing the needle after each stitch through the tear line. The person on the port side would push the needle through to the person on the other side, who would then pull the needle through. Then we would repeat the process. We could each use only one hand for the needle, as the other hand was for holding on – around the mast, to hand holds on the dinghy, to the other person, to anything that would help us keep our balance. We were both crouched awkwardly on top of the dinghy.

It took an hour and a half of concentrated work to do about a half-metre of the 2.2-metre repair.

"Do you want to rest or shall we do another length?" asked Paul, as he waited for the right moment to free both hands to tie off the thread.

"I'm going to crawl back to check on the kids and give them a new game," I said. "After that, let's keep going but change sides. I don't know which arm is sorest at the moment – the arm I'm hanging on with or the one that's sewing. They need a change."

I crawled along the deck and into the cockpit and opened the companionway hatch to clamber into the main cabin. I knew exactly where I had hidden our mid-passage treat, a game of Ludo (Parcheesi to North Americans). It seemed more important to give it to Penny and Peter now. They were delighted at the unexpected present and much too interested in it to worry about what was happening outside. In my misery I had to smile. Children sure normalize any situation.

"Same instructions," I said. "No one in the cockpit. Stay below." But the kids were already immersed in their new game.

I crawled back out again, closed the hatch and looked over the same angry seas and listened to the same wind. Perhaps it had lessened a fraction.

Paul had not stopped working since I had left him, but he had not accomplished much as it really was a problem for one person to get that needle through the multi-layered material. In spite of our anxiety, I couldn't help feeling a special closeness as we worked together, each of us doing our part to get things in order. In an emergency like this, I thought, there isn't another person I would choose to be with. We were also getting into the rhythm of the sewing. It was going a bit faster.

But we were both tiring.

Suddenly an out-of-pattern wave hit the boat and I saw Paul clutching at the air as he lost his balance on the dinghy and plunged towards the sea. He hit the lifelines as his safety-harness line came taut and that stopped him.

"Close," he yelled up at me cheerfully, waiting for the boat to roll to port so he could scramble up again. This time he sat almost astride the dinghy so that he could also hold on with his knees as well as his one "free" hand.

"I think we need a break," I said, taking the needle from him. "We've done half. How about a drink of orange juice?"

We had been working for over three endurance-testing hours after a sleepless night and no breakfast. Another large wave hit the boat and this time it was I who spun off, landing, however, on deck on my feet.

"Not quite so close," I echoed. "But really time for a break."

We both crawled back into the cockpit where Paul lay flat out with his eyes closed. I went below. It was too rough to put on the kettle.

"Now can you play with us?" asked Peter. "And how about breakfast?"

I had to laugh. Fizzy vitamin drinks and chocolate cookies for everyone.

We got back to the job with renewed energy. The worst part was reinforcing the head of the sail where the tear had started. With an additional two layers of new webbing there, it took all my strength – shoulders, arms, and thighs – to push the needle through, and I could feel the end of the needle grinding into the metal reinforcement on the leather sewing palm. Those twenty or so stitches took us an hour and a half.

At 1300 we returned, shaking, to the cockpit. We had been sewing for seven hours. Paul lay down, and I sat with my head between my knees. The wind had eased.

"Now what?" I said finally.

We could go back to New Zealand – back into cold and probably heavy weather – or we could press on to the tropics and presumably warmer weather. But Vanuatu was some distance with a repaired sail . . .

"Let's get the sail up and see how it looks," said Paul slowly.

I eased the sheet as Paul pulled up the sail. One panel. Two. Three. Four. It looked good. Five. Six. And *Lorcha* was moving. She was also headed south.

"I don't want to," I said quietly, "but I suppose the safest thing is to head the shortest distance, back to New Zealand. That's what the wind is telling us."

"I don't want to either," said Paul. "But I'm too exhausted to beat into the wind. We'll just leave her heading south."

By 1400 *Lorcha* was eating up the miles on a fast broad reach towards New Zealand. Paul was sound asleep in his bunk, the kids were still Ludo-engrossed and I was dozing in the cockpit, squinting occasionally at the sail.

At 1600 Paul came up, new colour in his face and looking ready to take on the world. As he climbed into the cockpit, the wind shifted 180 degrees, taking the boat with it. Paul gave me a look and eased the sail.

"The forecast is southerlies for two days," he said quietly. "It looks as though they've just arrived."

"The sail looks okay," I added.

There was a silence.

"We can make it to Vila," said Paul. "If we have two days of southerlies, we'll get into the trade winds. And once we get to the half-way mark, it will be much easier to keep going – and less risky as we get into warmer waters."

We looked at each other and smiled. We let the sail out some more, heading north.

The gods were with us. *Lorcha* scudded on her way, covering 117 miles by noon the next day. Everything was holding and everyone was feeling rested and relieved. And how could we not feel optimistic with a fair wind, a repair made good, and Peter's incessant chatter about his birthday the next day.

There were no frights, no mishaps, no repairs, and we celebrated with a supper of corned beef hash and a dozen lus-
cious green kiwi fruit.

I hadn't realized just how stressful our passage had been
until dawn ten days later, when I wiped tears of relief from
my eyes as we sailed into Vila, the sun rising over the hills and
magically burning off an early-morning mist while we tied up
to the bright yellow quarantine buoy.

We had made good a difficult passage and we knew we
would enjoy the next six months, cruising in new islands in
tropical waters. Although we couldn't know it at the time,
there was a big price to pay in terms of my future health, but
that would not be until we reached Australia.

VANUATU 16

To cruise the oceans of the world – daunting bodies of water – is to meet the challenge of self-sufficiency while seizing the opportunity to visit far-flung and remote islands, many unapproachable in any other way. It is to take responsibility for the people one is closest to with no idea of what tomorrow might bring.

Being part of the voyaging community is something much appreciated on the world's oceans. We felt that bond with our fellow peripatetic yachtsmen strongly during our months of voyaging in Vanuatu, the Solomon Islands, and Papua New Guinea. This is island cruising at its best. All the yachts are headed more or less in the same direction, in more or less the same time frame, so our paths crossed and recrossed and we had more opportunity and time to spend with more people. Engrossed though we all were with the different cultural aspects of the areas we were sailing through, we enjoyed the constant companionship with the other cruising yachts. For Penny and Peter it was a few months spent exploring a different aspect of childhood as they met and mingled with more children than during any other period of our passage-making.

It started when we made that dawn entry into Port Vila.

A community of voyagers . . . discovery of boat children . . .
shared lessons . . . the Reed family . . . speaking Bislama . . .
shark tales . . . crab hunt . . . waterfall anchorage . . .
volcanic crater anchorage.

"There's children on that boat," Penny said excitedly. "I can see two girls in the cockpit."

"I think there's a boy on that one," chimed in Peter, pointing to another boat.

"And there's nappies over there," shouted Penny. "Gosh, Mama, there's *lots* of children here!"

Indeed there were. And so many the same age that no time was lost in organizing a general morning school ashore. This meant that in a week of lessons, each teacher had to work only one morning. And the children loved it. They looked over each other's lessons (Canadian, Australian, and New Zealand correspondence courses), compared work, and helped each other. It was more than interesting to watch them test each teacher, to see how much they could get away with. We could see and appreciate what was going on, however; the one-to-one relationship between the teacher and the one or two pupils per boat makes it difficult to rebel for very long.

"You're a good teacher, Mum," Penny informed me one day. "But I think the best of all the boat teachers is Aggie."

Dear Aggie. She and her husband Don Reed and their two sons, nine-year-old Danny and seven-year-old Adrian, were to become our closest cruising friends. If we enjoyed cruising with four, it was double the pleasure with eight. We were like two close-knit suburban families, always running in and out of each other's boats, with the added advantage that we all spoke the same jargon and our "work" consisted of cruising and exploring.

161

It didn't take the Reeds long to move their mooring place to raft up beside us. As soon as they were settled, I called over to invite them for dinner that evening.

"Why don't all the kids eat on *Moonraker?*" suggested Aggie, "Don and I will eat with you." The children shrieked with glee. They would likely have preferred the same arrangement for sleeping and probably even sailing!

Our plans for sailing through Vanuatu were slightly different from the Reeds, but we met up again at Epi. After one night in the uncomfortable anchorage there, we both elected to move on – with Penny and Danny as crew on *Lorcha* and Peter and Adrian on *Moonraker*.

The village children at Paami were out in force to greet us as we sailed near that small island, but once we were ashore they became strangely shy, backing away and refusing to shake our hands. Penny solved the impasse. She started jumping up and down, and the silently staring group of Vanuatan children could sustain themselves no longer. I suppose they realized this strange white person was a child just like them. In no time, about twenty children were enthusiastically holding our hands and taking us through their village. It was time for the boat children to be impressed when a twelve-year-old girl scaled a very tall palm tree to hack down refreshing green drinking coconuts for all of us.

We managed to communicate haltingly with these children in our newly learned Bislama. It is a kind of pidgin English, but actually a language in its own right. Our walk turned really hilarious when we found that one of the children's favourite songs was "You Are My Sunshine." We must have sung it together at least twenty times, more uproariously each time as we enjoyed one of those hard-to-understand cross-cultural jokes: they thought it really funny that we should be saying "sun*shine*" while they sang "sun*sine*."

We enjoyed Port Sandwich, Malekula, for its naturalness and its people. No guided tours, ruins, or museums, just walks from village to village, trying to find the local bakery and discovering how the island people lived. Don and Aggie shared a kava-drinking evening with a local chief. Though women cannot drink kava on a ceremonial occasion, it is seemingly permissible in private. We traded T-shirts and children's clothes for fresh fruit.

We got up at first light to watch the fishermen cast their nets, anticipating the small schools of bonita tuna that came inshore at this time of year. The fishermen hooked the fish's gills on their fingers to carry their catch ashore, carrying ten to fifteen fish in this way. We needed fresh fish for supper and traded a stick of tobacco, a standard trading item, for three nice ones.

The villagers had a great fear of sharks. We met one man with extensive scars from a shark attack. We were told several stories about other attacks on people, as well as tales of dogs being taken from the surf on the beaches just in front of the villages. There were tales of children being lost from yachts, too many perhaps for all to be true, but it was certain that one eight-year-old had gone swimming from his family's boat in recent times and had never been seen again. We were warned again and again not to swim or wade in the surf, or to play in the shallows.

"We never used to have a problem with sharks," said Chief Didier Nally, "until there were lots of yachts coming here to visit. We think the sharks follow the yachts into Port Sandwich, perhaps because the yachts throw their garbage overboard."

There were a great many shared sails, shared suppers, and shared anchorages between *Lorcha* and *Moonraker*. We seemed to imbue each other with more energy than we might normally have had on our own, and Don and Aggie introduced us to some new experiences. One was crabbing.

Twenty-eight miles further up the coast on the east side of Malekula Island lay Crab Bay, and the Reeds insisted we sail there to go crabbing one night. There was no one about as we went ashore at dusk. It was just as well, as, armed with torches, gaffs, sticks, and buckets, we looked more like a marauding party than friendly tourists.

163

Eight of us crashing through the undergrowth and running on the sand gave the crabs plenty of warning of our arrival, especially when the kids ran on ahead, giving little shrieks when they saw a large crab or when a branch brushed their face. The night was dark and moonless, so they were both scared and exhilarated at the same time.

Surprisingly, the crabs weren't frightened of us when we met them head on. They reared up and waved their pincers threateningly. We held out a stick, the crab grabbed it, ready to do battle – and we put crab and stick in a bucket. Hey presto, Mr. Threatening Crab found himself trapped. It's hard to believe we did this for about three hours, but we did, and it was a great adventure for the children, who were fiercely competitive about who was catching the most.

With twenty good-sized crabs between us, we walked about three kilometres back to our dinghies and shared yet another pleasant dinner.

Our first shark-free anchorage was Palakula Bay, Santo, so we stayed for five days, barbecuing ashore at night with the other five yachts who had reached the spot before us. This was a perfect bay for Penny and Peter to go out on their own board boat, *Penepete*, and they were soon confidently sailing across the bay and back, about three miles, with one another or Danny or Adrian as crew.

In town one day we met yachtsmen Gordon and Carmen Heath, originally from Edmonton. They and their three children had sailed here two years earlier on their yacht *Pisago*. Gordon was now managing a soft-drink factory in Santo, and, understanding yachtie that he was, he took us home for an evening of laundry and dinner.

Time was running out on our two-month visas and there were still two anchorages in the Banks Islands we very much wanted to visit.

The first was one hundred miles north, Vanua Lava, or, as the yachties called it, the waterfall anchorage. A hundred miles is my least favourite distance to sail, as we have to sail

164

overnight. We leave in the early afternoon and arrive some-time after noon the following day. I'm usually pretty tired when we arrive as my stomach does not cope well with these twenty-four-hour sails.

We don't usually fish during an overnight sail, but we put out a couple of lines just before arriving at the waterfall anchorage. At about 0800 the line went taut; Paul had a big yellowfin tuna.

"Bring in the other line, so we don't get tangled," he said to Peter. Peter grabbed the line and a look of surprise crossed his face. "I've got a fish on my line, too," he said.

Luckily it was a small one, and he hauled it alongside himself while Paul landed the larger fish. We had fish for every-one at the anchorage now, always a good way to arrive.

The twin waterfalls were visible from sea, so there was no trouble in identifying the correct cove. The anchorage is in an open bay, and it was rolly, but not so bad that we couldn't enjoy a few days here.

The boat children would pick each other up in the dinghies and be ashore as soon as breakfast was over. The pools and rocks below the waterfall made for a great imaginative play area and soon there were dams and new rivulets running all over the place. The water was cool, but refreshing in the hot sun and laundry at the water egress was the order of the day, as well as daily fresh-water baths and shampooing. When you're living in a salt-water environment, you can't get enough of fresh water.

Too soon we were on our way to our next anchorage, Urapa-rapara, where we sailed into the crater of an extinct volcano which had an opening to the sea on one side. It was an eerie feeling to head *Lorcha* through that rough and current-stirred opening and enter a lagoon surrounded by the high steep sides of a volcano. There was no mistaking what it was we were in, and we quickly reduced sail to cope with the heavy gusts of wind hurtling down the rock face. There was no problem in anchoring, though the water was twenty metres deep.

The four yachts which had sailed from Waterfall Bay had each had a catch of large tuna or dorado on the way in, so we took the extra fish ashore for the villagers. These gifts of fish are always appreciated as, though fish is a staple in these fish-rich waters where everyone owns a canoe, the larger pelagic fish are difficult for the locals to catch with their basic gear. Usually the recipient of a gift of fish will return the next day to reciprocate with some coconuts or papaya.

The Reeds decided they would anchor only one night here, but we wanted to watch the rebuilding of the village church. The villagers fashioned the beams using adzes and primitive tools and prepared the palm-frond thatch for the roof.

It rained in short heavy tropical downpours on the three days we were there, with a heavy veil of mist hanging right around the inside of the crater so that you couldn't see the top of the ridge. We were enclosed in our own time capsule, enjoying the community spirit of the village and getting involved in a project that was central to their lives.

Those idyllic three days were in sharp contrast to the difficulties we had in leaving the crater. The opening to the sea is not directly into the brisk trade winds. The wind swirls around the steep island before it hooks into the opening. It then swirls around the inside of the crater. Boats headed out of the crater find it rough going, with heavy gusts accelerating down the slope and the surge rolling round the rim. One has to stay mid-channel, too, as there are fallen rocks where the sea has worn the hole to form the lip of the break.

With reefed sail and the engine at full revolutions, *Lorcha* hardly breasted her way over the foam-crested waves. It was wet and uncomfortable for two miles before we burst through the narrows into a calm (by comparison) sea. We shut off the engine and made full sail, headed for the Solomon Islands.

166

SOLOMON ISLANDS 17

"**D**o you mind if we follow you?" asked Ross Cook, skipper of *Murbah*, an Australian 9.7-metre motor-sailer ketch.

We had been sailing at about the same rate as the Cook family through Vanuata. There were several other Australian yachts around, but Ross had found that his under-canvassed motor-sailer couldn't keep up with the larger, faster yachts. "This is our first offshore voyaging," he explained, "and we don't have a SatNav to help with position-finding between island groups."

I was hesitant to agree. Different boats sail at different speeds even in the same wind strength. Skippers operate their boats according to their personalities. Some like to press on with full canvas, trying to minimize the time on passage. We sail "by the seat of our pants," meaning that we adjust our boat speed according to the situation to maximize our comfort. If the seas are rough, we may slow down, even though we know we could push on faster. Also, we adjust our course to suit our self-steering gear. If it keeps a steadier course ten or twenty degrees off the plotted course, we often let it go, making up the difference later. We have always taken the attitude that cruising by boat should be enjoyable, not an endurance trial.

Shepherding a neophyte voyager, whose skill in

The Cook family . . . night arrival at Ndende . . .
money and trade . . . Penny's deep dive . . . fishing floats
and hooks . . . rain tank repair . . . food shopping at
Mbili Pass . . . trading a sail for carvings . . . war history of
the Solomon Islands.

---

boat-handling or navigation I knew little about, wasn't appealing. I am willing to take responsibility for my own boat and family, over whom I have some control, but looking after someone else is another matter, so when I agreed it was reluctantly.

"We will sail as we want," I told them. "If you want to follow us, that's okay with me. It will be about a two-day passage to Ndende. We'll leave the VHF radio switched on and we'll check with one another through the day, but, please, no night-time calls unless absolutely necessary. I'll leave the masthead navigation light on overnight for you to watch for." (In areas where sighting cargo ships is unlikely, we often sail at night with only a dim kerosene lamp rather than the masthead light to save the drain on the batteries.)

The wind was strong, up to 30 knots, and we were making the passage faster than expected.

"*Moonraker, Moonraker, Moonraker,* this is *Lorcha.* Over," I called on the VHF early the following evening.

Don and Aggie had left Ureparapara a day ahead of us. We were headed for the same anchorage at Ndende, our first harbour in the Solomon Islands, and I had told Don we would call on the VHF when we neared the island. It was now early evening, so we would not approach the anchorage until after dark. It is not our practice to enter unmarked anchorages during the night. We usually heave-to, stopping the boat's movement through the water, but leaving some sail area up to steady *Lorcha* from rolling too much. We then enter harbour at first light.

169

"Stay about one mile offshore as you come up from the southern headland," Don's voice crackled over the VHF. "The coral doesn't extend very far from the coast. I'll leave our masthead light on. When it bears northeast head for it and anchor behind us. There are no lights ashore to confuse our light with."

Don is a good sailor, and, having sailed in *Moonraker*'s company, I trusted his judgement.

As we got in the lee of the headland we slowed down in calmer waters to wait for the Cooks, who had monitored our conversation with *Moonraker*. The two of us sailed the few miles up the coast, watching the waves crashing on the reefs near the shore by the light of a three-quarter moon, only occasionally obscured by clouds.

Soon *Moonraker*'s light was in view, and we slowly sounded our way to within thirty metres of her before letting go our anchor at about midnight. We were a bit nonplussed, however, as we neared the headland, to find our SatNav giving us a position which put us up on shore! We checked the position of the anchorage the following day to find that the charted position of the island was about 2.3 miles southeast of the position registered on our SatNav.

"It's about eight-and-and-half metres deep here," said Don, the next morning "and I can't dive that deep."

We had been snorkeling around the coral heads near the anchored boats, and had gone over to *Moonraker* to find that Don, while disassembling his dinghy outboard motor, had dropped the propeller overboard. Fiona, who is a better swimmer than I am, said she would get a weight belt and try to dive for it.

"If you look down just below *Moonraker*," said Aggie, "you will see a large triton shell. Some kids from shore wanted to trade it, but dropped it from their canoe. The propeller should be just beside it."

Penny looked down through the clear water. She is an excellent swimmer, though we were unsure how deep she could dive. "I'll dive down a bit and try to see it," she said, as she took a deep breath and swam towards the bottom.

It seemed only seconds later she broke the surface of the water, holding the triton shell. "I didn't see the prop, but here's the shell," she said helpfully.

"But that was my marker for the prop," said Don in exasperation, quite overlooking Penny's remarkable free dive.

The propeller remained underwater, despite more dives by Penny, until Ross, a superb swimmer, came over from *Murbah* and easily brought it up on his first try.

The three yachts in the anchorage: *Murbah*, *Moonraker*, and *Lorcha*, made the forty-hour sail to Santa Anna Island in company. We all arrived at about the same time, sailing into the lee of the island before dawn. We trolled back and forth along the fringing reef, having our own fishing contest (a tuna and a coral cod for *Lorcha*; a mackerel and a travelly – the largest fish – for *Moonraker*; and a bonito for *Murbah*) while we waited for the sun to come up so we could find the unmarked reef opening for Port Mary.

Once inside the lagoon, we anchored the boats in a line off the landing beach in front of the village, easily recognized by the villagers' canoes hauled up there. Fiona made breakfast while I cleaned the fish, and I looked up when I heard the bump of a dugout canoe coming alongside.

"My name is John Bob Wasia," said the man in the canoe, "and I am the official welcomer of yachts. If you need anything, just let me know."

We invited him on board for a cup of coffee, well laced with sugar, something the islanders always enjoy as they rarely can afford coffee and anything sweet is a treat.

"We'd like to see some of your carvings," I said, for we had heard that Santa Anna and its close neighbouring island, Santa Catalina, were the only islands in the world where the wooden fishing floats were carved. The fish float motif usually involved Tararamanu, a male figure with a fish's head. The figure sat on the upper end of a twenty-five-centimetre-long

171

shaft. The lower end had a stone ballast weight laced to it. The villagers believe that the much-feared Tararamanu resides in an underwater reef cave between the two islands (sightings are occasionally reported), and that he has often caused the death of people either wicked or naïve who do not honour his being. He is a bridge between the human and the fish world, so fish trust him and approach his image. He is also half human and understands that men must eat fish to survive. Tararamanu mediates the balance. Traditionally the fish float is set free in the lagoon, with fishing line and baited hook attached. When a fish bites, the carving bobs about on top of the water and a canoeist retrieves it and the catch.

When we went ashore that afternoon we found that John Bob had alerted almost the entire village, and most houses had carvings to show us, including many different fishing floats, dancing sticks that women carried during ceremonial festivities, and food bowls, used only during harvest festivals, inlaid with nautilus shell. The pieces were intricately carved with incised patterns and with culturally significant motifs, such as the frigate bird, thought to be a good fisherman and good provider for his offspring, and tuna and bill fish, important food sources; execution of the carving was primitive. There was another item we highly admired: hand-made fish lures and hooks fashioned out of bone or tortoise or clam shell; some of them were very old as they were made by fathers and grandfathers of these villagers. Not many people fashion these work-intensive hooks today, when the islanders are able to get modern lures and hooks, especially from passing yachties.

Items on the top of the list for trade were sharp knives and almost any carving tool, as well as sandpaper of all grades, especially very fine sandpaper. I felt I was contributing to the islanders' cottage industry when I went back to *Lorcha* to get an extra set of auger drill bits. There was only one drill brace on the island, and until I produced my set of bits, the islanders had never known the bits could be changed in the brace

172

for a different-sized drill. The bits were traded for a fishing float and a dancing stick, to the satisfaction of everyone.

"Chief Francis Sao of Santa Catalina Island is here visiting some relatives," John Bob told us the following morning when he again paddled out to *Lorcha*. "He would like you to go to his island to trade with his people."

We thought we had done our quota of trading for this area, but John Bob told us that we would see different carvings on Santa Catalina, as well as some unusual shells which had been washed ashore by Cyclone Namu.

"Besides," he added, half afraid to ask a favour of us, "the Chief needs a lift back to his island."

Santa Catalina was only ten kilometres away from Santa Anna, but it is rarely visited as there is no pass through the fringing reef, except for a dinghy or a canoe; it is only safe to anchor in settled weather for a few hours.

Different carvings and unusual shells were enough of an attraction, and we told John Bob that, weather permitting, we would take the Chief over the following morning.

At 0800 *Lorcha* was heavily loaded as John Bob, who would act as interpreter, Chief Sao, and Aggie and her two boys, plus the four of us headed into the brisk easterly trade winds. It was nearly two hours later before *Lorcha* was anchored off the break in the reef with the thatched roofs of Aorigi Village visible through the palm trees.

"You are only the second yacht in memory to anchor off this island," said John Bob as we helped the Chief into our dinghy, surrounded by dozens of curious island children swimming round us.

"The Chief would like to take you for a walk around the island," said John Bob, as soon as we got everyone ferried ashore.

Cyclone Namu had passed quite close to these islands in her recent destructive path. Many of the gardens were ruined, and several houses were roofless, or the thatch roofs were hanging at precarious angles. But worst of all, one of the two tanks that collected rain water from the school roof, the only metal-roofed building on the island, had been badly damaged. As Santa Catalina is a low island, wells are brackish and rain water is the only source of drinking water, a commodity currently in very short supply. Water was being ferried over from Santa Anna which, being a high island, had good wells and springs.

The real reason for our invitation to visit this island was becoming clear. The Chief said something to John Bob, who cleared his throat.

"Would you be able to help us repair this tank?" he asked.

Though the islanders are self-sufficient in their traditional lifestyle, they had no experience with fibreglass, a material well-known to every yachtie. We carried spare fibreglass cloth and epoxy resin, as we used it from time to time to repair *Lorcha*'s dinghy, and I was glad to help.

Meanwhile, Penny had identified the mysterious shells swept ashore by Cyclone Namu as bubble cones (*Conus bullatus*), a rare shell usually only found in seventy metres of water. Penny and Aggie and Fiona were trading furiously for them, the exchange being worked out at two pieces of children's clothing and/or a small bag of rice for each shell, depending on its condition. As far as Penny was concerned, the day's trip had been worth it just to add this unusual orange-and-red-coloured shell to her collection.

While they were trading, I worked with several men to clean and sand the cracks in the tank. I accelerated the resin so it would harden quickly, enabling us to put several layers of material on the cracks throughout the day.

While we waited for each layer of epoxy and fibreglass to set up, the villagers entertained us in various ways, taking Peter, Danny, Adrian, and myself to the Custom House, a large enclosed thatched building where their sacred religious objects are kept. We were allowed to go inside to see and photograph some of the objects, but Fiona, Aggie, and Penny were not allowed within thirty metres of the building. Had they seen any of the sacred objects, forbidden to the eyes of

174

women, they would have broken ancient tribal tabus. Peter and Adrian were given bows and arrows like those used by the villagers to shoot birds, mostly large pigeons common in these islands, and then were taught how to use them. His bow and arrows are still among Peter's most prized souvenirs of the trip.

By way of payment to us for repairing the tank, the island men who do the ceremonial dancing dressed in their costumes and allowed us to photograph them. They explained that they were not able to give us a dancing demonstration, as a child had died the previous day, and the village was in mourning.

The sun was setting as we returned John Bob to Gupuna Village on Santa Anna Island, and Aggie, Adrian, and Danny to *Moonraker* after a hectic day.

With its half-moon beach, shallow anchorage, and almost enclosed bay, Santa Anna was a perfect place for the kids to row ashore on their own. They were popular visitors as only about twelve yachts a year visit the island and only a small proportion of those have children on board. We could hear the cries of excitement as soon as Penny, Peter, Danny, and Adrian were spotted rowing towards the beach where twenty to thirty children waited to help them drag the dinghy ashore. The island and boat children would spend hours together, walking around the village, playing on the beach, looking for shells, and swimming and diving. Sometimes they would just sit on the sand and sing songs to each other.

Two days before we left, one of the island children, a friendly girl called Anni, shyly pressed a shell necklace into Penny's hand. We rowed ashore that evening with a return present for her – half a bar of chocolate. The next morning when Penny and the others went ashore, there were twelve children lined up with shell necklaces for Penny. Anni had shared her gift with her friends, and it was the first taste of chocolate any of these island children had ever had! Now everyone wanted some. But with our supplies down to our last half bar, we were not able to do any exchanges. What we had done was please one child and disappoint twelve others, which was definitely not our intention, and we resolved to be a little more thoughtful in our future gifts to island children.

Some days later, we were anchored further west at Marovo Lagoon, in front of a house which, it transpired, belonged to Luten Hilakolo, the chief of the area.

We had sailed from Honiara where, because of the devastation of Cyclone Namu, little fresh food was available. There were five yachts in the anchorage here at Mbili Pass, all wondering where to replenish their fresh food supplies.

Nonetheless, the snorkeling was good here and the water still and clear. We saw several lion fish, highly venomous though exotic and beautiful, and the children chased crayfish among the coral heads.

There were Second World War relics nearby – a four-engine plane lay half-in, half-out of the water at the shore only a hundred metres away from *Lorcha*. And Chief Luten came to talk and showed Penny and Peter how to carve ebony and kerosene wood Solomon Island style.

But there was no shopping nearby. The land was flat and sandy, with no fertile soil for gardens. There was a small trade store a couple of miles away from the village, but our own stock of canned and dried goods was better than his. What we wanted was pamplemousses, oranges, limes, papayas, snake beans (a half-metre-long string bean), pumpkins, yams, pineapples, and other fruits and vegetables which grow well in the fertile soil of the higher islands.

"We can go to the gardening area and get some," said Luten. "If you can give me $15 for petrol, I will arrange for one of the men in the village with an outboard motor on a large canoe to take you to there. And I will go along as guide."

Early next morning, then, the four of us, along with the four from *Moonraker*, and two adults from an Australian boat named *Windy*, clambered into the canoe with Luten and two village men. What followed was one of the longest, but most

176

interesting, food-shopping expeditions we have ever gone on.

We motored about three kilometres across the lagoon to one of the higher islands, then poled the canoe two kilometres up a river until we could go no further. We then hiked another kilometre to the top of a ridge overlooking the sea and along a foot path until we came upon a village. There were few people about as most were out in the fields. Luten led the way to some pamplemousse trees loaded with fruit.

"This woman says there are about ten ripe fruit. Would you like them?" said Luten. And so a bargain was struck, the fruit carefully poked with a stick and caught before smashing on the ground, and off we went to another field or plantation.

Luten, chief of this island as well, often stopped to chat with his people. Good-natured banter, then an inquiry as to whether there was surplus produce to sell. We would choose what we wanted, and Luten would buy for his needs. Soon we were loaded like donkeys with all our knapsacks and carrying bags full.

"Don't worry," said Luten. "The Marys will carry for you." *Mary* is a general term in the Solomon Islands for a woman. Soon a long line of bearers followed ten white people, with Luten marching at the head of the column. I began to feel as if we were in an old African safari movie. We hiked through the dense bush between the farming plots, loaded with as much as we could carry in the tropical heat, our female bearers balancing sacks of yams or stalks of bananas on their heads, some carrying armloads of snake beans like fire wood or struggling with large pumpkins. And everyone chattered and laughed, thinking it as much of a lark as we did.

When we were thirsty, drinking coconuts appeared. At one point, Luten called a halt and children gathered nuts. We all sat in the shade of a large tree at intersecting foot paths while nuts were cracked and passed around. The well-placed stones and piles of broken shells were proof that this was a popular stopping place.

When we returned to the canoe we feared that all our produce wouldn't fit. But the carrying capacity of this large canoe was truly amazing. All those sacks and bundles were placed around, we perched on top of the less fragile produce, and Luten made a huge pile of his own purchases. After an hour's journey back down the river and across the lagoon, it was late afternoon by the time we arrived at the anchorage.

Though the shopping in these western Solomon Islands is still primitive, the islands and islanders are much more sophisticated than their eastern counterparts. The carvings here are fashioned from dense and beautifully coloured ebony wood and some, especially the "Spirit of the Solomons," an intricate carving comprising a number of marine animals carved from an ebony root, may cost hundreds of dollars. The carvers are able to take their work to the not-too-distant capital city of Honiara to sell in the tourist trade there.

Hundreds of yachts might come through these islands in a cruising season and the carvers have set up a "half-trade, half-cash" system with the yachties. But the trade items wanted are watches, radios, top-of-the-line carving tools, cameras, or solar panels. We did not have any of those items, but we came up with a winning trade – a large sail. This was a spare fore-sail which we had replaced with a new light drifter in New Zealand. The old sail was of interest because islanders who had invested in outboard engines for their canoes in previous years were now finding it difficult and expensive to get spare parts – and there was a move back to sail. Our sail was too big for a canoe, but we soon solved that problem by cutting it in four. We traded one part for a carving in the morning, and that afternoon had three visitors one after the other also wanting to trade goods for a sail. Which is why we have so many carvings from the Solomon Islands.

The western Solomon Islands saw much action during the Second World War, and memories of that time are still very much alive in the area. The island naval base in Rendovo Lagoon where John F. Kennedy, then a lieutenant, was stationed on the torpedo boat PT109, has been made into a small museum with a thatched hut holding some relics. We sailed

178

past Pudding Island, one of the motus near Gizo, to which Kennedy swam when his craft was sunk during a battle.

There are still Japanese gun emplacements overlooking passes between islands. One lagoon held a sunken Japanese ship with its masts projecting above water. Snorkeling over it we saw a truck swung over the side, still hanging in the slings for off-loading, just as it was when the ship was sunk.

The Solomon Islands were the scene of fierce battles on the islands themselves, in the air, and on the sea around them. The local people have many stories to tell of the coast watchers they aided. We were shown caves where whole villages hid from the Japanese when they invaded. These people were very loyal to the Allied forces, and, it is said, never delivered any Allied personnel to the Japanese, no matter what the consequences were to themselves.

War relics are everywhere: there are downed planes in the bush, artillery batteries, sunken ships, and 1940s Coke bottles on the beaches.

We spent two-and-one-half months in the area, and would willingly have spent much more time there. With their friendly and interesting people and great history, as well as virtually hundreds of excellent anchorages in a tropical setting, the Solomon Islands are one area of the world we would gladly return to.

PAPUA NEW GUINEA 18

A natural extension of our season's cruise through Melanesian Southwest Pacific was our plan to visit Papua New Guinea (PNG) after the Solomon Islands. But nothing works according to plan, and here we launched into a long tale proving that this is so even when one tries to follow proper procedures.

We had planned to leave the Solomon Islands in late September. Had we successfully acquired two-month visas for PNG, we could have spent eight weeks there, still arriving in Australia before the onset of the cyclone season in December. At Honiara, the capital of the Solomon Islands, we applied to the Australian Embassy for PNG visas, as recommended in our guide book. But it seemed that PNG no longer asked the Australians to act for them.

We visited the Air Niugini office and asked their advice. They telexed Port Moresby, PNG's capital city, for advice. We were sent back a telexed message giving customs and immigration officials at any port of entry permission to issue us a two-month visa on arrival.

We were eager to visit the eastern-most islands of PNG, the Louisiade Archipelago, especially the two eastern-most atolls of that area. We had hoped to spend the whole two months exploring these little-visited islands to see the many sailing canoes still in use there, and in general to experience the life of

The best-laid plans of mice and men . . . Misima Island . . .
outrigger sailing canoes . . . luxury on Tempo II *. . .*
a burial ceremony . . . skull cave . . . under surveillance . . .
a fishing accident . . . Samarai at last . . . the wind
swings northeast . . . across the Coral Sea.

---

one of the more primitive areas of the world.

We were told there was a new customs and immigration office on the island of Misima where a gold-mining operation (Canadian Placer) was being established, and much equipment and many expatriate workers were coming in. This sounded great, as it was just next to the Calvados chain of islands, where we hoped to spend much of our time.

As we sailed from our last port in the Solomon Islands, the trade winds were strong and blustery. I lost my favourite sun hat during the first hour of that passage. The stronger trade winds in this area tend to be more southerly in direction, and these winds were true to that rule. Would the loss of my hat be an omen?

We were in rough seas, with *Lorcha* sailing as close to the wind as she could. She sometimes made good our course, but was often forced by the winds to a more northerly course, with sharp blows from the advancing waves, and a quick shower as the spray leapt over her bow.

We approached Misima Island during our second night at sea, but dared not come too close. There was a reef nearby, covered at high tide and with no navigational lights on it. I feared that if we hove-to we might be swept on to the reef if the current around the island was as strong as it is around many other islands in this area. So we came about, and sailed away in a safe direction until near dawn, when I again headed us towards Bwagaoia Harbour.

"Yes," said the Chief of Police, the only official I could find at the government offices at 0930 the next morning, "There is a new customs and immigration office, but the man is not here."

"What time will he arrive?" I asked, thinking he meant the official was not yet in his office for the day.

"In truth," he said, "although the office was officially opened five months ago the customs officer hasn't yet arrived at this island."

Hearts sinking, we showed him our papers and explained what we wanted. We knew that if we were not allowed to clear in here, we would have to go two hundred miles to either Samarai or Alotau from where it would be nearly impossible to return to the islands we wanted to visit, as it would mean going directly against the trade winds and dominant ocean current. It could also mean a more difficult passage to Australia. If the southeast trade winds remained strong and more southerly we wouldn't be able to lay the course to Cairns, the northern-most port of entry on the Great Barrier Reef coast of Australia.

The genial Chief of Police offered to radio Port Moresby to ask if we could be issued a provisional clearance. That way we could visit the Louisiades at will, even if it did mean a difficult passage later. Meanwhile Bwagaoia Harbour was a pleasant anchorage.

There were several outrigger sailing canoes, up to nine metres long, bringing people and produce from the nearby atolls to this government and trading centre for the area. Their sails were mostly made from a mixture of rice or flour sacks, and some had plastic tarpaulin sails. These canoes were double-ended, so that when they changed direction they didn't have to turn around: the former stern would become the new bow, and the sail and mast were angled towards the new bow. It was entertaining to watch them tack out of the narrow reef entrance right into the blustery trade winds. I sometimes held my breath as it appeared they were being swept onto the reef as they changed tacks, but they always made it.

182

"We're waiting for the supply ship to come in," said Ron, skipper of *Tempo* II, a large Australian catamaran with five adults on board, and the only other yacht in the harbour. "It was supposed to arrive yesterday. We left Australia three weeks ago and we need supplies."

Thinking back to when we began cruising, we remembered how many times we had run short of supplies. Now, when we stock *Lorcha*, we load up with enough food and supplies to remain independent for four to six months. But even so, our supplies seemed not quite on the scale that these people expected.

"We've run out of bacon and can't even have a good breakfast," Ron continued. "And the freezer is just about out of steaks and chops. I just hope that supply ship is well stocked."

Fiona and I looked at each other, sharing a thought we dared not express. We hadn't seen a steak or a chop, let alone bacon, for months. As diplomatically as we could, we asked if they didn't think replenishing such things in this remote outpost a bit far-fetched. Had they tried any of the local fish or produce?

We invited the skipper and his wife, Teri, over for coffee. Fiona showed Teri how to make quick bread in the skillet, and how she bakes bread in the pressure cooker. She explained how we get by with only one cooked meal per day. Teri was grateful, as she had felt she was letting her family down by not preparing the kind of meals she would in her land-based home.

We returned to the police station three days later to find we had been refused provisional clearance. We were to proceed to Samarai or Alotau.

We chose Samarai, but I refused to sail there non-stop as the passage was through an area poorly charted and littered with reefs and islets. I said we would sail only during daylight hours and fair weather, and estimated we would arrive in Samarai about one week after leaving Misima. The police chief agreed it would be foolhardy for us to try to sail through the reefs at night, and said he would notify his superiors to that effect.

"But you don't have to leave immediately," he told us. "Stay a few more days here in Bwagaoia."

We were glad we had taken him up on that suggestion, as we met Joanne, a local woman who was well educated and spoke excellent English. She was from one of the important families of the region. Her relatives in a neighbouring village were having a second burial ceremony for one of the chiefs who had died. Would we like to come see some of the ceremony?

In this hot and humid place, when someone dies they are buried almost immediately. A month or two later, when the family has had a chance to spread the word and relatives can gather, they have the official send-off.

We followed the foot paths to find the village. Joanne showed us around, introducing us to people, as well as showing us the food being prepared. One group of women was making sago palm pudding by splitting a type of palm tree, taking out the pulpy interior, then boiling it and straining it into a thick pudding. Pigs, taro, and yams were cooking in the underground ovens, and soup boiled on open wood fires. The soup ladle was a sea shell called a bailer shell (*Melo broderipii*), common in these waters and also used for bailing water out of the open canoes.

Joanne took us into one of the larger houses in the village where many people were assembled, and introduced me – the headman of our family – to Leitu, the new headman. As we sat together, he told about his father, the deceased chief. The man had lived a long life – into his seventies, a great age in this area where short life spans are the norm. He had served as a local government official, and had married wisely to a woman from another important family from a nearby island. She bore him seven children, four of them strong sons, all well educated. His father would always be remembered because not only was he fair in settling disputes, but he had started poultry farms in the village, giving the people a cash income.

True to their oral traditions of honouring the life of an ancestor and preserving his memory by story-telling, Leitu was telling me about his father so that I in turn would be able to pass on the story of this man who had led a productive life.

As we made our way back to *Lorcha* at dusk to avoid the descending mosquitoes in this malaria-prone area, we discussed with Penny and Peter the similarities between this small ceremony, with perhaps 150 people, in a Melanesian culture, and the large funeral in Polynesian Tonga, and how people everywhere have their own ways and traditions of dealing with death.

"We've arranged with a driver to take us up to the top of the island to see the skull cave," said Ron. "Would you like to come along?"

The four-wheel-drive pick-up truck took us up a nearly non-existent road, winding through trees, sometimes following a foot path, sometimes over rocks and ridges. We then walked with a few local people along some foot paths until we reached a ridge overlooking the sea on the windward side of the island. To get into the small hole that was the entrance of the cave we had to crawl over the edge of a sheer cliff with the waves crashing against its foot about sixty metres below. A local man in charge of watching over the cave entered first. After he was inside, we took turns crawling over the edge and lowering ourselves into the cave. Inside, by the light of our flashlights, we could see well-ordered stacks upon stacks of skulls. Some skulls were balanced upon a pile of bones, others simply one upon the other. They were piled almost to the entrance of the cave, which was said to be very, very deep. We were told the skulls were the booty of head-hunting expeditions, which were common throughout Melanesia until about the turn of the century, when European missionaries and colonial governments teamed up to eradicate the practice.

It was said that the skulls were placed in this sacred and dramatic setting to honour the bravery of the opposing warriors.

Fiona and I took our turns first to view we-knew-not-what grisly scene before allowing Penny and Peter to enter. Because the setting was so majestic, almost other-worldly – the white-capped waves marching towards us from the distant horizon, the thunder of the breakers crashing below, the buffeting of the brisk trade winds as they lifted in gusts over the cliff edge and whistled at the mouth of the cave – the skulls imposed an image not of deceased people, but rather of a surrealistic mural. They seemed somehow anonymous, and we had no hesitation in allowing our children to witness this cultural relic. Penny and Peter were thrilled more by their daring at lowering themselves over the edge of the cliff – one hand clamped to an adult's – than they were frightened by the cave's contents, though they soon scrambled out again. It was the grandeur of the setting, not the death symbols, that left the biggest impression.

"We are leaving this morning," I told the Chief of Police as I shook his hand. "Thank you for your efforts on our behalf."

I hadn't told him our destination for that day, as we hadn't yet made up our minds. I was tempted to sail to Tagula Island, then head through the nearest reef pass and on to Australia, but we sailed first to the Deboyne Lagoon, in the direction of Samarai, to anchor behind Nivani Island. At only twenty-five miles from Misima, it was an easy sail, and we were soon ashore trading with the locals for some excellent nautilus shells. There were several sailing canoes around the lagoon, and a few were being built on the beach. We decided to spend an extra day here, thinking we might not get another chance to visit such interesting and friendly villagers.

Early the next morning we were again ashore walking the foot paths and visiting many local people employed in their common tasks. They wove baskets, mended fish nets, and there was a crowd constructing a thatch hut. Penny and Peter were enchanted with a pet parrot who strutted around his master as he worked. I watched as one man carved a *lagim*, a ritual canoe splash board, intricately patterned in curvilinear designs. The new canoe it would decorate was just beside him, nearly complete. Others worked to finish the sailing rig.

Late in the afternoon, after we were back on *Lorcha*, a large fishing-trawler-type vessel entered the lagoon and motored slowly towards us. We were anchored in shallow water so a skiff was launched for the trawler's occupants to approach us. These were several men dressed in military uniform.

They were a government patrol, and could they check our documents?

I explained our situation to the three men as they sat in our cockpit drinking coffee served by Fiona. They took down the particulars and returned to their vessel to radio the authorities and check our story. We were to remain on the boat, they said, at anchor, until they returned.

A couple of hours later the skiff approached again. The men told us that they understood the situation, though they were disappointed that we were not moving along a bit faster.

I was fed up with trying to accommodate the officials in this situation not of our making. I wanted to head towards the Jomard Pass in the outer reefs, about forty miles away, and make for Australia.

Fiona feared the surveillance vessel might stay near the pass and apprehend us if we ran for Australia. I felt we had done nothing wrong, and if we did head for Australia, we would simply be saving the other officials some paperwork.

Fiona's persistence won out, and for the next three days we sailed on, only anchoring overnight. The water inside this reef area was crystal clear, with lots of coral banks, but it was nerve-wracking to look down and see coral heads flying by. Even though there was up to fifteen metres of water below us, the clarity and colours made it appear only a metre or so deep.

"My hand! My hand!" shrieked Peter as we sailed along one day trolling for fish.

He had wrapped the trolling line around his hand to get a better grip so that he could "jig" the lure as *Lorcha* breezed along at about 5 knots. A large fish had struck the lure, and the line was cutting into Peter's hand. The fish was large enough to create a strong drag as it fought the line, nearly pulling Peter over the side.

I threw the tiller over to let *Lorcha* fly into the wind, slowing her pace and easing the strain. I grabbed the line in front of Peter's hand and was able to pull in enough slack to ease the line from around his hand. The one-hundred-kilo test monofilament line had made deep creases in Peter's skin, and the skin was broken and bleeding in a couple of places. It was painful for several days afterwards.

The fish was a big trevally, a sort of jack, weighing about eighteen kilos. Not my favourite eating fish, but we took enough for a couple of meals and gave the remainder to some people at Tubetube village on Slade Island where we anchored late that afternoon.

One week after leaving Misima we arrived at Samarai on the China Straits, so named because when first discovered it was thought to shorten the route from Sydney, Australia, to China. It was never a popular route, as the strong currents and many reefs and islets make it hazardous.

"Yes," said the man at the customs and immigration office, "I know all about you."

I asked if there would have been a problem if we had sailed for Australia after the surveillance vessel checked our documents.

"It would have meant nothing to us," he told me. "But for now there is a problem of issuing visas. I advise you to accept only a temporary visa, as I can stamp that in your passports. Otherwise I will have to send your passports to Port Moresby where they may get lost. But the temporary visa is only good for ten days."

Samarai is a dying town. It was formerly a government centre as well as a trading centre, but the large storehouses were falling into disrepair, many stores and workshops had closed down, and there was a rumour the few remaining government offices would soon leave, too.

We sailed to nearby Dagadagabonalua Island for a few days to sort out what to do. By now it was early October, the time of year when the trade winds ease in strength, and we could hope for some northerly winds for a few days at a time. I prayed for a wind shift. But meanwhile we had a nice time here, with lots of village children coming out to the boat. Penny and Peter paddled about in the dugout canoes and swam with the local youngsters.

Three days after our arrival at the anchorage the wind swung to the northeast during the night. Though that shift made the anchorage uncomfortably rolly, the wind rolling waves in from an unprotected direction, I was glad to have it. During the morning the wind strengthened. We sailed back to Samarai to clear out of the country.

"I thought you might be coming in today," said the same immigration official. "I have these four passports from people on an Australian yacht. They gave up waiting for them to be returned from Port Moresby. Can you carry them to Australia? I don't want to trust them to the mail service."

I set a course due south from the China Strait, for I knew the northerly wind would last for two, perhaps three days at the most. It would then likely shift back to the southeast and blow more strongly than ever. If I could get us far enough south on this wind, we could still have an easy passage to Australia when the blustery southeast wind returned.

With full sail up and fingers crossed, I set the self-steering gear to maintain a fast broad-reaching course, heading across the Coral Sea.

AUSTRALIAN AMBLING 19

"The wind is going to the east," I told Fiona as I came off my morning watch forty-eight hours after leaving Samarai. "It will probably continue to shift as the sun gets higher in the sky."

In those two days we had sailed 250 miles. Though we had headed nearly due south, sailing at 5 knots, we were being set to the west by a 1-knot current. I had known from the current arrows on the pilot charts that this would happen and had allowed for it. We were now in an excellent position to make for the Grafton Passage of the Great Barrier Reef.

On passage we always try to stay up-wind and up-current of our destination. We sometimes sail more miles than a direct-line course, but I avoid heading straight for a destination until I know I can run downwind to it. I began sailing in this manner after reading about old-time voyagers whose sailing ships could not efficiently sail against the wind.

By following commercial sailing ship routes, or planning passages using the same philosophy, we rarely have the wind forward of the beam. This assures comfortable passages and increases the likelihood of our making our destination.

During the night of our fourth day at sea we sighted the eleven-mile-range light, flashing four

Sailing up-wind . . . Grafton Passage . . . enter bureaucracy . . .
Lorcha ashore . . . we buy a car . . . gypsying on land . . .
kangaroos and kookaburras . . . friends at Noosa Heads . . .
gold-panning . . . cyclone coming.

---

times every twenty seconds, marking the Grafton Passage. A metal framework tower holds the light thirty-two metres above the water.

But where was the Great Barrier Reef? We could see nothing except the tower. No crashing breakers, no motus with palm trees. And where was the largest inhabited island, the smallest continent in the world? Grafton Passage was about twenty miles from the mainland. There was a morning haze, and even though we should have been seeing a sector light on Fitzroy Island (it has a range of thirty-two miles) there was nothing visible.

But soon we made out Cape Grafton, and then we saw charter boats speeding towards us. These were tourist boats from Cairns, heading for the Great Barrier Reef, closer to the mainland here than at any other major city. Sport-fishing boats, scuba-diving charter vessels, and tour boats are up early, chasing the tourist dollar. Before long a thirty-metre military vessel also roared towards us at high speed. This coast is closely patrolled for drug smugglers and illegal immigrants, and we were surprised we hadn't seen a patrol vessel earlier.

Once inside the Great Barrier Reef – and we never did see any actual reefs – we sailed for seven hours before arriving at Cairns harbour. I called the harbourmaster on the VHF to announce our arrival and ask where to go for clearance.

"As you sail in, you will see a jetty with *Aurelia* IV, a white cruise ship, tied to it," said a voice with a sharp Aussie twang.

191

"Tie up at the jetty and the officials will be there to board you and clear you in."

There were only barnacle-encrusted pilings about four and a half metres apart for us to lay alongside, and a gap of about six metres from the planked walkway to the water. A back eddy from the tidal race nearly swept us under the jetty. Full revolutions in reverse narrowly saved the day. The three officials waiting impatiently on the pier again motioned for me to come alongside. I swung around in the current, and cutting across it, threw the tiller over at the last minute. Along with a lot of throttle in reverse, this put us alongside. There was no way we could keep *Lorcha*'s rub rail from grinding against the pilings. The wood groaned and the swirling current kept *Lorcha* shifting about.

The waiting officials came down the ladder to assemble in *Lorcha*'s now-crowded cabin.

"We'll have those passports you brought from Samarai," said the customs official, an officious and brusque young woman. She carefully inspected the seal on the envelope to check it hadn't been opened.

"How long will you stay in Australia? Can you show us proof of funds to support yourself for that time? You are here on a tourist visa, no working allowed."

"How much is your boat worth?" asked another official.

"I have no idea what the value of *Lorcha* would be in Australia," I replied. "Nor what the rate of exchange from Canadian to Australian dollars would be.

I was fixed with an icy glare, as if I had ridiculed some tenet of Australian bureaucracy. If a foreign-built vessel is sold in Australia, the seller is liable for a 50 per cent duty. Pleasure boats are, as a rule, less expensive in Australia than in Europe or North America. Thus, if the owner is asked at entry the value of the vessel, he is likely to state a higher value than the potential selling price in Australia. The duty would be payable on the higher amount.

"List all electronic or other removable equipment you have on board, complete with serial numbers, on this form. The list will be compared with what you have on board when you check out of Australian Territory."

"Let's have a look at your food stores," said the agricultural officer.

Because Australia is an island, they can closely guard against plant or animal diseases which might be unknowingly imported.

"I'll take this Singapore canned chicken, and these tins of South American beef," he said putting the confiscated items in a large plastic bag. "You can crack and cook those eggs, and I will take the shells. Peel a couple of those onions for your omelet. I will take the skins and the remainder of the onions."

He searched further, taking such items as popcorn, lentils, all fruit and vegetables, mung beans, and even a soup mix which had some whole grains which he said might sprout and grow, and could be carrying a plant disease.

"Let me see your first-aid kit," said the customs officer. Her eyes lit up as she rummaged. "I'll take these antibiotics and these Lomotil diarrhea tablets. They are prescription drugs here. When in Australia you will follow the rules like everyone else who lives here."

The questions and paper-signing continued for what I thought was an unreasonable length of time. I had had little sleep in the previous twenty-four hours, and was more than a little put off by the demanding officiousness of it all. *Lorcha* grated her rail on the pilings, irritating me even further, as I wasn't allowed the time to properly protect her topsides.

I promised to take to the customs officer, within the demanded forty-eight hours, a detailed list of the times and dates of the anchorages we would be at for the next months. I was told to go to the harbourmaster's office to get permission to anchor in one of the designated areas before leaving the jetty, which we were to clear in fifteen minutes time.

Welcome to bureaucratic Australia!

We established ourselves in the anchorage up Smith's Creek. The Cairns Cruising Yacht Squadron is nearby, with a club house complete with laundry facilities and showers. We paid a reasonable fee for a temporary membership and had use of all the facilities.

Other international cruising yachts were arriving daily, many that we knew. Some were staying the cyclone season here, while others would only clear in here and then continue sailing further down the coast.

We didn't plan to sail south down the coast. It is against the predominant wind and would be a hard and slow slog. At the end of the cyclone season we would have had to sail back up the coast, repeating those same miles. Nor did we want to stay in Cairns where the gnats, mosquitoes, and flying cockroaches were worse than at any other place in the world we have visited.

We decided to do some inland touring and put *Lorcha* ashore at Safe Anchorage Marina, run by Joe Vendable, an Australian who had lived in Sarnia, Ontario, for several years.

Lorcha was still in excellent condition after all our work on her in New Zealand and required little repair or maintenance. Left in the care of Joe, we knew she would be safe, even though she would be stored in a cyclone area.

"If you can get her certified," I told a man who sold older cars from his home, "I'll give you your asking price of $900."

The fifteen-year-old station wagon looked a bit tatty, but seemed mechanically sound. Australia has strict rules for roadworthiness and older cars are well maintained. In the seven months and twelve thousand kilometres we drove it, we only replaced the muffler and two tires on that station wagon.

Australia is a marvelous country to camp through. The campsites in national or provincial parks are free, as are some owned and operated by municipalities. Most have toilets and showers, water supplies, as well as the necessary (for every Australian) picnic table, "barbie" (barbecue pit), and firewood.

We found the itinerant life ashore was not that much different from our life afloat. We travelled slowly, as the old wagon, loaded as she was with all our camping gear and some basic stocks of food and water, would overheat if we drove at more than eighty-five kilometres per hour. We would set off in the early morning to avoid the worst of the Australian summer heat, stopping at lunchtime at a municipal park, always with shade trees and a water spigot. We'd do another hour or two of driving before we pitched our tent and let the children run around while we built our fire for the evening meal.

The national parks of Australia are well organized, and the sites have all been chosen to preserve something special at each one. Eungella National Park was the first visited, and it remains one of our favourites. It was here that Penny and Peter were introduced to some of Australia's fabled animals.

Kangaroos grazed placidly around the tent site as we made camp. The children were more timid of them than they were of the children, but soon Penny and Peter tried to match the hopping of the kangaroos, and they seemed to have found new playmates.

A stream flowed just beside the campsite, and in it lived many platypuses. Standing quietly by the banks in the late evening or early morning one could see the bubble trails as these small brown creatures hunted for food. If you were quiet enough, they would slowly float to the surface for a breath of air, and pause to look around before diving again. Penny and Peter were up at the crack of dawn every day to watch the platypuses.

But who could sleep late anyway, with the kookaburras calling so raucously? These birds are known as the bushman's alarm clock – with good reason. Their loud laughing calls are territorial warnings and can reach fever pitch. The birds are related to the kingfisher and closely resemble a brown version of one of the larger species. They can be real characters, and their antics are always entertaining. They were constantly hungry. Kookaburras would jostle one another for a vantage point as the breakfast fire was started. Once the bacon was sizzling in the pan, it was every man – or bird – for himself. One might swoop down to snatch a rasher of bacon right from the pan on the fire. Landing nearby, it would give the bacon a few healthy wallops on a rock before gobbling it down. The kookaburra's usual fare in the wild is small lizards and snails, hence the wallops. Successful habits are hard to break.

But it wasn't only the kookaburra birds that entertained us. The Australian bush contains a profusion of bird life which has to be seen to be believed. Imagine waking up to the sight and sound of a thousand brightly coloured wild parrots! We bought the children bird books, and all of us became avid birdwatchers.

Overland travel in Australia is always interesting – sometimes for the similarity of mile after mile of low and sparse bush, sometimes for the tall and dense forests, but always for the land and what grows on it. It is very different in colour and texture from what we North Americans are accustomed to.

Away from the coast, you are quickly into the hot and dry countryside. The green areas of Australia are merely an outline of verdure following the coast. The further inland, the hotter and drier it is.

After several days of tent camping we would stop for a night or two and rent an "on-site van." This is a caravan in a commercial campground, fully furnished with cooking utensils and everything but bed linens and towels. There are usually laundry facilities, swimming pools, and barbies. They are less expensive than renting a motel room, yet make a comfortable break from tent camping.

By the time we reached Noosa Heads, part way down the east coast, our friends, Don, Aggie, Danny, and Adrian Reed of *Moonraker* were there, established back in their waterfront home. In this same small town, only one block away, lived Anita Aarons and Merton Chambers. Anita had been the director of the art gallery at Harbourfront, the waterfront complex Fiona had worked at up to the time of our sailing from Toronto three years earlier.

When we had left Toronto, Anita had invited us to visit her "if we happened to get to Australia." Though she had lived

196

and worked for many years in Canada, Anita is Australian, and she had returned to her home country for her retirement years.

Over Christmas and New Year's we divided our time between these two households. Penny and Peter liked playing with Danny and Adrian, but Anita's grandmotherly attentions (and her guinea pig, which gave birth to a litter of offspring on Christmas morning), had certain attractions.

Our lives were as mixed and varied as ever. We visited Sydney and then Canberra before we were back in the bush cooking over an open fire and sleeping in a tent.

We panned for gold in Ballarat, where gold was first discovered in Australia in 1851. Thereafter Penny and Peter wanted to pan for gold in every stream we crossed to add to the few gold particles they had found.

We were on a free-roaming amble around the eastern portion of Australia, but we did have a time limit, the change of seasons when we should be back in Cairns to rejoin *Lorcha*. We also had a destination in southern Australia, a turn-around point. Fiona had last seen Kate Obst nearly thirty years earlier when they had been classmates for ten years at Cranley School in Edinburgh, Scotland. After they had graduated from school, Fiona had moved to London, England, with her family before emigrating to Canada. Kate had eventually emigrated to Australia.

Our travelling now allowed the opportunity for these two roaming Scots to renew their friendship and share the divergence and similarities of their lives on two different continents, both former colonies of the Empire, from the perspective of a common education.

"You might make it through on the road today or tomorrow," said the Park Ranger at Carnarvon National Park, "but there's a cyclone up in the Gulf of Carpentaria which will dump a lot of rain on us in the next few days. It could be a week or more before you get out again."

We were at Roma, 280 kilometres from a park said to have

some of the finest examples of aboriginal cave drawings, as well as spectacular scenery. Like many roads in Australia's interior, this was not an all-weather road. When it rains, the road turns to mush.

We decided that perhaps the next time we were in Australia we would visit there. That is the attitude one must take when travelling overland or by sea. You can't do it all, so why risk getting into a potentially dangerous situation when there are so many other fascinating places to visit?

THE CORAL COAST 20

I n Cairns the international cruising boats were in a positive orgy of preparation. The well-organized yachts which had spent the season in Cairns and environs had, to our envy, already left. They would take their time on the 450-mile northwards cruise of the upper reaches of the Great Barrier Reef, stopping at isolated anchorages on the mainland and on the reef itself and perhaps also exploring some deep mainland rivers. Other international cruisers were still making their way north up the east coast of Queensland and would be leaving Cairns even later than us. A solid core of us were in the middle ground, neither early nor late, but feeling that we had to get moving.

You would be forgiven for thinking that we were such old hands by now at the getting-ready-for-passage game that the necessary preparation would be second nature for us. But no matter how experienced you are, there is always a lot of work to do to get ready for weeks or months of sailing.

In Cairns we would stock up for the voyage up the Great Barrier Reef coast and then west to Darwin, and also for the upcoming Indian Ocean crossing. We also needed to apply anti-fouling paint to the bottom of the boat, paint the decks, repair our dinghy outboard engine, service our inboard diesel, check all lashings and fittings of *Lorcha*'s sailing rig,

Maintenance . . . our new life-raft . . . the "Careful Coast" . . .
coral formation . . . Captain James Cook . . . lice attack . . .
booby bird . . . chocolate rationing . . . anomalies at
Portland Roads . . . a gift of prawns . . . great groupers . . .
Ashymakaihken.

---

fit the new sail (our old one was worn out after 22,000 miles),
and it was time to have the life-raft checked – its last inspec-
tion had been in Panama two years earlier.

We couldn't expect to pass muster unscathed and we were
not disappointed. First we found that our new sail had been
sewn with one panel too many and as there was no way we
could make it fit, we had to take it to the local sailmaker to be
recut. Then, to our utter astonishment, our five-year-old life-
raft was condemned.

"Look here," said Bill Rutland, the manager of the RFD life-
raft servicing depot in Cairns. "All those dark spots (there
were at least a hundred) are where the rubber has dried. Just
rub them with your finger and they'll turn to dust. Your life-
raft won't hold air for long. Just thank your lucky stars you
had it checked."

We had to agree, even as we unhappily dug deep in our
pockets for the $3,000 we needed for a new life-raft. Our situa-
tion caused consternation among our cruising colleagues,
some of whom had not had their life-rafts checked for five
years.

Our own life-raft had been two years old when we had
bought it. It had been inspected on purchase and again
twenty months later in Panama. We kept it stowed in *Lorcha's*
cockpit, protected with a specially fitted cloth cover over the
canister.

"I can't see that there was any negligence with your raft,"
said Rutland. "We don't expect life-rafts in the tropics to last

more than five to seven years. You've just hit the lower edge of the scale."

We displayed our condemned raft at the Cairns Cruising Yacht Squadron for other yachties to inspect before slashing it with a knife so that no one would be tempted to take a chance with it. The nice ending to the story is that we drowned our sorrows with Joy and Ken Bryce of the Australian yacht *Mischief* and their two children, ten-year-old Cameron and eight-year-old Andrea, and found ourselves wonderful cruising companions for the next year, as the Bryces were also headed across the Indian Ocean.

We dubbed the Coral Coast the "Careful Coast" for this is not an easy coast to travel. It is that part of the Queensland coast protected by the Great Barrier Reef, a reef extending about twelve hundred miles from Gladstone in the south to the Torres Strait off the northern tip of Australia. In truth, the Great Barrier Reef is a series of thousands of individual reefs so close to each other that they are known by one name. There are many charted entrances through the reefs ranging from wide and major to small and difficult. The navigable channel between the mainland and the reef is well marked.

Coral is formed by millions of tiny animals which secrete a lime covering. Each animal's shell is connected to the lime shells of the animals above, below, and beside it. Live coral reefs are filled with a rich variety of marine life, for though the coral consumes most of the plankton, seaweed and the coral polyps provide food for small fish, which in turn attract the larger fish. Live coral is brilliantly coloured, and the fish which inhabit the reefs, to protect themselves, have adapted by also becoming brilliantly coloured.

Disappointingly, that world was not reflected in the waters we explored. Though there were still plenty of fish, much of the coral we saw had lost its glitter because of the predations of the crown-of-thorns starfish (*Acanthaster planci*), which eats living coral organisms. The natural predator of that starfish, the triton trumpet (*Charonia tritonis*), now protected in northern Australia, has had its population so depleted by

202

collectors that the crown-of-thorns starfish population is out of control. The Great Barrier Reef is in need of attention.

We decided to day-sail the Coral Coast, anchoring in the late afternoon.

On June 9 we sailed out of Cairns harbour on our first voyage since we had arrived in Australia the previous October. We made a short sail to the Low Isles on day one and to the Hope Islands on day two. On our third day we made a passage to Cooktown, named after Captain James Cook.

When I think of the care we had to take on this coast with the benefit of modern charts and navigational aids, I can only imagine with horror what it must have been like for the early explorers. Captain Cook, who first sailed through here in 1770, was sailing these waters unaware that the Great Barrier Reef existed! Cook's vessel, *Endeavour*, ran onto a reef, now named Endeavour Reef, east of the Hope Islands and south of Cooktown.

The coral reef which almost destroyed the ship also saved it. After a calamitous twenty-four hours on the reef, the ship was at last refloated and was found to have a piece of coral plugging the hole in the hull. This actually saved it from sinking. *Endeavour* was then towed by rowboats manned by Cook's crew to a safe careening beach up a river, now the present site of Cooktown.

Cook and his crew camped here for six weeks while they made *Endeavour* seaworthy, making them the first Europeans to spend any time along this coast. They are often credited with being the first Europeans to see a kangaroo, but in fact, the animal had been recorded more than a century earlier by the Dutch Captain Pelsaert (1629) and later by the English explorer, William Dampier (1685). Cook and his naturalist team of Joseph Banks and Dr. Daniel Solander were the first to take specimens of this strange beast. Cook reported that "its progression is by hopping or jumping . . . it bears no sort of resemblance to any European Animal I ever saw . . ." Cook called this strange beast a kangaroo after consulting with some aboriginals. Banks brought back a stuffed kangaroo skin

203

to the English painter George Stubbs, and the first ever painting of a kangaroo was presented to the Royal Academy in 1772. Cook was, however, the first European to make contact with the aboriginal people of Australia, of whom he wrote in his journal: ". . . they may appear to some to be the most wretched people on earth, but in reality they are far more happier than we Europeans; being wholly unacquainted not only with the superfluous but the necessary conveniences so much sought after in Europe, they are happy in not knowing the use of them. . . . They seemed to set no value upon anything we gave them, nor would they ever part with anything of their own for any one article we could offer them. This in my opinion argues that they think themselves provided with all the necessarys of life." Two hundred years later, life is not quite so simple.

At Howick Island, we wondered why Penny and Peter were scratching their heads so much. Sure enough – head lice. And we had no lice shampoo on board. It is perhaps noteworthy that while the kids never got lice in the many South Pacific islands where we often saw islanders examining each others' heads for the little critters, they got infested with these pests on mainland Australia. I washed their heads with a medicated shampoo, hoping to control the parasites until we could get to a town with a pharmacy – and that wouldn't be on this isolated coast.

During our port- and island-hopping north, we often anchored but did not launch the dinghy to go ashore. We were tired after the day's sail, but also shark warnings and crocodile stories made us apprehensive about swimming. We were glad to row ashore at Flinders Island where our chart indicated there were fresh-water springs, but it was not be one of our most pleasant stops: the sandflies were fierce, and, on the way back to *Lorcha*, Penny's glasses fell from her nose to be lost forever in deep water. Losing glasses is a hazard for cruising families and one which must be budgeted for. A string definitely helps, but Penny wasn't wearing the one we had bought for her. She had a reserve one-ear-piece-broken-off pair which she had to make do with until Darwin. We know of one cruising family which bought six pairs of glasses at a time for their ten-year-old daughter.

We had an unexpected catch on our trolling line near Hannah Island – a booby bird. Penny and Peter added their frantic cries to the pained squawks of the hapless bird as we tried to haul him in, impossible to do without dousing him under water and nearly drowning him. But he was still crying loudly when we pulled him on board. Paul donned gloves to free him, as our fierce captive was still lively enough to put his pointed beak to vicious use. The hook wasn't deeply embedded, and once free the booby bird was able to lurch away under his own steam, gathering strength as he went till we could see he was going to be all right.

Later in the evening another booby bird was determined to settle on *Lorcha* for the night despite being chased off. At one point, as Paul was gently shooing him away, he toppled off our stern and into the water. His clumsy ineptitude verified his name and caused us much laughter.

We were not counting the days to Cape York, Darwin, or South Africa, but at anchor off Night Island Penny wanted to know when we could eat the twelve large bars of chocolate we had stocked up with in Cairns.

"We left Cairns in June and we plan to be in Richard's Bay, South Africa, by the beginning of December," I told her. "You work it out."

We each had our first piece of chocolate after supper that night, Penny having decided that we could share out two bars each month for the next six months.

The following day we saw a tanker steaming up from the south behind us at the same time as a freighter was charging down from the north ahead of us, their speeds quite obviously such that they would pass each other and us at the same time. They decided to pass one on either side of us, their respective crews waving cheerily from forty-five metres to port and to starboard. We felt like a mouse between two elephants.

Portland Roads was nothing more than a straggle of isolated houses, but it was memorable for a number of reasons, not least its friendly, get-away-from-it-all inhabitants who told us that at least a yacht a day, sometimes two or three, had been anchoring there overnight for the past few weeks.

"You're welcome to get fresh water from that big tank," said inhabitant Bill indicating a large tank just down the hill from his house. "It's supplied by a natural spring." Under a tree beside the tank stood an anomaly we had never seen anywhere else – a gasoline-powered washing machine.

"Yes, it does work," laughed Bill. "But it has its idiosyncrasies. You're welcome to have a go. Just fill it up with your own gasoline. It doesn't always fire, but it's never blown up. We all use it!"

Portland Roads had another anomaly – a barge moored in the bay which acted as a floating supply depot for the trawlermen who ply this coast. The mother ship offloaded supplies such as beer, cigarettes, fuel, and other necessities once a month in such quantity that the barge's decks were awash.

And talk about crocodile scares! The night before our arrival, the barge manager had come down the steps from his caravan aboard the barge and begun wading through the water sloshing on the decks to his rowboat to row ashore for the evening. Suddenly he noticed movement in the water on the deck at the end of the barge. He had been joined by a crocodile! This had put a sudden end to his night-time shore-side visits until the barge was fully afloat again, and its unwelcome visitor was clearly seen to have departed. The threat is not an imagined one. An Australian government publication, *Crocodiles – A Few Simple Facts!* states that the male estuarine or "salty" crocodile (*Crocodylus porosus*) matures at sixteen years of age at three to four metres long, and "the salt-water crocodile is a known predator of man."

At Cape Grenville the following night we anchored near a couple of trawlers.

"Are you one of those world-travelling yachts?" shouted the skipper as he nosed his vessel's bow near *Lorcha*. "Good on you, mate. Here's a present for the children."

He passed over a huge bucket of magnificent prawns. I had nothing freshly baked, so we handed over a bar of chocolate (leaving Penny to calculate the consequences!) in thanks.

"Now don't be afraid of the big groupers you might see around here," the skipper continued. "But don't go after them with a speargun either. They've been coming here for their share of prawns ever since we started anchoring overnight five years ago. We consider them our special friends."

Peter immediately set up a grouper watch, and it wasn't long before he spotted one, two, three of them – enormous fish swimming lazily between and around the boats, quite at home and unafraid. They must have weighed about 150 kilograms – each! – and were the same species of giant *mourou* that we had seen captured and tethered to mooring buoys at Ile Royale, French Guiana, waiting to be served up for dinner. It was fine to see them in a freer environment and to watch the friendly trawlermen throw them a breakfast of net-damaged prawns at dawn the next day.

After a couple of quiet overnight anchorages at Hannibal Islets and Escape River, we were on our last day's sail to our most northern stop, Mount Adolphus Island. An Australian coastwatch plane called us to check our identity, and then we got a call from another Canadian yacht, *Ashymakaihken*. They had overheard our conversation.

"We're expecting to get to Mount Adolphus this afternoon, too," said the skipper, Ashley. "Brenda's from Toronto; let's get together when we arrive. First to catch a fish cooks supper."

A few minutes later we had an enormous tug on our trolling line. Unfortunately it was a large barracuda, reputed to carry the sometimes fatal ciguaterra poisoning, so we threw it back, but we still enjoyed cooking dinner for Ashley and Brenda as we were able to collect a bucket of oysters ashore. We were amazed and impressed to hear that they were on their second circumnavigation of the world, having left Toronto fifteen years previously.

Mount Adolphus was a pleasant stop for a few days. It was full of unusual marine life, including a sea hare, our first close look at this large (twenty-five-centimetre-long) slug-like creature with ruffled skirts and eyes on stalks. This one rewarded Peter for rescuing it from the beach by squirting red ink over the rock pool he had gently placed it in. In the pristine tide pools here we also saw a sea cucumber, another slug-like animal which can grow to half a metre long, and one-third that in diameter. Sea cucumbers will jettison their inner organs when disturbed and regrow them later. Many-coloured abalone shells were abundant, as were giant clam shells wearing gardens of colourful algae on their fleshy lips. These were embedded tightly in the coral reefs.

The idyllic days passed swiftly and sweetly, giving no indication that on our next passage, the 750-mile voyage across the Gulf of Carpentaria to Darwin, we would face our most fearful incident at sea.

NEAR COLLISION 21

There's no accounting for the thoughts that go through your head at times of danger.

The night we almost died, I thought: I must be dreaming.

I thought: This is how *Mainstay* went down.

I thought: Let the children sleep. There's no point in waking them if we're going under.

We had sailed out casually from our comfortable anchorage at Mount Adolphus Island for the long passage across the top of Australia to Darwin. There was no running around or flurry of last-minute shopping. We would make do with what was on board. We were well stocked with basic foodstuffs, though a little light on fresh fruit and vegetables, our only fresh produce being apples and cabbage. We waved *au revoir* to *Ashymakaihken* – they had decided to relax for another day. We'd see them in Darwin.

Sailing over the top of Australia is complicated by the constriction of the Torres Strait. The tides of the Pacific Ocean and the westward flow of her currents try to squeeze through this seventy-five-mile-wide body of water, miles further divided into many channels as a sprinkling of islands and reefs further complicate the passage.

The tides and currents of the Indian Ocean on the western side of the islands of the Strait have a

Sailing problems at the top of Australia . . . seasick again . . .
supertanker from nowhere . . . collision course . . .
emergency! . . . hit by the bow wave . . . bridge deck
deserted . . . back to work.

---

different pull. Within a few miles the mariner might go from a high tide in the Pacific to a low tide in the Indian Ocean. The currents rush first one way then another as the water tries to seek an equilibrium. There is a lot of turbulence, and not all of it is predictable.

We studied the tide tables and the phases of the moon, looked over the charts, and decided not to go to the main shipping channel, the Great North-East Channel, which flows past Thursday Island, but to take the shorter, but shallow and unmarked Endeavour Strait, which passes just south of Prince of Wales Island. This is only possible at certain phases of the moon, as the tide and daylight must be in proper synchronization.

There was a light tidal flow against us as we sailed from Blackwood Bay to round Yorke Island, just north of Cape York, mainland Australia's northern-most point. Then the pull of the tide had us racing along with about 3 knots of current sweeping us towards the sandbanks at the other end of Endeavour Strait. Six hours after leaving Mount Adolphus Island astern, we were past Red Wallis Island, itself a mere sandbank a couple of metres above the high-tide mark.

Now it was 630 miles of plain sailing to Cape Don and Dundas Strait.

I had not put my usual Scopaderm seasickness patch behind my ear as I hoped that with all the day-sailing we had done coming up the coast my body would be attuned to the sea.

I began to feel queasy in the late afternoon and had a

couple of vomiting sessions that night. The lightship marking Carpentaria Shoal and the last of the less than thirty-metre-deep water was abeam at 0410.

By the following night, I was quite ill, but this had happened before, and I came up for my 0200 watch as usual. It was now over forty hours since we had left Mount Adolphus and as I'm usually over the worst within forty-eight hours, I assumed I would get through my watch all right.

But, huddled under our cockpit dodger on a black night with a light following wind and feeling sick and tired, I dozed off. At about 0300 hours, I was shocked awake by a loud, growling rumble. It seemed threateningly near, and, completely disoriented, I jumped up to look over the dodger. The mammoth, rearing bulk of a supertanker was only a few hundred metres away – perhaps not even two hundred metres. It was headed straight for us. Was I dreaming? The noise of its thundering engines was horrific, and for a few valuable seconds I couldn't take in the fact that I had neither heard nor seen the vessel until this instant. It was as though it had appeared from nowhere.

It moved inexorably on.

Shocked into alertness, I at first gauged that the monster, riding three storeys high out of the water, was going to slide past us, even though I could clearly see its huge bulbous bow and the phosphorescent wave it was pushing in front of it. At the same time, my mind was registering the light configuration. Green. White. Red. The position of the lights tells you the heading of a ship. If you see two white lights above each other, one on a low mast forward, another higher up further aft, as well as the red sidelight on the port (left) side and the green sidelight on the starboard (right) side, you must be in the direct path of the ship. We were on a collision course. She was going to hit us.

"Paul!" I shrieked down the companionway. "Emergency!"

The wind was light, which meant *Lorcha* was moving slowly and would be sluggish in turning, but I tore the tightly fastened ropes off the tiller to shove it to port with all my

212

strength. Anything to move *Lorcha* just a fraction off the path. Those two huge waves the tanker was throwing to either side of her enormous, bulging bow seemed two storeys high and sounded like Niagara Falls. She was still headed straight for us.

As I had never panicked on the boat, Paul knew that my use of the word *emergency* meant just that, and he bounded up the companionway not even pausing to pull on a sweater. I'll never forget the look on his face as his calm, phlegmatic personality took in the situation. He said "Holy shit!" followed by "Didn't you see it?"

There was no answer to that. Our entire world now consisted of one small and one monster vessel. I can remember the blackness completely surrounding us as I concentrated on the essentials: the sea, the sky, the stars, and the world simply did not exist – only *Lorcha*, her occupants, and the huge freighter.

About two minutes had passed since I had first seen the tanker. Before Paul had finished speaking, the tanker was so close we were in the shadow of her bow and could no longer see her deck lights – now there was just a wall of black and two creaming waves bearing down on us.

Thoughts were racing through my mind much faster than I can write. I had that instantaneous vision that seems to occur in moments of frightful danger.

My first thought was that this was what had happened to our friends on the New Zealand yacht *Mainstay*, which had gone missing in the Pacific. A roll-over by a freighter and straight to the ocean floor would account for her sudden and complete disappearance with no sign, radio message, or wreckage.

The second was that though Penny and Peter were within arm's length in the aft cabin, there was no point in waking them. Best they die in their sleep if the freighter ran us down and swept us under.

"Do you think she'll hit us?" I said in a tight and wobbly voice.

213

"I don't think so," said Paul in measured tones. "But it will be close."

There was no time to enjoy the first glimmer of hope. There was a final rush of sound and the tanker's port bow wave crashed deafeningly into us, filling the cockpit with water and drenching me, but also throwing *Lorcha* out of the direct path of the behemoth.

We didn't worry about the water – it wouldn't sink us – we stood there, frozen in place and gripping the dodger as *Lorcha* sheared about in the turbulence. Then we were clear of the bow wave and mesmerized by the solid wall of threatening metal sliding past, so close I felt I could reach out and touch it. Only by craning my neck backwards could I see the ghostly and deserted bridge deck.

The length of the ship seemed to slide past us forever, but suddenly the black threat was gone and the tanker, blind and uncaring, churned relentlessly forward on her unwavering path. Her crew hadn't seen us.

I sat down, shaking and ice-cold, my legs still in the water draining out of the cockpit, and pulled the stopwatch out of my pocket. I wanted to know how long I could see the tanker's lights before she disappeared over the horizon. *Click* went the watch and then *click* again twelve-and-a-half minutes later.

Twelve-and-a-half-minutes! Normally we scan the horizon every fifteen minutes. Even if I had been normally alert, we still could have died.

There were no words of recrimination from Paul. He simply gave me a quiet hug and went below to get what rest he could. I was left to continue my watch. We were still on passage with a few days to go before we could reach port. We might make mistakes, but we still had to depend on each other, each of us still had to do our share of work.

I vomited over the side and looked at my watch. Ten minutes had passed since Paul had gone down the companionway. It was time to scan the horizon again.

214

DARWIN 22

D arwin is a city with a bad reputation in the international sailing community. Everyone writes about the shallow, rough anchorage and how far from shore you have to anchor, how long a row it is to reach the beach, and how your muscles will develop from dragging your dinghy half a kilometre up the beach at low water on a spring tide.

We had read that the last crocodile attack *in the streets* had been a scant four years previously, and we heard lurid rumours about a crocodile that had tried to board a vessel at anchor. (What can you expect if you persist in hand-feeding a crocodile from a boat, as it transpired that this particular boater had been doing. One day he had nothing to throw to his new-found pet, so naturally the hungry monster had tried to climb closer to what he perceived as his source of food.)

We found Darwin to be a terrific city and though the reports about the anchorage were more or less true, the city and its amenities are so attractive that the trials are worth it. But this is one anchorage where there is absolutely no question about whether one needs an outboard engine for one's dinghy! Yes, yes, and yes!

The people of Darwin are laid-back and friendly. The yacht club members enjoy meeting the international sailors who pass through, and they go out of

Penny and Peter with a giant tortoise on Santa Cruz Island, Galapagos Islands. Eleven of the original fifteen species of the giant tortoise live in the Galapagos Islands.

Penny and Peter get a close look at a young sea lion on a black lava rock beach on Isabela Island, Galapagos Islands.

Paul and Penny on the anchor of the original *Bounty*, the ship that carried the mutineers and their wives here in 1790. The anchor was raised from the sea in 1957 and brought to the courthouse square at Adamstown, on Pitcairn. Peter struts around the square with his stick, while Brian and Kari Young's two children look on.

Together with Gail and Richard and their children Stacy and Andrew of *Gai Charisma*, we hiked to the top of the volcanic ridges overlooking Cook's Bay, Moorea, in the Society Islands.

Ian Conners puts the final few dabs of anti-fouling paint on *Lorcha*'s bottom as she is about to be launched after a complete refit and the addition of an aft cabin and sugar-scoop overhang.

At Santa Ana Island in the Solomon Islands, Paul talks with Ross Cook, skipper of the Australian yacht *Murbah*, as he sits on the transom of his dinghy. His wife Sandra and children Melanie and David are behind him. Penny and Peter are in *Lorcha*'s dinghy while the island children look on. The yachts in the background are *Lorcha*, *Moonraker*, and *Murbah*. Santa Ana Island, Solomon Islands.

Peter with one of his favourite hermit crabs.

Don and Danny Reed of *Moonraker*, with Peter behind them, prepare to go snorkeling over a Japanese ship sunk during the Second World War in Mbasroko Bay, western Solomon Islands. The derricks at the forward end of the ship are visible in front of Peter and other derricks stick up at the right of the picture.

Somewhere in the Indian Ocean, Fiona helps Peter with his school lessons in the early-morning sun in *Lorcha*'s cockpit.

Penny helps winnow the rice crop in northern Madagascar, as Peter looks on.

Fiona and Peter sit on a rock at the base of the Grande Cascade at Montagne d'Ambre nature reserve in northern Madagascar.

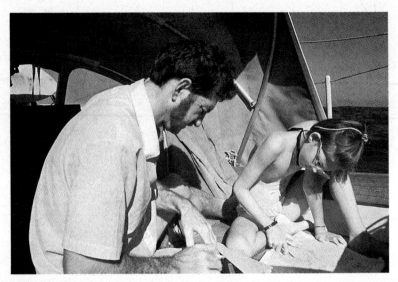

Paul and Penny doing some plotting in *Lorcha*'s cockpit.

A family portrait celebrates the completion of our circumnavigation, as our home-bound track crosses our out-bound track at Fernando de Noronha Island, with its distinctive finger rock in the background.

Darwin's reputation . . . outboard anchorage . . .
international barbecues . . . Red Sea or South Africa? . . .
my painful problem . . . the children are changing . . .
opening the "special package" . . . flying gybe . . .
Cocos Keeling Atoll . . . children's paradise . . .
Penny turns ten . . . Peter feels guilty.

---

their way to provide information and hospitality. As well as lifts into town and to various attractions such as the Thursday-night Asian Sunset Market and the unusual experience of hand-feeding free-roaming ocean fish at Doctor's Bay, we were taken on a three-day camping trip to spectacular Kakadu National Park, only a few hours' drive away.

On another visit to Australia, we would make Darwin a major stop. I'd like to live there!

The only area where I would have trouble in keeping up, however, would be in the phenomenal amount of beer drunk – a few beers for lunch, more for dinner, maybe a couple of cans for breakfast! Two people invited for a simple meal on board would bring twenty-four cans of beer with them – and drink the lot. These northern Australians have an enormous capacity – and the head for it as well.

There were nightly barbecues ashore, gatherings of twenty, thirty, or forty international yachties who watched the spectacular sunsets and planned their passages across the Indian Ocean. A handful of the international cruisers had opted to enter the annual Darwin to Ambon Race as a means of getting a visa for Indonesia. The rest of us were fairly evenly divided about whether to make for South Africa (as we were) or going up the Red Sea to the Mediterranean. With political problems and unknown factors on each route, it was a case of deciding which would be the least troublesome. I think it's fair to say that fewer boats are opting to sail around South Africa, the once-favoured route to the Atlantic Ocean.

I had other things on my mind.

That incident with the torn sail off New Zealand a year earlier had resulted in a painful problem in my right shoulder called capsulitis. As I understand it, this is a little-understood swelling inside the shoulder cap which is triggered by some sort of strain, in my case the sail incident. It takes about six months to develop, followed by six months of intense pain and an arm that can't be raised, six months of lessening pain and the beginning of movement, and six months of "getting better": a two-year project.

My shoulder had started seizing up in Cairns and I had gone through the painful period while we were touring overland and then sailing to Darwin. I had counted on it starting to feel better for our challenging passage across the reputedly harsh waters of the Indian Ocean. But now my left shoulder was seizing up, and Paul and I were facing a series of long and arduous passages during which I would be incapacitated, in severe pain, and not in a fit physical condition to cope with an emergency.

Our options were: to put off the passage for another year; to sell the boat and give up our voyaging; or to carry on. We decided to keep going. It wasn't the decision I might have made a couple of years earlier, but though ocean voyaging is always challenging and each passage is hard work, we now had a lot of sea miles and experience behind us.

We stocked the boat with fifty kilos of potatoes, thirty kilos of onions, and twenty dozen eggs, filled the watertanks, and checked the SatNav.

"Careful of that special package, Mama," called out Penny.

The package had been sent to us from Don and Aggie in Noosa. Now living on land and working hard to prepare for another voyage a few years down the road, they had taken the time to think of us and had sent a "Not to be opened until crossing 70°E longitude" package.

"See you at Cocos Keeling," yelled Ken and Joy from *Mischief*, as we sailed away from the friendly Darwin Yacht Club with 25 knots of wind behind us. "We'll only be a couple of days behind you."

Just like two families arranging to drive off in separate cars and rendezvous for a friendly lunch – only our "drive" was two thousand miles long!

It was surprisingly cold on this passage, and both Paul and I donned our long-sleeved running suits as soon as dark fell, Paul also incongruously sporting his old woollen Canadian toque here in the tropics, only twelve degrees south of the Equator.

A week later and six hundred uneventful miles nearer our destination, I thought how good it was to see the children developing during these long passages. A few days previously, Penny had sat down with a book on crochet, something I had never mastered, and with a hook and some cotton thread she had proceeded to teach herself the basics. Already she had made two pretty mats.

I also no longer helped her with her schoolwork. She supervised her own schooling, only giving me a week's completed work to look at. An independent step for a ten-year-old.

Always preferring to be active or at least doing something with his hands, Peter's surprise of this voyage was his sudden interest in reading and his ability to read a full-length book.

Our physically close lifestyle was once again permitting us to enjoy milestones in our children's maturity, and I was more than happy to encourage Peter by letting him open our "one week at sea" present – seven paperback volumes of C. S. Lewis's Narnia books.

I was more tired and tense than usual on this passage, with intense pain from both shoulders. I could not pull a shirt over my head, reach round to wash my back, or even mix a batch of bread dough. I could not lie on either side to sleep (the best way to sleep when underway as you don't roll around as much), but had to sleep on my back. In the dark privacy of my bunk I sometimes cried from the pain.

Our boat was heading steadily west, though there were a

few days when the wind was light and Paul put up our red-and-white drifter, his concession to my shoulders being that we didn't leave it up overnight as I wouldn't have been able to get it down by myself if the wind got too strong.

Making it to 70°E longitude was a reason to celebrate and Penny and Peter tore into their surprise package – magazines (old), chocolate (melted), stamps (stuck together), and a second-hand game. But never was a gift more joyfully opened or lovingly appreciated than that package in the middle of this lonely ocean.

On the second half of our trip the winds increased to 25 knots and the seas grew more turbulent and stayed that way for three days, making cooking difficult and sleep elusive. My left arm began to ache from the strain and during our thirteenth day out there was an explosive crack as the boat spun completely around and the sail whipped over.

"Paul, we've hit something!" I yelled wildly, looking frantically around.

But we hadn't. The self-steering gear had slipped, throwing the boat into a flying gybe. With my weakened left arm, I had not screwed the adjusting knob down tight enough when I had last re-set it. Apart from fright, there was no damage. Just a sharp reminder that we were hundreds of miles from help and on our own.

But our challenges, though worrying to us, were light in comparison to others'. That night we heard on the radio that tornados had killed a hundred people in Edmonton, Alberta, and the city had been declared a disaster area.

After the changeable weather, the trades began to blow steadily and *Lorcha* settled into her stride. We had our best day's run ever – 144 miles over the bottom.

The constant pain in my shoulders and the inability to move my arms had made me apprehensive about my ability to cope in an emergency on this passage. The worry was invading the rest of my body as I now had a mild case of haemorrhoids – usually associated with pregnancy and constipation – but I can directly associate the onslaught with stress. I could also feel my tension easing the nearer we came to Cocos.

The rest of the passage passed quickly and on our nineteenth day, we saw land at dawn and headed for the entrance through the reef. There were eight yachts in the anchorage including our speedy friends on *Mischief*. I could not raise my arms to wave to Joy, but I could feel the tension draining out of my body as Joy called out:

"What took you so long? Never mind – you're in time for lunch and a swim. Only four thousand miles to South Africa!"

As long as there are far-flung islands to visit and boats to sail, yachties will ply the oceans of the world. For to escape from the madding crowd and to visit remote islands like Cocos Keeling is what all this joyous voyaging is about.

"If there is a paradise on this earth it is Keeling," wrote Joshua Slocum in 1897. Almost a hundred years later, nothing much has changed – a few more yachts in the anchorage, perhaps.

Cocos Keeling Atoll is not just one island, but a cluster. The islands were settled and developed by Australian John Clunies Ross, but the Clunies Ross's interests are currently being bought out by the Australian government, with some dispute from the family as to the fairness of the government dealings.

The yacht anchorage is behind uninhabited Direction Island where the trade winds sing lustily in the green fronds of the palm trees, whisper along the brilliant white sand beach, and swirl around the clear blue and turquoise waters. They usher the cruising yachts into shelter with caressing touches, adding a beguiling message to stay awhile.

Lorcha needed no urging. We were ready for all of that and spent long lazy days with the other yachtsmen enjoying sand, sun, and surf.

It was a children's paradise. Penny and Peter literally moved off the boat with Andrea, Cameron, and the children from three other yachts. They built their own camp and stayed overnight, cooking simple meals on their fire at night, running wild with the other children during the day, only joining us when we came ashore to go for a swim in the "rip."

At the east end of the island the sea came over the coral reef to run straight and deep between two islands. The water surged through, creating a current of 3 knots in the steeply banked channel. We would all meet there at some point during the day, throwing ourselves into the fast-flowing water, which would carry us over what looked like the world's largest aquarium. There were brightly coloured damselfish only five centimetres long darting among the coral heads; bright red squirrelfish with large round eyes hovering near their holes. Parrotfish in the colours of the rainbow, some nearly one metre long, crunched the coral with their parrot-like beaks, and the similar-sized blue wrasse hovered in schools near the bottom to feed on whatever the current brought them. Moray eels as thick as my arm poked their heads out of their holes looking for edible morsels among the debris sliding past. We were not considered a danger by these fish, as there were strict rules against using spear guns in the rip area, and they only had to worry about being taken by their natural predators. It was thrilling stuff for the youngsters; the fierce current took them mercilessly in its grip, only to spit them out safely into the still lagoon at the other end before the younger ones could start to panic.

We celebrated Penny's tenth birthday with a hermit crab race, a sport some of the islanders had explained to us. You draw a small circle within a larger circle in the sand. Each person puts his or her hermit crab in the inside circle. When word is given, the crabs are released. The first crab to scurry past the larger outer circle is the winner.

Poor Peter had a terrible experience and learned the meaning of loss. After dire warnings not to let any crabs loose on the boat because they could scurry into a dark corner and die, Peter lost his favourite crab in just this way. As fate would have it, some of his schoolwork for that week was to write on the death of a friend. Poor Peter. He could no more write that essay than fly to the moon. Three times he had a go at it and three times he gave up, heaving loud sobs. He had been care-less over the safety of his little friend, and we decided to let his guilt run its course.

But three days later, there was a wonderful reprieve. Who should appear from somewhere deep in Peter's clothes locker but his crab! Peter's face, his life, his very being was trans-formed with joy. He quickly put his little friend in a bucket with water and seaweed and rowed him ashore.

The lessons and challenges of life are there to be experi-enced whether you're living in a big city or travelling round the world in your own small yacht.

COCOS KEELING TO MADAGASCAR 23

"It will be Joy's fortieth birthday in two weeks," said Ken, Joy's husband and skipper of *Mischief*. "If we leave now we can be in Chagos by then and do some great partying in those uninhabited atolls."

"We'll meet you there later," I told Ken while I watched him take down *Mischief*'s sun awning in preparation for leaving Cocos Keeling.

We had arrived only six days earlier, and wanted to stay for at least ten days. The following day we waved good-bye to several of our cruising friends. *Mischief* (Australian), *Mash* (New Zealand), and *Contour of Cuthill* (New Zealand), all were headed for Chagos. *Tangara* II (Australian) and *Gamin* (French) left for Mauritius.

The anchorage behind Direction Island seemed almost deserted. But, in addition to ourselves, there were still nine boats here, four of them under 9 metres long. *Asia* was an American, 8.8-metre, home-built wooden cutter with newly married Jim and Gina on board. Seven-metre, steel-hulled, Dutch *Anna* was the smallest. Wim (whom we had first met in the Netherlands Antilles) had sailed from Holland single-handed, but had been joined by Karen, his Swedish girlfriend, in Tonga. *Tarka the Otter*, a Vancouver-registered, 8.2-metre, fibreglass sloop, carried a couple, both former school teachers in their thirties. And then there was *Lorcha*.

Farewell, friends . . . mixed bag of boats . . . wintertime
trade winds and doldrums . . . Fiona's shoulders . . .
change of course . . . flying fish . . . the green flash . . .
another complication . . . surfing into Madagascar.

There were four medium-sized boats. *Mona* II, a 10.5-metre, home-built, fibreglass French boat was sailed by a retired merchant marine ship captain and his wife. Eleven-metre *Asynja* from Sweden was a popular boat, with Jonas and his French-Canadian wife Sylvie, and their son Daniel, a bouncing blond toddler born in Australia one year earlier. Jonas, a sailmaker by profession, was much in demand to repair sails. Daniel was such a charming and beautiful child, with an adventuresome and even disposition, that there was never a lack of baby-sitters available to look after him. They also had Mark, a young Australian, to act as crew across the Indian Ocean. *Potlatch*, a 12.5-metre, production fibreglass American boat had a couple on board. The wife gave palm readings and did fortune telling, an unusual occupation. A home-built, fibreglass, 13.5-metre, *Carly Adam*, had a couple from Australia on board. The owner had taken early retirement from his oil-refinery engineering career to build their boat, and they had lived aboard for eight years. They were just beginning their second circumnavigation of the world.

There were also two larger vessels: *Charisma*, a German-registered Swan 65 (20-metres long), was on her way from Australia to the Seychelles with a wealthy couple aboard, accompanied by an Australian professional crew of three. *Koatka*, a new, 20.5-metre, Taiwanese-built motor-sailer, had an Australian delivery crew of five on board sailing her to the Mediterranean.

We were a mixed lot, in a small anchorage mid-ocean on the

trade-wind route around the world, but a typical cross-section of the fellow cruising yachtsmen one is likely to meet.

Eleven days after arriving at Cocos, we let slip the mooring lines to sail out of Port Refuge into the brisk trade winds.

We were sailing into the area of the central Indian Ocean where the wind blows at an average of 17 to 21 knots from the east to southeast 89 per cent of the time. But gale-force winds can be expected for at least two days every month, and the wind can blow at over 30 knots for weeks at a time. Waves are three-and-a-half metres or higher for up to 30 per cent of the time.

The crossing is made at the height of the winter-time trade winds, which build up a strong and steady wave train. South of the 35° south latitude the dominant wind blows from the west, and gales are common at this time of year. The wave train from those southern storms crosses the wind-driven waves in the tropics to make freak waves, the odd one being up to twice the height of the average. But even in the average cross-swell the ride is a rough one, and many rudders and self-steering gears are damaged.

The Chagos Archipelago is part of the British Indian Ocean Territory and has fifty-five islands. The Diego Garcia Atoll has a large American military base, but remains under British sovereignty through a 1966 agreement between the two governments. The former inhabitants of the five clusters of islands which make up the group were bought out and they voluntarily moved to Mauritius, the Seychelles, and other nearby islands. There are abandoned villages on the islands but no people, except for the military base personnel and the British ships which regularly patrol the area.

We were headed for the Salomon Islands of the group, located at about 6° south latitude. Cocos Keeling is at about 12° south, so we would be angling to the north during this fifteen-hundred-mile passage. On our fifth day out, at about

8° south, the trade winds began to fail us as we moved into squally doldrums-type weather.

Because of Fi's arms, she couldn't raise the sail, but she could lower the sail to reef as the squalls came through. The wind would blast us for twenty or thirty minutes, shifting perhaps ninety degrees then failing altogether. The sail would flap and rattle as *Lorcha* rolled in the persistent swell. The wind would slowly gain strength until about one hour later we would again be sailing in 15 to 20 knots of wind. Then another squall would pass.

Each time the sail was reefed, it had to be raised again when the gale-force squalls passed. Thus I was up and down like a jack-in-the-box, perhaps fifteen times a day, to raise the sail. I would wake up in the night during Fi's watch to help her, as it was impossible to sleep with the sail rattling when it was deeply reefed in light winds. With full sail up there was enough area to hold *Lorcha* steady and keep her driving at speed through the water.

After three days of this and with another 700 miles to go, I told Fi I wanted to skip visiting the Chagos and head directly for Madagascar. Though it would turn this passage into a 2,900-mile marathon, the advantage would be that we would again go to the south, finding the brisk but steady trade winds and not having to endure the tiring doldrums conditions we would likely experience the remainder of the way to Chagos.

"I'm not sure I can survive till we get to Madagascar," Fiona said tearfully.

Though I had no fear for her survival, I knew that just hanging on with her injured shoulders in the rough seas was tiring and painful. But I was also becoming exhausted keeping the boat driving towards our destination. Once back in the trade winds I could get my required number of hours of sleep. It was a difficult decision, but I felt that for the safety and well-being of all of us, it would be best if we got back into the trade winds.

Once below 10° south the winds steadied and we made

some of the longest day's runs of our circumnavigation. We had several days when we sailed 135 to 140 miles through the water, with up to 155 miles over the bottom, the extra miles being gained by a favourable ocean current.

We also had more flying fish than we had ever had before winging around us. They took off like flocks of sparrows from the wave tops. They would launch themselves into the wind, and then glide round to coast downwind, remaining airborne for up to three hundred metres.

During the day they could easily avoid *Lorcha* plunging headlong in their midst, but at night, especially in the darkness before moonrise, they would often turn to head back towards us. These Indian Ocean flying fish were very big, with forty-five-centimetre-long ones common. That is a hefty fish to have flying towards you. Many's the time during my night watches my hat would be knocked off by an errant flying fish. They would come crashing into the dodger and lie gasping on the deck. I kept a piece of wood in the cockpit to flip these fish back into their rightful medium, as trying to grasp the struggling creatures was impossible.

Now that we had sailed in all the oceans, I began to get a sense of the moods of the different bodies of water of the world. The Indian Ocean has strong winds and large waves, but the air is crystal clear. It is an ocean strong and testing, but with a bright disposition.

Eric and Susan Hiscock wrote about their three circumnavigations of the world. They wrote of the "green flash" at sunset, and said that it was easiest seen on the Indian Ocean. What is the "green flash?"

As light from the sun passes through the atmosphere, it is refracted or bent because of the moisture in the atmosphere. The amount of bending is slightly different for each colour of the spectrum (think of the colour spectrum seen from light shining through a prism), and maximum refraction occurs at the horizon where one's line of sight passes through the most moisture. The sun must travel through the ten seconds of arc of the curved surface of the world to make the colour spectrum go from violet at one end to red at the other end. (The world makes one revolution every twenty-four hours, making the sun appear to have made a 360-degree circle around it. One degree of arc of that circle equals sixty minutes; one minute of arc equals sixty seconds). The red image of the sun is the least bent by refraction (the red ball of sun easily seen as it nears the horizon), and is therefore the first colour to set, last to rise. The shorter-wave blue and violet colours are scattered most by the atmosphere, giving the sky its characteristic blue colour. Thus the green image of the sun may be the last of the colours to drop out of sight. The sun by this time is below the horizon, but the green flash occurs just as the last bit of upper rim disappears, and one sees a segment of a green circle around the rim of the sun. The green flash may last for up to ten seconds, but is usually less than two seconds in duration.

The ideal conditions to observe the green flash, no matter where in the world you are, is the sun setting over a clear horizon over the sea with clear air, conditions often present in the Indian Ocean during the wintertime.

We would shield our eyes from the sun as it began to disappear below the horizon, looking directly at it only as the last bit of the rim slipped out of sight.

"I saw it!" Peter would boast.

"I didn't see it," Penny would moan. "Are you sure you saw the green flash, Peter?" she would add, scrutinizing Peter's face to see if he were telling the truth.

But we all managed to see the green flash several times on this passage.

Watching the sun go down from the cockpit became a regular time of family togetherness on this passage. Much of the day and night Fiona and I are either sleeping, working, or resting. Penny and Peter sleep regular shoreside hours, and play or read during the day. With an adult always on watch, one of us is always accessible to the children, but it is rare, even in our restricted space, for the four of us to be gathered together for leisure time.

The sundown ritual seemed to signal a time for sharing confidences and intimacies. We would sit together as darkness settled around us, gradually growing quieter, until Fiona would go below for a nap before her evening watch.

"Paul!" shouted Fiona down the companionway.

There was no need for her to shout, as I was already nearly in the cockpit. Nothing rouses the skipper from his off-watch sleep in the middle of the night faster than a loud crash and a few heavy thumps.

We had been sailing deeply reefed for the last two days, with winds in the 30- to 40-knot range. We were also closing with the coast of Madagascar, and I expected to make good our landfall the following day. But at 0030 came the heavy crash as the lazy jacks, the lines which held up the reefed portion of the sail, broke and the sail bundle crashed on to the dinghy, then rolled to the deck.

There was still some sail up, but it and the reefed portion were unmanageable. Fiona hove *Lorcha* to, to stop her headlong rush through the waves and ease the motion. I donned my foul-weather gear to protect me from the stinging spray, the splash of the waves, and the strong but warm wind. I struggled into my safety harness and passed Fiona our powerful torch as I put one of the smaller torches in my pocket. Scrambling forward to the mast, I clipped my safety line round it, then tried to sort out the several bits of loose line flying about in the wind.

The whipping holding a thimble (a grooved plastic or metal ring which prevents wear in a rope loop) had chafed through at one end of the multi-part arrangement of the lazy jacks. There was no possibility of my going part-way up the mast to re-rig the lazy jacks. But I saw that if I got a spare block and shackled that to the part of the lazy jacks I could get hold of, I could use the spare halyard to raise the sail bundle off the deck so we

230

could control the sail and continue on to port. I knew this arrangement would soon wear through the lines in the rough seas, probably not lasting longer than twenty-four hours.

As the dawn sun rose it gave definition to the outline of the hills of Madagascar. I had plotted a SatNav fix about two hours earlier and knew we were approaching the coast about fifteen miles south of the opening to Diego Suarez Bay. With the strong wind and fast current flowing up the coast, this is the only safe way to assure you are not swept past this harbour at the northeastern tip of Madagascar.

I began to angle along the coast, running downwind in the steep waves. The self-steering gear was having a hard time steering a straight course in the humping-up waves, so I disengaged it and took over steering duties.

At 0730 Fiona poked her head out the hatch to catch her first glimpse of Madagascar.

"The waves are getting pretty steep," I told her. "There should be another fix soon on the SatNav. The detailed charts are under the bunk cushion."

"Change course to due north," Fiona shouted to me through the partially closed companionway as soon as she had plotted our position.

"Is 340 degrees okay?" I called. "I'd rather not have to gybe over just now in these steep seas."

"Go to a 360-degree heading immediately," came a sharp retort. "We are less than one mile from a shoal with a depth of only two metres over it."

Little wonder the seas were so steep – these monsters were humping-up in the shoaling water. I immediately gybed the sail over to take the new course.

Moments later *Lorcha* was rolled by a breaking sea until her cockpit coaming was underwater. But we were already headed towards deeper water, where the waves would not be so steep and breaking.

As we sailed up the coast we did our usual puzzling over the charts, trying to identify a few landmarks.

231

"There's the entrance," I announced as I made out the lighthouse on the cliff overlooking the narrow passage. "But it looks like it will be a thrilling ride."

"We must be doing 10 knots," said Penny.

"More like 12,' said Peter, not to be outdone.

I had no idea how fast we were going as *Lorcha* surfed down each succeeding wave front. The Indian Ocean swells were being pinched up in the narrowing and shelving channel. There were scattered rocks on the port side, with the lighthouse at the top of the cliff. To starboard was a jagged reef, with the breakers thundering on it in a welter of foam.

I would have liked to slow *Lorcha* down some more, but short of employing a sea anchor, which I was not prepared to do, I had done all I could. *Lorcha* kept her bow up and ran straight as she surfed in, a trait which endears her to me whenever I see her do it. We had once owned a wooden cutter which would bury her bow up to the mast in conditions like this, a potentially dangerous habit.

In no time we were in the calmer waters of Diego Suarez Bay, but the wind continued to blast at us as we sailed the final five miles to Port de la Nievre at Antsirananna.

We saw the national flag of the Malagasy Republic flying from the port captain's office, but it was Sunday afternoon and there was little activity in the port area. We slowly jilled about, wondering where to tie up or anchor.

We saw a woman waving a piece of red cloth from the second-floor balcony of the port captain's office. As we neared, she indicated that we should tie alongside an old pilot boat in a small basin just in front of the office. We did, 23 days, 4 hours, and 2,913 miles after leaving Cocos Keeling Islands.

MADAGASCAR   24

Madagascar, the fourth-largest island in the world, is thought to have separated from East Africa about 165 million years ago. It was uninhabited until the Christian era, when Indonesian seafarers discovered it. People from the Polynesian area of the Pacific and from neighbouring Africa also settled here.

There are eighteen ethnic groups, but only one indigenous language, Malagasy, of Malayo-Polynesian origin.

The Malagasy Republic, which became independent in 1960, has a colourful past. In about the seventh century AD, Arab traders established posts along the east coast. The Portuguese stumbled upon the island in 1500. It was a much-feared pirate lair during the late eighteenth and early nineteenth centuries. The French were well entrenched by the 1700s, and though there was a period of British influence, the French eventually established military control by battling the local population.

During the 1970s Madagascar underwent a turbulent time of realignment of its foreign relations. The country developed close ties with several Communist states and separated itself from some western nations, especially the United States. They expelled the American ambassador and five of his staff in 1971, refused a new ambassador in 1975, and nationalized two American oil companies in 1976. It

Madagascar's past . . . no visas . . . telephone trials . . .
a pleasant mooring . . . unique natural environment . . .
taxi brousse . . . *camping with friends . . .* Mischief *at*
Nosy Be anchorage . . . miserable Mahajanga . . .
blowing a gasket.

---

was not until 1980 that an American ambassador was welcomed, and since then a policy of aid and trade from or with all nations has been pursued.

Until recently the word on the yachting circuit was to steer clear of Madagascar, but we now heard glowing praise of this country as a destination.

"But you don't have visas stamped in these passports," blurted out the immigration officer in French, the official language of Madagascar. He sat on the starboard settee of *Lorcha*'s now-crowded cabin the day after our arrival.

He turned to his second, who muttered something in Malagasy, and they both shook their heads. The secretary, third in line along the settee, simply clucked her tongue in what we were to learn was a typical Malagasy expression when encountering a hopeless situation.

We had known there might be a problem over our lack of visas. We had tried to obtain visas in Australia, but there was no Malagasy Embassy there. We would have had to send our passports to another country where there was an embassy. We are reluctant to let our passports out of our hands, as many get lost, or are held for months before being processed.

We had written letters to the central government officials at Antananarivo, the capital city, as well as to the port officials at Antsirananna. We included a photo of the boat, as well as passport-sized photos of ourselves, and the usual information asked for when completing visa request forms.

235

These officials, now on board *Lorcha*, had received none of the above letters, but they were sympathetic and helpful. They were empowered to extend visas, but they were not able to issue the initial document. They said they would contact their superiors at the capital city, and suggested we also contact our embassy.

The officials could have restricted us to the port area, or even requested we stay on board our boat until visas were issued or an order was given for our expulsion from their territory, but they were not hard-liners. Their only restriction was that we not take *Lorcha* out of harbour, and we were asked to check with them every other day to see how the paperwork was progressing.

Fiona and I went to the PTT (Poste, Telephone et Telegraphe) to enquire about calling an embassy 725 kilometres away, a great distance in this third-world country.

There was no listing for a Canadian Embassy or Consulate, but there was a British High Commission and an American Embassy. Either of these might act on behalf of Canadians when there is no official Canadian representation in a country.

We got no answer at the British High Commission, but the American Embassy came on the line at the first try.

A woman took all the details amidst the crackles and whistles of the telephone line and I arranged to speak to Consul Bob White the following day. But the next day the phone lines were out. The following day the lines were said to be working, but I couldn't get through. Beginning to get worried, I tried every day, but it was six days later before I again got through to the embassy.

The immigration officials were having little better luck. They used the radio-telephone link of the National Police, but days passed with no definite word.

"If there is no word from the capital," said Desiré, *Chef du service immigration* in Antsirananna, "no one has made a decision and a positive response is still possible."

Unknown to us, Patricia Gates Lynch, American Ambassador to Madagascar, had already personally spoken to the President of the Malagasy Republic on our behalf. And though it took more than two weeks for the authorization to be passed along to this provincial outpost, we were eventually issued visas.

Consul Bob White later told us we were the first North American yacht he had heard of to sail to Madagascar.

Rafted alongside the derelict pilot boat, we were in a basin perfectly protected from wind and sea surge, and also within the walled compound of the port captain's office. He and his extended family lived on the second floor of the building, providing Penny and Peter with ready playmates.

There were shower and laundry facilities ashore, and it was only a short walk to a bus stop and a short inexpensive ride to the central market area, full of high-quality and inexpensive locally grown foodstuffs, as well as interesting handicrafts such as wood carvings, baskets, and semi-precious stones. After all that sea time we were glad to find such comfortable and colourful surroundings and, visa problems notwithstanding, we were in no hurry to move on.

Madagascar, at sixteen hundred kilometres long, is nearly a continent in itself, with many plants, animals, and insects having evolved into species found nowhere else. Four-fifths of the plants growing in Madagascar are found only here. Most of the ten thousand kinds of flowering plants are unique to this island. Only a dozen of its four hundred species of amphibians and reptiles exist elsewhere. Half the world's chameleons, those colour-changing, eye-swiveling lizards so superstitiously regarded by primitive peoples, live here. More than half the island's birds and virtually all its native mammals are solely Madagascar's.

One of the two Malagasy national parks, based around an extinct volcano called Montagne d'Ambre, was nearby. We packed a lunch, our water bottles, and sweaters to take a *taxi brousse* the thirty-two kilometres to Ambohitra, the end of the road. We hiked up the side of the mountain, another seven kilometres, to walk through a rain-forest area full of flowering plants, ripening fruit and berries, as well as many of the one thousand species of orchids which grow in profusion here.

Once through the rain-forest area we were in the pine forests of the upper altitudes and soon the Grand Cascade came into view. This waterfall plunges in a sheer drop to a lava rock basin 79 metres below. At an altitude of 1,127 metres there is a definite change in the feel of the air from down on the coastal plain: the air was cool and the water felt frigid. Colourful butterflies flitted from flower to flower. Bird calls rang all round us and there was always some interesting sight or sound to attract our attention.

Late in the afternoon we hiked to the road end to wait for a *taxi brousse* to take us back into town. These Peugeot pick-up trucks with a canvas cover over the back are licensed to carry twelve passengers and their baggage. There was a line-up, and the driver couldn't resist cramming all thirty-one of us into the truck, with a precarious pile of baskets and bundles roped to the top.

Perhaps the most nerve-wracking of all, to save fuel the driver coasted down the steep mountain side, careening around turns and bouncing over the potholed roads. Just outside Antsirananna there was a police checkpoint which the driver didn't see until he rounded a curve and almost landed on it. He slammed on the brakes, accepting the inevitable, and slowly coasted up to the officers.

We disembarked so the passengers could be counted. The vehicle was given a cursory safety check with, I am sure, many faults found. A fine of about forty dollars was issued.

Providing transportation in Madagascar is a real dilemma, and our driver wasn't necessarily a wrong-doer. These taxis are the back-bone of rural transportation in this country. There are more people who want to ride in them than vehicle capacity at the licensed rate. Vehicles are poorly maintained because spare parts are very expensive, with all imports heavily taxed. Is it better to transport people in overcrowded and poorly maintained vehicles, or to let them walk with what they can carry?

Asma, a German-flagged yacht about the same size as *Lorcha* sailed in bearing acquaintances Clarke Stede and Michelle. We had first met them in the Solomon Islands about a year earlier, but had last seen them in Darwin, Australia. They had spent more than one month in the Chagos Archipelago, and had great stories to tell of the beautiful beaches and coral viewing, as well as of the prolific sea life.

Our own appetites had been only whetted by the natural beauty we had found at Montagne D'Ambre National Park, and it was decided that the crews of both *Lorcha* and *Asma* should share a car rental for a few days to drive around the northern part of the island.

We loaded the Peugeot station wagon with camping equipment for the six of us, planning to sleep in tents at any site we chose along the road and prepare our meals on campfires, and decided to head for the mountains, as we are always at the seaside and harbours.

We bought what road maps we could but had no luck finding a guide book. The maps divided the roads into three categories: the red roads were paved, but there were few of them; yellow roads were said to be passable in all seasons; and white roads were said to be only passable during the dry season.

The roads were poorly marked, as there were few private vehicles, with the *taxi brousse* being the most common, then many heavy cargo-carrying trucks. The vehicle most often seen was the ox-cart, lumbering along with up to four animals pulling any sort of cart at a snail's pace.

We soon found the red roads were badly potholed – *nid de poulet* in French, "a hen's nest," yet the locals joked the holes were more like ostrich nests. These roads led to the major market towns – interesting, but not adventure.

The yellow roads had been graded at some historic date, and the going was slow. The saving grace of these roads was that the bridges did seem to be intact. They led to mountain villages or made short cuts across from one red road to another – interesting, but not exciting. It was on the white roads we decided to travel.

They rambled through fields and over ridges, places more suitable to a four-wheel-drive vehicle than our station wagon. Their route and direction seemed to bear little resemblance to the charted route on the map we held in front of us. We would often get out of the car on a high spot to look over the surrounding peaks and puzzle over where we might be in relation to a landmark visible in the distance. Asking locals for directions was little help, as few knew how to read a map.

But we had a great time. We searched for and found some marvelous underground grottos deep in the bush. We waded in up the out-flowing rivers to see stalactites biased away from the direction of the dominant wind as they dripped from the cavern ceilings. Along the rocky ledges the bright red eyes of crocodiles shone in the light of our torches. We knew that there was little danger of attack from this small fresh-water species, yet it was spooky wading along through the dense blackness, hearing the sharp drips from the stalactites and the wind whistling from some vent in the distance, and being constantly reminded of the crocodiles' presence whenever one of our torch beams picked out their eyes.

The white roads might end suddenly in the middle of a mountain-top village. What a stir we made when our car disgorged its passengers and we wandered about admiring the view. The people were always puzzled about how we managed to get there and why we seemed to have no pressing reason for our visit.

In the evenings we would drive down a white road until we found a stream near a flat piece of ground, with some firewood nearby. We would pitch our tents, prepare our meal, and greet any passersby. Our only disturbance was from dogs

240

who came sniffing around for food scraps in the middle of the night.

After the thrashing we had taken sailing through the pass into Diego Suarez Bay, I feared we would have a worse time getting out. The port captain advised us to go out at dawn, as that was the calmest time of day. I put extra lashings on everything on deck, put covers over the hatches, and prepared for a real dowsing.

Nervously I steered *Lorcha* for the pass, only to find near-millpond conditions.

After several days in lonely anchorages surrounded by high and barren hills, we sailed into Nosy Be anchorage. We were pleased to find *Mischief* at anchor here, with our old friends Ken and Joy, Cameron, and Andrea aboard.

"Ten days after our arrival at the Salomon Atoll of the Chagos Archipelago we began to worry about you" said Joy. "We expected you to arrive every day. When you didn't, we began to think 'This will be their second day in the life-raft,' or third or fifth as the days passed."

We were sorry to have worried our friends because of our change of plans, but there was nothing we could have done about it. Although they do have a marine SSB radio for long distance communications, we had seen no cargo ships on that passage which might have been able to pass along a message to them. And we were never within range to use our VHF radio transceiver which, even under the best of conditions, is rarely heard fifty miles away.

We spent a few days at nearby Nosy Komba to see the lemurs, a primitive primate pre-dating monkeys. These animals, unique to Madagascar, reminded us of a sort of raccoon, opossum, and monkey mixture. They are protected in a nature preserve on this island, and are very tame.

Sailing in company with *Mischief*, we visited several anchorages along the coast until we reached Mahajanga, our last port in Madagascar. The anchorage here is the worst of any harbour we have been in. The tide races through at up to 4 knots. The trade wind blows from the east till noon, then, with the heating of the hills inland, air begins to rise and an onshore wind from the southwest begins to blow in the afternoon, reaching up to 25 knots. The afternoon wind blows directly against the ebb tide. Spring tide, the strongest tide of the monthly cycle, happened to be on the day we arrived. It was still relatively calm as we anchored, but soon piped up. *Lorcha* and *Mischief* swung around their anchors like crazed dogs tugging on their leashes.

The tide would swing us around to lie to the ebb, then a strong gust would blow us forward, slacking the anchor chain. As the gust lightened, we would shear away to be caught again by the tidal flow. We didn't launch the dinghy that afternoon as we feared we wouldn't make it to shore in the maelstrom.

Later in the afternoon the port captain came out in his launch to board us and check our papers. I refused to let his launch come alongside, fearing we would be damaged by his heavy boat as *Lorcha* swung around. I shouted to him that we had cleared into the country, and that we would come to his office in the morning.

The American Consul, Bob White, had invited us to visit Antananarivo, the capital city, as his guests. It was impossible to leave *Lorcha* unattended in this rough harbour, but Penny and Fiona flew there for Hallowe'en weekend. A few days after their return, we prepared to leave Mahajanga.

I had arranged with the nearby crab-meat-packing plant to go alongside their jetty at high tide to fill *Lorcha*'s water tanks with their hose. I started the engine, raised the anchor, and put the engine in gear. It began to smoke, sputter, then died and refused to start again. I checked the oil and found the crankcase over-full with watery oil.

I have no idea why the head gasket blew. The engine hadn't been overloaded or overheated. The Yanmar engine had been so reliable perhaps I was lulled into thinking it would run forever.

We visited the Japanese adviser for the fish-packing plant just down the waterfront from us.

"We do have some Yanmar engines," said Kazou Matsumoto, "but nothing under 100 horsepower."

That was little help for our 15-horsepower model. Kazou assured me there would be no possibility of finding parts for our engine in Madagascar.

"If you can dismantle the engine and bring in the head gasket," Kazou offered, "I can have my machinists make a new head gasket for you."

Matsumoto was true to his word, and though the new head gasket wasn't perfect (which he apologized for), it looked serviceable. He also furnished us with some other small parts, gasket compound, and engine oil.

A few days later, with our two-month visas nearly expired, we again headed for the crab-meat-packing plant jetty to fill the water tanks, this time successfully.

I was still fretful over the engine, as I knew the makeshift gasket might blow again at any time. I decided we would run the engine only at low revs, and no more than necessary. If the engine gave out, we would have no electric power for the VHF radio or for the SatNav, no lights and reduced manoeuvrability during what could be a trying passage down the difficult Mozambique Channel.

Fiona's shoulders were much improved after two months' rest in Madagascar. They were still far from normal, but she could lift her right arm above her shoulder while the pain was easing in her left one. She was looking forward to getting underway for our next destination.

MOZAMBIQUE CHANNEL

25

"What are you trying to be – some sort of heroine? Don't you realize our lives are in danger? Can't you understand this voyage is jinxed?"

Paul was sitting in *Lorcha*'s cockpit, back against the bulkhead, shouting accusations at me. Tears streaked his cheeks, his eyes were wild, and his voice shook with emotion.

Penny and Peter were staring at both of us. They had never seen Paul so upset (the only tears I could remember in fifteen years were tears of joy when Penny was born), and they had never heard us having a serious disagreement.

This was serious all right. We were four days out from Mahajanga, trying to head southwest down the treacherous Mozambique Channel to Richard's Bay, South Africa, a thirteen-hundred-mile passage.

The channel is a dangerous body of water; cyclones sweep through it, and it has unpredictable and wide-banded fast-flowing currents. We had been looking for the south-going Mozambique current for three long days. Instead we found ourselves in the grip of a north-going current and a headwind. We were being swept northwest.

We hadn't worried the first day as we headed west, though covering only sixty-four miles was a disappointment. On the second day, however, there was a 20-knot southwest wind. Towards the end of

Paul's breakdown . . . strong currents . . . off-course . . .
cyclone season coming . . . Lorcha's poor condition . . .
minor repairs . . . northerlies at last . . . the wrong key . . .
Zululand Yacht Club . . . reunion with Mischief.

---

the day I could see that no matter how we headed the boat, we were being swept northwest. The minutes of latitude were accumulating much too fast towards 15° south latitude. Paul made his first quiet comment that he didn't think we were going to make South Africa. I thought he was trying to be funny and didn't take much notice.

We had a nerve-wracking overnight passage trying to work the boat south, to no avail. We were in the grip of that fast-going northerly current and couldn't break free. To the west lay war-torn Mozambique, where, it was rumoured, trigger-happy gunfighters shot at vessels which came too close to coast. How close was too close? Not that I was too worried yet. We were still sixty miles off.

"Fi, we're never going to make South Africa," sobbed Paul. "I want to go north to Mayotte. We could be there tomorrow. I just want to stop sailing for a while."

I had never imagined my strong mate and captain would ever have a breakdown; it was hard to believe even as I looked at Paul, sitting white-faced and shaking in the cockpit. If I hadn't taken him seriously before, I certainly had to now, even though I didn't understand what was happening.

The passage had been frustrating, yes, but we were in no danger. To go north was, at best, a poor decision. We would be harbour-bound by the upcoming cyclone season and would be unable to round the Cape of Good Hope that season as planned. It would take us an extra year to return to Toronto, and that would mean we'd have to get our house rented again, give up the idea of getting Penny into Grade Six French Immersion, and we'd also miss the launching of our book about our Atlantic Ocean adventures, which was due to be published in the fall of 1988.

If we had been in a real emergency – a sick child, a terrible storm, a jury-rigged boat, I wouldn't have hesitated. I would have changed our travel plans for two years if that was what the circumstances had called for, but apart from worry and frustration we were not in a life-threatening situation, and the option of heading north at some point was open-ended.

"We'll give it another twenty-four hours to see if the wind and current will shift as we go further west," I said. "It's too soon in the passage to give up."

It hasn't been often that Paul and I have had wide differences on what we should do in a difficult situation. Some strange force has always seemed to be at work ensuring that we complement each other. If I was weak, Paul was strong, and when he had difficulty, I was usually able to cope. That force seemed to be at work again. Usually on the first days of a passage I am seasick and tired. That stress can lead me to make hasty decisions, but Paul usually copes well at this time. Yet, on this particular passage I had not been sick and was completely in control of my energies. I was confident we would eventually make our destination and was prepared to wait it out.

I tucked Paul into his bunk and fed him vitamins, wheat germ, brewer's yeast, and any other health-sustaining food I had on the boat. Then I sat the kids down in the cockpit and broke a bar of chocolate for all of us.

"Penny and Peter," I said, "Papa's having a tough time just now and isn't feeling well. He's suddenly frightened about this passage. There's no reason for any of the rest of us to feel that way. But we all deserve some chocolate and hugs to keep our spirits up. Okay? And let's look at the chart together and see exactly what's happening."

Later that day the wind started going more westerly, and I

changed course to the southwest to at least try to get some southing, which I thought would make us feel more optimistic. Paul stood his night watches, though every watch was preceded by a trying discussion.

In the morning we found we had made about twenty miles southing, but were now headed south*east*. We were virtually going back along our track. Nothing was giving us a break and Paul was still feeling, as he described it, "scared to death." He had a very strong premonition of disaster and our worst argument ever followed, with Paul bitterly accusing me of trying to be some sort of heroine. I could not see, smell, or feel danger, so I opted to go on, trying to understand what was happening with Paul.

I knew that Paul had been worried when we left Australia to cross the Indian Ocean, because of my weak shoulders. Certainly, I had been the weaker partner, and for the last six thousand miles of travel I had not raised the sail once as it was beyond my strength. Paul's sleep had been interrupted more than usual as we had been through a lot of squalls when I had had to lower the sail – and then had had to ask him to help me raise it again.

Lorcha, our stalwart vessel, was in her poorest passage-making condition since leaving Toronto. The blown head gasket in Madagascar had been a complete surprise to us, and Paul was worried that the makeshift gasket might not hold.

There had been some minor challenges, bringing on a worrying feeling of "too many" and "what's next." Paul had repaired the trailing log and had got the SatNav going again when its lights had unaccountably gone out – both relatively minor problems, but perhaps accumulating in Paul's mind.

Now the strong west wind was falling off and we had to hand-steer through the night. We changed course again, deciding we had to go still further west in an effort to find that south-going current. We would have to close with the dangerous Mozambique coast.

As I was cooking supper that night, our cooking gas bottle ran out. We had a limited emergency supply, but we would now have no more coffee, tea, or baked bread, and we would be cooking one-pot meals once each day.

"Don't you see," pleaded Paul as he competently put the emergency supplies into place. "We're just never going to make it to South Africa. Let's turn the boat around, Fi. I'm a nervous wreck."

"We have plenty of food that doesn't need cooking," I said. "If something else breaks, I know you'll fix it. I'm just not ready to give up. Our luck will change soon."

It wasn't to be that night, though. We hand-steered again, once more heading west but still being swept north, though at a slower rate. I thought that grounds for optimism, but all Paul could see what that we were still headed in the wrong direction, however slowly.

We had a difficult day of discussion, though the kids were coping well. They did not like seeing their father in this upset condition, but were willing to accept my explanation and, as the weather was not rough, they could carry on merrily with their usual games and projects. I didn't have to cope with any extra anxieties on their part; they were taking the situation in their stride.

The following night the wind came up out of the west, and a stray wave breaking over the cockpit drenched the radio, though Paul tried to shield it with his body. It seemed to me I was travelling with two Pauls – the one spooked, scared, and a self-confessed nervous wreck, and my competent partner, who calmly took apart our precious radio, sprayed it with WD40, and put it together again.

In the morning, light northerlies at last. So light that we had to motor and hand-steer, but it was the first positive sign that we had had, and I found myself praying that this wind would stay. The seas were calm and for the first time, we were making some real southing. The calm conditions continued through the day, and the cloud of gloom weighing *Lorcha* down lightened, though we did have another set-back that evening.

Paul was casually looking at the engine starter switch when he did a double take. I had used the wrong key to start the motor! God knows how it started at all, as it is usually impossible to start an engine with the wrong key, but I seemed to have done just that. Now the key just came away in Paul's hand and wouldn't go back in. We couldn't turn off the motor!

"This is just an ill-fated voyage," muttered Paul, but at least there was resignation and not panic in his voice. I may have been keeping my cool on the voyage, but it was Paul who kept the boat together, however pessimistically. He had to take the switch apart and fudge the broken mechanism before we were once more able to turn the engine on and off . . . with the correct key, of course!

On our sixth day, the north wind strengthened and we continued south, not sure if we had found the south-going current yet, but glad to be out of the grip of the north-going one.

This was the turning point of the voyage. By evening we realized we were picking up 1 knot of current and at last we could count on making a hundred miles a day in the right direction. There was no celebration. We all felt relieved we could get on with our voyaging in a normal fashion. And reading, schoolwork, playing chess with the kids, showers, and cooking supper became the order of the day. Paul, though perhaps quiet, was completely whole and participating.

Fourteen days after we left Madagascar, we motored slowly through the Richard's Bay breakwater into the Zululand Yacht Club.

"How was the passage?" called Joy from *Mischief*, which had sailed away from Madagascar ten days before us.

"Not bad," we called back as we came alongside. "Nothing we couldn't cope with."

"We had a terrible time!" said Joy. "We ran out of drinking water and Andrea fell overboard when we were making 7 knots. We missed her the first time we went back, but don't worry, she's just fine."

Everyone on *Lorcha* felt good. We had come through a major personal crisis, but the strength of our small family had overcome the passing weakness of one of its members.

And who knows, perhaps we were all the stronger because of the experience.

KRUGER

26

M ost travelling yachts still elect to make the city lights
their first port of call in South Africa and tie alongside the International Jetty in Durban. And why not?
It's convenient, if crowded, and the Durban Yacht
Club is located in the centre of the city.

But a growing number of voyagers are electing to
do what we did, heading first for the Zululand Yacht
Club in Richard's Bay, eighty miles north of Durban.
The overwhelming friendliness of its members
makes up for its somewhat isolated locale. We
instantly became a part of the community and were
whisked off to morning coffee and *braais*, the South
African equivalent of a barbecue. Nearly all the
cruising boats with children aboard made Richard's
Bay their first port in South Africa, so there was a
solid community of families who looked forward to
spending a few months together.

The only black South Africans we met, however,
were the men and women who swept the docks,
worked on the boats, and stood on the other side of
the bar. But what did we expect? We were white
people on white yachts staying at a white yacht
club in South Africa.

There was only one incident of note. The club
had a wonderful Christmas party for children, and
all the kids from the visiting yachts were invited. We
were moored alongside a yacht that had some

*Zululand's family atmosphere . . . children's Christmas party
. . . on safari . . . Kruger Park . . . a frightened elephant . . .
young male lions . . . orphan animals at Tshukudu
Game Park . . . Swaziland . . . thanksgiving ceremony . . .
respect for their culture.*

Indian visitors on board, including an eight-year-old boy. He was watching wistfully as Santa Claus greeted the other children on the lawn to the left of the moored boats. As a shore visitor to a visiting boat, he had not been invited to the party, but I did what I would have done for any child on the sidelines. I checked with the commodore that an additional child would be welcome and then took him along. He had a grand time.

After the party, I thanked the official Santa Claus for including Penny and Peter.

"South Africa is going through changes," he said to me. "Now take that little Indian boy at the party. That's wonderful to see. It's the first time we've ever had a coloured boy at a function here. I wonder where he came from?"

"I invited him," I said, realizing only then that I had invited not just a child, but a "coloured" child.

The yachts were divided into three groups: those who would be heading down the Wild Coast in January, staying in South Africa for only a few months; those who would be staying for another season and taking the time to explore the country, perhaps buying and fixing up an old four-wheel-drive vehicle to travel through the border countries; and those who would apply for work permits and work for a season. We were rather sorry to be in the first group, as we would have liked to have driven north and spent a few months camping and visiting.

But Richard's Bay was well-suited to local exploration.

There were many game parks within easy driving distance. We could visit a nearby park for a day, or we could elect to stay overnight, either camping in a designated area or staying in an African *rondevaal*. We could barbecue our own evening meal or have someone cook our food for us. We could buy supplies or eat in a restaurant. Accommodation could be simple, medium-priced, or luxurious. And the parks ranged from the general to those that specialized in rhino, giraffe, lions, elephants, or zebra. Wildlife was abundant.

But it was the 20,000-square-kilometre Kruger Park, located about four hundred kilometres northeast of Johannesburg in eastern Transvaal, that attracted us. It is the largest of Africa's game parks, with the reputation of being home to the greatest variety of animals. We decided we had time to visit Kruger for a few days, to take in a small private park, and also to spend a week of driving and camping in nearby Swaziland.

Peter could not imagine seeing a giraffe at close quarters, nor could Penny visualize a lion softly padding by the car. "Will we see heffalumps and woozels?" asked Winnie-the-Pooh *aficionado*, Peter.

Switzerland was the first country to establish a sanctuary where hunting was prohibited – in 1592! It was not until 1872 that the United States proclaimed its first national park at Yellowstone. Kruger National Park, first named the Sabi Game Reserve and three times the size of Switzerland, was founded in 1898 by then-president, Paul Kruger. The first tourists did not drive through its gates, however, until 1927.

We decided to hire a free-lance guide for our four-day trip through Kruger. We could thus combine interest with education and be better equipped to visit other game parks on our own. We found Fred Bester, a burly, knowledgeable man with a minibus in which the five of us spent twelve hours every day, viewing an astonishing variety of birds and animals.

We drove through Kruger's southern gate with great expectancy. "There's a hippo," said Fred. "And some impala," he added almost immediately, pointing in another direction.

Only five minutes later we saw four cars stopped at the side of the dirt road we were following. A giraffe lay tumbled on the ground just off the road.

"He's been killed by a lion, probably early this morning," commented Fred, eyes combing the undergrowth. "Most people don't realize it, but giraffe, where available, are the main kill of lions."

Friendly South Africans in a neighbouring car told us where to train our binoculars. A well-fed male lion was eying us sleepily through the grass, his mane and blinking eyes clearly visible through the binoculars. The kill was recent; there had been time for vultures to gather in the nearby trees, but not enough hours for them or the smaller predators to be allowed by the lion to approach the kill.

All this in our first fifteen minutes!

It was a day of keen observation as we drove along winding roads, windows down and staring hard at the lush green bush and clearings, eyes straining to be the first to see a new animal. Shapes and colours blended against the greens and browns of trees and scrub so that often an animal – even a large one – was impossible to spot until some movement gave him away. Time and time again, it was Fred's trained eye that saw the first wildebeest, duiker, or hyena.

And then we spotted our first elephant. He was aiming to cross the road in front of us, and Fred drove the car very close.

"He looks upset," said Fred quietly, keeping his foot on the accelerator. "He may come at us, but don't be nervous. I can easily accelerate the car away from him."

At that moment, the elephant charged, pulling up short about ten metres away to stand, flapping his ears, and angrily uproot a small tree in his path. Slowly he backed down, then stopped, and, putting his trunk down his throat and into his stomach, seemed to draw out water which he sprayed over his ears.

"I've only seen an elephant do that once before," said Fred. "Something's frightened him badly." Fred had been to Kruger some five hundred times, and, he told us, "That's what keeps me coming back to the parks. You never know what you'll come across."

Our first three hours in Kruger passed quickly as we spotted many animals with young, including a breeding herd of elephants with three little ones; a troup of baboons with red-faced, black-haired babies only a few hours old; a warthog who let us have a good look at her four piglets before she disappeared down a culvert; and impalas with frisky babies born during the previous ten days.

We developed a pattern in Kruger: we were on the road by 4:30 A.M.; we drove slowly around for three to four hours before having breakfast at one of the eighteen rest camps; then another three-hour drive and we broke for lunch between noon and 1:00 P.M. After napping for a couple of hours, we drove around from 4:00 to 6:30 P.M., when the camp gates closed for the evening. We saw animals on every outing, though not every period of the day was equally productive. Early morning was the time to see jackals and hyena, while we saw the big cats in the evening. It was an intense schedule and very different from our life on the ocean, where we threw only cursory glances at the seascape, but patience learned during those long hours at sea – and their natural love of animals – now stood Penny and Peter in good stead: hour after hour they sat glued to their respective windows, drinking in each new experience. Every bend of the dusty road promised a fresh sighting, and they could hardly wait to round the next corner, and the next, and the next.

We saw a giant hippo lumbering along a bank before sliding into the river to challenge the other hippos already there. Early one evening we spotted another recent kill: a leopard had hung a dead impala in the forked branch of a tree to keep it from roaming scavengers, waiting for dark – or for us to go away – before he began to tear apart his evening meal. Crouched under a bush about thirty metres away, he eyed us malevolently.

But the thrilling highlight was the sighting of three young lions. Fred explained that they would be brothers about two years old, leaving the main pride to form their own group until it was time for them to mate. Through binoculars we watched them playing beside a waterhole and nuzzling each other affectionately. We paralleled them in the car as they strolled, lolled, and padded past the water. Waterbuck stood stiff-legged a hundred metres away, never taking their eyes off the potential death threat and ready to leap away at the first threatening gesture. Baboons barked warnings from nearby trees. The very undergrowth seemed alert and listening, and waves of fear and apprehension hung almost palpably in the air.

After about an hour, the lions began to make their way up the hill towards our car. "Close your window, Peter," said Fred, softly.

The first lion crossed the road in front of the car, walked around it, and stood at the back bumper. We stared at him – a scant six feet from our noses. He turned and walked slowly into the bush.

Interesting though it is to see these rare creatures in zoos or on television, the adrenaline can only pound through your veins when it's you who's in the cage, and the animals who are stalking, prowling, and padding all around.

Appetites whetted by our experiences in Kruger, we headed for more game-park viewing.

A few miles from Kruger, near Hoetspruit, also in the Transvaal, is Tshukudu Game Park, a five-thousand-hectare reserve filled with giraffe, sable, kudu, nyala, rhino, duiker, waterbuck, and impalas. But it's the nuzzling, friendly animals nearer the farmhouse that are of more interest.

The privately owned park is run by a ten-member extended family. Owner Lolly Sussens, a well-known big-game hunter in Botswana for over twenty-five years, has now turned conservationist, and he and his wife Ala have made a reputation for themselves taking in and raising orphaned baby animals.

Gerry the giraffe, whose head was inside the car window before we even had time to open the door, was two weeks old when found after his mother had been killed by lions.

After being bottle-fed every two hours for eight weeks, he regards himself as one of the family. Now five and a half years old and nearly five metres tall, he visits with the other giraffes in the park for a week at a time, but always comes back to the farmhouse for a friendly pat. He's careful about the swimming pool – having once had to be hoisted out of it inelegantly with block and tackle.

There have been three sets of baby warthogs. The latest newcomer, only ten days old when we were there, was named Maggie the Third. She was minuscule and still being bottle-fed, but like all the other tame animals, she had the run of the farm, although all are fenced in at night because of wandering predators from nearby Kruger. The first Maggie was named after Margaret Thatcher by a British tourist who could see that the baby pig was determined to survive. Many of the animals bear well-known names. Ronnie, the young kudu, was named after Ronald Reagan, while Pik, the sable antelope, is called after Roelof (Pik) Botha, South Africa's foreign minister, and if you're lucky, when you tour the reserve in an open truck, you'll meet Charles and Di, the more-or-less tame rhinos.

Numerous animals brought here as babies – wildebeest and hyena among them – have been successfully returned to the wild. We added to the menagerie by bringing in a colourful European roller bird which had been hit by a car and had a broken wing.

Our short visit to Swaziland once again underscored for us the importance of getting off the boat from time to time to travel inland. We always returned to the boat with some new knowledge and insight, and the few days off the boat recharges the batteries for future voyaging.

The Kingdom of Swaziland became a sovereign state in 1968 after one hundred years of British rule. It is a country rich in history and custom; there is evidence that it has been inhabited from early Stone Age times. Between 1840 and 1868, a loose confederation of clans ruled by Mswati became a nation. The Kingdom of Mswati was about twice the size of present-day Swaziland, which has an area of about 17,362 square kilometres. *Swazi* means "the people of Mswati."

With mountains, river valleys, fertile rolling grasslands, low veldt, gorges, and impressive escarpment, Swaziland is a stunningly beautiful and varied country. We had timed our stay there to coincide with the national thanksgiving festival, the Incwala. Swazi warriors from all over the country made their way to the Royal Palace near the capital of Mbabane, where the week-long festivities would take place. Dressed in their traditional costumes and carrying spears, knobsticks, battle-axes, and cowhide shields, the tribespeople blended superbly with the grandeur of the scenery. These were not people "dressed-up" – they were simply and naturally celebrating an ancient custom. We picked up many hitch-hikers as we drove, and, seated between Penny and Peter in the back seat of the car, they willingly told us where they had come from (some had walked for a week) and what the significance was of the cow tails or feathers they wore for ornamentation.

In all the countries we had visited, we had never met people so proud of and so steeped in their traditions.

The main ceremonies of the thanksgiving festival were to take place near the Royal Palace in a special enclosure built like a stockade – a *kraal* – with thousands of stripped branches woven together into an impenetrable wall. A few openings allowed people in one at a time.

We had visited the tourist office in advance to get permission to take a camera inside the kraal. The Swazis regard the taking of pictures as an intrusion and a debasement of customs and sacred traditions, and photography is only allowed under rigidly controlled conditions – how rigid those conditions were we were to find out.

Paul and camera and a small group of other photographers were allowed inside the kraal. I was not. The reason? I was wearing trousers, regarded as a sign of disrespect at any time – women in Swaziland *never* wear trousers – but especially rude in the presence of royalty. Such an outrage had never been allowed in the presence of the king and an ignorant tourist from Canada was not now going to break that tradition.

I was disappointed, but acknowledged my gaffe – there could be no argument. Penny and Peter and I waited outside the enclosure, interesting and colourful enough with the thousands of milling participants waiting to enter. A friendly warrior told me I could take some photographs outside, but that if anyone objected I should immediately refrain. The few white tourists stood out in the crowd, and every tourist carrying a camera was barred from entering the enclosure unless the camera was surrendered, to be retrieved later.

Inside the kraal with about ten other photographers, Paul was facing the unusual (for westerners anyway) situation of only being able to take photographs when allowed.

"You may take photographs directly in front of you, but you are not allowed to turn to either side," said the Swazi protocol officer. When one photographer, seeing some interesting action to one side of him raised his camera to take a shot, the camera was confiscated. "If anyone disobeys our wishes again, we will smash the camera," said the protocol officer calmly. "You are privileged guests. Please respect our restrictions."

After about three hours of thousands of tribespeople milling about the kraal and various government people being acknowledged, the king made a brief appearance. Immediately afterwards, all white people and all photographers were asked to leave. No one except Swazis would be allowed to participate in and witness the sacred ceremonies.

While this was a disappointment, we understood and respected the wishes of these proud people. They wanted to keep their culture intimate and intact. Having seen what the heavy, greedy, and voracious hand of tourism has done to other cultures in the world, we admired these independent people for their stand, perhaps all the more appreciating the small glimpse we had had of their private world.

WILD COAST

27

Abnormal waves – Under certain weather conditions, abnormal waves of exceptional height occasionally occur off the south-eastern coast of South Africa, causing severe damage to ships unfortunate enough to encounter them. In 1968 S.S. *World Glory*, of over 28,000 gross tons, encountered such a wave and was broken in two, subsequently sinking with loss of life.

These abnormal waves, which may attain a height of 65 feet (19.8m) or more . . .

The above is an excerpt from the *Africa Pilot*, Vol. III, published by the Hydrographer of the Navy, British Admiralty. It is the beginning of a treatise explaining why waves of exceptional height are generated along this coast.

The Agulhas Current flows south along the coast of South Africa at up to 5 knots. When the northeast wind blows strongly, which it often does, the waves generated by the wind travelling with the current build up. Every two to three days the cold front of a depression comes through, with winds blowing strongly, often at gale force, *against* the flow of the current. It is the sudden 180° change in the direction of strong winds coupled with the fast-flowing current which generates the freak waves that makes this coast so dangerous.

Abnormal waves . . . Agulhas Current . . . dangerous coastline
. . . Durban . . . East London . . . touching bottom . . .
surfing into Port Elizabeth . . . Thursday's Child
and Shambles *. . . Mossel Bay, a Scottish*
village in Africa . . . around the Cape . . .
Atlantic again . . . a friendly voice.

The other complicating factor is that there are few protected all-weather harbours along the coast. Distances are
such that it is impossible to day-sail around the lower tip of
Africa.

Low-pressure cells come from the south and head up the
coast. A low-pressure centre generating southwesterly winds,
the violent wind of this area, moves from just south of the
Cape of Good Hope up to Durban in about three to four days.
Small but violent coastal low-pressure cells can also develop
between the larger cells to play havoc with what looks like a
promising forecast.

And as you sail south you are meeting the bad weather as it
comes towards you. It is similar to racing a train to a crossing,
with similar potentially disastrous results.

We had spoken to Winston and Caroll Bushnell of Elliot
Lake, Ontario, whose yacht was capsized, pitch-poled, and
dismasted along this coast. In Tonga we had met a New Zealand couple whose yacht had been capsized and dismasted
here, too. When we had arrived in Richard's Bay the notices
were still posted requesting information about a U.S.-regis-
tered yacht which had disappeared off this coast the previous
sailing season. And while we were in Richard's Bay we listened to radio reports as a South African yacht was first
posted missing, then searched for and presumed lost. A week
after the search was called off a freighter picked up the crew
from their dismasted and badly leaking vessel. A summer

storm with winds of up to 60 knots had rolled their ill-prepared boat through 360 degrees and they had been blown out to sea.

We left Richard's Bay with a forecast of a favourable northeast wind of 20 to 30 knots, about average for this area and season. It is eighty miles down the coast to Durban, but allowing another ten miles to get away from the coast and the same again to get back to it on the other end makes a passage of about a hundred miles. This would normally be about a twenty-four-hour sail, though with the strong current it could be much shorter.

Because the northeast wind is considered the fair-weather wind, all the harbours on this coast are open to the northeast. Just getting out the harbour mouth into the teeth of this brisk wind was a challenge. *Lorcha* first buried her bow in the chop generated by the tidal outflow and the opposing wind, then reared up like a fighting stallion to throw the waves along her deck, first to douse us in the cockpit, then to roll back to their rightful place.

I was drenched repeatedly as I tried to hide behind the dodger, but I had to keep a good watch – there was a large bulk carrier coming out of the harbour behind us, with another manoeuvring to come in as soon as the exiting ship cleared the way.

It was with great relief that I made sail as we bore away down the coast. The waves were steep and splashy, with some spray coming over the aft cabin. As we neared the hundred-fathom (two-hundred-metre) depth contour the Agulhas Current accelerated our progress.

We had expected a fast ride, but at midnight the wind fell light. A small coastal low cell had formed and the wind changed to the southwest, but it didn't blow hard, perhaps 20 knots maximum. We motor-sailed into Durban harbour, tying up at the International Jetty near the Point Yacht Club where hundreds of international sailing yachts have lain over many years.

It was here that Joshua Slocum, the first sailor to circumnavigate the world single-handed, stopped for a rest in 1897. He was visited by three Boers who wanted to collect evidence from Slocum about the world being flat.

> . . . and they seemed annoyed when I told them that they could not prove it by my experience. With the advice to call up some ghost of the dark ages for research, I went ashore, and left these three wise men poring over the *Spray*'s track on a chart of the world, which, however, proved nothing to them, for it was on Mercator's projection, and behold, it was "flat."

Later Slocum was introduced by a judge to Paul Kruger, President of the Transvaal, as a round-the-world sailor.

> "You don't mean *round* the world," said the President; "it is impossible! You mean *in* the world. Impossible!" he said, "impossible!" and not another word did he utter either to the judge or to me.

Slocum describes them as "these Transvaal geographers" who sent him a pamphlet "proving" the flat-Earth theory before he "sailed on from Africa on my last stretch around the globe."

Perhaps the Boer of South Africa is slow to pick up on "new" theories, with today's examples more likely based on theories of racial supremacy.

"We'll sail tomorrow," some of our colleagues would say. "There is a high-pressure cell in position according to the weather map."

With that they would head for the port office, the customs office, and the immigration department, all three of which must be checked into and out of at each harbour visited in South Africa. It is a time-consuming procedure, requiring a few hours to make the rounds and complete the forms. The clearance is only good for thirty-six hours – if one does not leave within that time, the procedure must be gone over again.

But if four boats were preparing to leave, by morning perhaps only two would sail.

"I called the meteorological office this morning," would be the excuse; "they said a coastal low might form sometime today."

Some would leave, others would delay, and time would pass, with all of us fretful and apprehensive of sailing down this coast. All of us had sailed many thousands of ocean miles to arrive here, yet most were nearly catatonic when it came time to head out of harbour.

Durban to East London, a passage of about 250 miles, is along the part of the coast where the Agulhas Current flows very fast. There are no harbours between these two ports. The usual drill is to wait until the end of a southwest gale, and when the barometer has risen to 1020 millibars, check out with the officials to clear the harbour mouth with the last dying puffs of the southwester. You head offshore about eight miles to the one-hundred-fathom (two-hundred-metre) depth contour where the current flows fastest and make as much speed as possible. You listen to the weather forecasts and, at the first mention of a change in wind to the southwest, you head inshore, back inside the one-hundred-fathom line, to get out of the main current and into shallower water where the monster waves do not form.

It is then your choice: you can heave-to and wait, or bash into it and keep heading towards your destination in the case of a coastal low; or you can run back to your port of departure if the contrary wind turns into a "southerly buster."

If luck is with you, you may be spared the contrary wind. But the best you can hope for is to enter the next harbour as a southwester begins to rev up. The changes come too close together for medium-sized sailboats to comfortably make the passages between cold fronts.

After two weeks in Durban, Fiona, who had kept meticulous track of the weather charts, announced it was time to get going. I checked out with the officials while she did some last-minute shopping.

We had a 10- to 15-knot wind overnight, but the barometer began to fall. Less than twenty-four hours out from Durban the southwest wind came in at about 20 knots. We slogged on, motor-sailing into the rough chop, but still making 7-plus knots over the bottom with the strong current.

It began to rain and turned foggy, with visibility down to a hundred metres or less. We plotted every SatNav fix and carefully altered course when called for. We occasionally saw a coastal light for a few minutes, but could identify nothing.

At 0515 we plotted a SatNav fix which put us one mile offshore and three miles from the breakwater. It was beginning to get light, but we still couldn't see a thing because of the fog. Plotting a course on the chart, which showed no obstructions to the harbour mouth at East London, I slowly motored on. But moments later we were in breaking surf, with a large breaker curling just beside us. *Lorcha* settled in the trough and touched bottom. I put the helm hard over, and as *Lorcha* rose to the next swell she breasted her way over it, lifting off the bottom, and made her way to deeper water.

"Call the Harbour Control on the VHF," I yelled to Fiona. "Describe our situation and see if they have any suggestions."

"They said they're in a tower near the harbour mouth," Fiona called to me from the navigation table near the VHF radio. "They're above the fog, and we might see them. They can't see us, but they can make out a ship anchored about a mile off the breakwater. Leave that ship on our port side and head southwest, and we should be in the channel."

We continued to grope along, eventually finding the ship at anchor, and then the breakwater with the channel markers, and at last we motored safely into harbour in the drizzling rain.

Later in the afternoon I called the met. bureau for the next day's forecast. We assumed the coastal low would pass overnight. Would there be enough time to make good the 140 miles to Port Elizabeth before the next strong southwesterly?

The wind was forecast at 25 to 30 knots, perhaps gusting to 40 knots the following night. But the easterly direction was right, even if there were to be near gale-force winds.

At 0630 I again called the met. bureau and received the

267

same forecast. At 0800 we were casting off the lines and heading out of harbour. The wind was brisk but manageable, though the waves were splashy with much spray in the air.

At about noon we had two SatNav fixes almost exactly one hour apart. We had made just over nine miles over the bottom in that hour. *Lorcha* usually sailed at about 5 knots, so the current was pushing us along at an additional 4 knots.

The wind was strong and gusty overnight, and we approached Port Elizabeth harbour at about 0200 the following morning. The near gale-force wind was dead aft, and though the visibility was good, it is nerve-wracking to run downwind towards a harbour mouth in these conditions. If you make a mistake, you are on the break-wall or beach before you get a second chance.

I slowed *Lorcha* to give us extra time to be sure of our approach. We could make out all the entrance lights from a few miles off, so we decided to head in.

One-half mile off the break-wall I began to feel the waves hump up, and I closed the companionway, fearing a breaking wave might fill the cockpit. Suddenly we were lifted by a real monster, perhaps nine or ten metres high. *Lorcha* surfed down the front like a California teenager. I hung on to the tiller, knowing the real test would come at the end of the ride.

Would *Lorcha* be overwhelmed by a breaking crest as she was overtaken by the top of the wave? Would she broach out of control as she exceeded her manageable speed? As she settled in the trough behind this monster, would she be overwhelmed by the following wave?

The overtaking crest was steep and foaming, but not breaking, so we passed that test. A bucket of water to the face of the skipper to keep him alert was the wave's parting gift.

Turning my attention to what was ahead of us, I shot *Lorcha* through the breakwater into calmer water. My knees were weak and shaking, but we were otherwise unscathed. We had made a fast passage, 140 miles in nineteen hours, harbour to harbour.

The southwest winds whistled around us for the next few

268

days, but we were content in harbour, with the hospitable Algoa Bay Yacht Club at hand. We renewed acquaintance with the crew of *Thursday's Child*, the British-registered yacht we had first encountered in Venezuela nearly four years earlier. We had met Malcolm and Mary often over the ensuing years, and always enjoyed their company. Malcolm had been a lecturer at Cambridge University and had a wonderful selection of books, so we tried to exchange books with him whenever we could.

We also got to know the crew of *Shambles*. Uli and Manfred were German-born South Africans headed towards Europe on their 13.5-metre steel ketch. They had a Morse code decoder connected to their short-wave radio receiver and could decipher the international shipping forecasts. We consulted them for the weather patterns coming up, as Uli meticulously plotted the highs and lows on her weather maps.

The 195-mile passage to Mossel Bay was made in very mixed weather. Light easterly winds, some rain and fog and calms. We motored about half the distance, rather than sailing slowly, as this coast is definitely not a place to wait for the wind.

Mossel Bay, a delightful fishing village with stone cottages, resembles Fiona's native Scotland. Seals swim about in the harbour, and the fishermen throw them net-damaged fish. Penny and Peter also tried to attract them with their meagre handouts.

It was five days before we again got a favourable forecast. Winds easterly, 25 to 30 knots, gusting to 40, sounded familiar, but manageable. Jonas, skipper of *Asynja*, summed up sailing along this coast with, "The best you can hope for is that the bad weather comes from behind you."

Our final 250-mile passage along the coast to Cape Town was trying. We had the usual brisk winds and choppy seas, but also encountered a lot of shipping. Cargo ships seemed to come at us from all directions. Fishing boats trawled along the coast and caused us a lot of confusion as they turned and stopped or circled.

As we sailed, we listened to the weather forecasts, and were stunned to hear that 50 knots of easterly winds were being recorded at Cape Point (the Cape of Good Hope). We were about ninety miles east of there, and worried about sailing into that weight of wind. Luckily, the wind was decreasing, and I don't think we encountered any wind over 40 knots.

"We're about fifteen miles from Cape Point according to a recent SatNav fix," I told Fiona at our 0200 change of watch. "Keep at least three miles away from the Point, as there are lots of reefs and rocks there. I'm going to get some sleep."

When Fiona called me for my 0500 watch I was surprised to find the powerful current had so accelerated our progress that we were well past the Cape Point lighthouse.

We were in the Atlantic Ocean!

The wind was easing as we headed north up the coast, and the sun was rising along a clear horizon.

"Is that a shark over there?" asked sharp-eyed Peter. As we closed with the animal in the water we realized it was a seal floating on his side with one flipper raised to the wind. It seemed he had his sail set to drift along the coast.

"Are those ducks?" again asked Peter. They were flocks of penguins. They sat on the water like ducks until we sailed almost up to them. Then, instead of taking flight, they dove. We could see them through the clear water, flapping their wings just as if they were airborne.

We also saw several albatross, recognizable by their wing span of up to three metres. They glided and banked around the boat, seeming never to flap their wings. We had last seen albatross near New Zealand, at about the same latitude south.

We entered Table Bay between Green Point, a park and picnic site, and Robben Island, site of the penitentiary where civil rights activist Nelson Mandela was incarcerated.

"*Lorcha, Lorcha, Lorcha,*" came over the VHF radio, "this is *Ashymakaihken,* do you copy?"

We acknowledged the call from Ashley on *Ashymakaihken,* and changed channels. Ashley continued, "I just spoke to Malcolm on *Thursday's Child* on the ham radio. He is in some heavy weather near Cape Point, but said you were ahead of him."

"Tell Malcolm the wind will ease as soon as he rounds Cape Point," I replied. "We're just off the breakwater, and will be entering soon. Where shall we tie up?"

"Come into the Royal Cape Yacht Club basin," said Ashley. "I'll be standing at a pier end to direct you."

SOUTH ATLANTIC SAILING

28

Tropical Cyclones – As compared to previous months, warmer sea temperatures in the southern latitudes during June increase the probability of tropical cyclone development. Over an average 10 year period, 7 tropical cyclones of force 8 or greater will take up residence in the North Atlantic with 3 of these reaching hurricane strength (force 12).

> *Pilot Chart of the North Atlantic Ocean for the month of June. Prepared from data furnished by the Defense Mapping Agency, U.S.A.*

I t was late March by the time we were prepared to sail north from Cape Town up the Atlantic Ocean. We were eight thousand ocean miles from our first North American landfall.

There is no hurricane season in the South Atlantic Ocean, but the hurricane season of the North Atlantic Ocean would begin sixty-eight days after we left Cape Town. There was no chance that we could make good all those miles before then, but we would hurry along as best we could.

"There won't be any wind along the coast tomorrow," said the forecaster at the met. bureau. "But if you motor about fifty miles off the coast you should run into a light southeasterly."

Thick fog blanketed Cape Town on the morning

Heading towards hurricane season . . . days of flat calm . . .
on-board treats . . . encountering Ishi . . . the Royal Mail
St. Helena . . . a French sailor in a tanker . . . arrival at
St. Helena . . . Jacob's Ladder . . . Napoleon's exile . . .
moonset . . . Fernando de Noronha.

of March 23 as we groped around trying to find the outer breakwater. Once clear of the harbour we could catch only the odd glimpse of the famous landmark, Table Mountain, as we powered along at just over 4 knots. We motored for thirty hours over a sea so flat and calm we could see our reflection in it. And then we were able to sail slowly for only five hours before again resorting to the engine.

It wasn't until the afternoon of our fourth day at sea that the wind steadied and we felt we were truly on our way. But in that time the engine alternator belt had broken, even though it was nearly new. I installed the last new spare, though I had some worn but still serviceable belts on board. The impeller for the engine-cooling water pump had also broken. I had replaced it just before leaving Australia, less than one year earlier, and was surprised to have it fail. I replaced that with my last new one.

One afternoon Fiona noticed that the trailing log was not registering. Pulling in the line, she found the spinner had been bitten off. I replaced that with my last spare – we had lost one to a fish off the coast of Madagascar, too. We decided not to put the spinner in the water again, but to estimate our speed, and let the SatNav calculate our distance sailed. We would save the log in case the SatNav failed and we had to revert to celestial navigation.

"Stop eating so many cookies," Fiona scolded as I munched.

"I hope twenty kilos of cookies will be enough to get us to Bermuda," I replied unabashedly, "I wasn't that fond of Brazilian cookies."

I find that much of the food we prepare at sea is soft in texture, and I like nothing better than to have a handful of crunchy cookies on night watch. It helps me stay awake, and I had insisted that Fiona stock up on cookies in South Africa.

Fiona is fond of chocolate during night watches, so buys a box of large chocolate bars for her stock of treats.

Treats become important, as there is so little to break the routine of life at sea. Other treats include dry-roasted peanuts (the oil-roasted kind are too greasy for sea-going stomachs), candied ginger (especially as ginger is said to help prevent seasickness), and dried figs, especially the Turkish ones, which we buy in ten-kilo boxes and ration carefully to make them last. Jars of olives and tinned fruit cakes are also high on the list.

We're not alone in our need for sea-time treats. Clarke Stede single-handed his vessel for several years. He buys tinned butter by the case – he needs it to make his favourite chocolate cake. He says he bakes a big cake, complete with frosting, twice a week when at sea.

Jim on *Becky Lou*, also a single-hander, complains about the quality of chocolate chips found in many countries of the world. He prefers to bake his own cookies, and he gave us several good cookie recipes.

We also carry fruit juices and fizzy drinks, such as cola, ginger ale, and tonic water to ring the changes for a different taste. Ascorbic acid tablets, which make effervescent vitamin C drinks, are refreshing and healthful and are rationed out when at sea. Neither Fiona nor I drink coffee or alcoholic beverages while at sea. Both are diuretics and can cause dehydration, but that's not why we abstain; we simply seem to have no taste for them, although we are fond of a coffee or a drink when at anchor or ashore.

Other small things become important, too. Fiona and I take turns sleeping in the same bunk when at sea. After I get up

274

she insists I shake out the sheets and blankets, turn over the pillows and make the bunk up again before I come on watch. Thus she has a freshly made bunk, without the hot sweatiness I might leave behind.

It is also important to have some solitary time during the day, be it for taking a nap, quiet reading time, or just off-watch day-dreaming. Off-watch solitude seems very important, even though night watches bring plenty of on-watch solitude. Four people on a thirty-foot boat may make solitude sound impossible to get, but it can mean as little as that no one makes demands on you or talks to you; you are free to occupy yourself as you will.

We were nearing the end of our ocean voyaging, and I was already getting nostalgic about it. I became intensely aware of the colour of the water and clouds. Even though the central South Atlantic seemed to have little bird or fish life, at least out where we were sailing, the water was beautifully blue, the sky was usually clear, and sometimes the puffy cumulus trade wind clouds sailed along with us.

I enjoy watching the changing shapes of the clouds, and liken them to sailing ships as they drift across the sky. When the clouds are small and regularly spaced the wind is stable at a moderate rate. When the clouds are larger, the wind is blustery and changes direction. When there is only flat greyish cloud, there is little wind.

The wave pattern is annoying in the South Atlantic Ocean. Just as in the Indian Ocean, there is an overlying southwesterly swell. It rolls us beam on, but is not so violent as in the Indian Ocean. This overlying beam swell lasted until we passed the bulge of Brazil. Once in the lee of South America, the swells rounding Cape Horn could no longer reach us.

"Fi, can you make a call on the VHF?" I shouted down the companionway only ten minutes after taking over watch at 0500.

I had been facing aft, adjusting the self-steering gear, when a light suddenly came on. It was high off the water and not very far astern of us. It took a few seconds for me to realize it was the masthead light of another yacht.

"This is *Ishi*," came the immediate reply from skipper Buzz Taylor. "We've been sailing without lights, and just saw yours. Is that a kerosene lamp? We left Cape Town the day after you did. The sailing is so slow it seems like we've been out here forever."

As the first light of dawn slowly overtook us I could see *Ishi* gybe to the other tack, then parallel our course as she, with her sixteen-metre length, gradually sailed away from us.

This mid-ocean chance encounter was the first time we had ever seen another yacht when we were well offshore.

The following night, at about midnight, I saw a ship approaching us from dead ahead. I switched on the masthead light to augment the kerosene lamp. The ship came near us, then began flashing the Morse Code letter K ("Wish to communicate with you" in the International Code of Single Letter Signals) at us with a bright light.

We usually sail with the VHF radio turned off as the chatter from passing freighters and fishing vessels can disturb the sleeping off-watch person.

"Fi," I woke up my sleeping mate, "can you call a ship signaling us? He is nearby, just at our beam. I want to stay up here to watch him."

"Yacht headed toward *St. Helena*, yacht headed toward *St. Helena*, come in please." It was the captain of *Royal Mail St. Helena*, the ship that makes a regular run to Cape Town for supplies and mail for that island. Seeing our light, he had decided to chat for a few minutes, as well as telling us about anchoring and clearance procedures at his home island.

The following night I sighted the steep, fortress-like island of St. Helena by the light of a three-quarter moon. We were coming too fast upon it, as it would still be dark when we arrived off the anchorage if we kept going. I stopped us sailing, heaving-to.

I headed *Lorcha* away from the island, then hauled the sheet in, to bring the reefed sail nearly mid-ships. I angled the

276

tiller about fifteen degrees off to the side, then set the self-steering gear as if we were sailing on a close reach, about seventy degrees from the direction the wind came from. *Lorcha* then lay nearly dead in the water, steadied by the wind on the sail. But this imparts a short rocking motion, much different from that of a boat moving through the water. The change in motion will wake an experienced sailor, and Fiona began to stir.

"I'll keep us hove-to for a couple of hours," I said down the companionway. "We'll get going again before your watch."

"Fi, time for your watch, but could you make a call on the VHF?"

A large tanker had appeared, coming around the south side of the island. I had got *Lorcha* sailing again, headed for the anchorage on the north side of the island. But this cargo ship was travelling fast, and appeared to be heading us off.

"I am the captain of this ship," came a heavily French-accented voice over the radio, "and the owner of a twelve-metre ketch I keep in Marseille. I am just coming over for a closer look. Is that a junk sail you have on your boat?"

It was a blustery day for our arrival at St. Helena, with a few quick rain showers to rinse us off as we headed into the anchorage at James Bay. No sooner was the anchor down than a heavy rowboat was pulling towards *Lorcha* with casually dressed island officials on board.

"Welcome to St. Helena," the three men chorused. "May we come aboard?"

The clearance procedures were informal, and we chatted to the men as we served them coffee.

"You must run up Jacob's Ladder, the 700 stone steps which go up Ladder Hill," said the harbour master, indicating the hill over his shoulder. "It has become a tradition amongst visitors to time themselves, and then record the time at Ann's Restaurant."

Our first day ashore saw us struggling up the hill on weak

sea legs, as Penny and Peter, like eager puppies, wanted a run ashore. Peter was the first up the steps, but his time at over ten minutes was nowhere near the four-minute record set by a visiting U.S. Marine two years earlier.

On all the island of St. Helena, there is only one sea landing place, and no airport. The stone quay steps are the place where everyone not born in Saint Helena must come ashore. It can be a thrilling landing depending on the sea's state. As the dinghy rises in the swell, you must grab a rope hanging from an overhead beam and swing in. Be prepared to have your feet covered with waves as the surge rolls up the steps! There is a mark on the stone ramparts where, in 1878, phenomenal rollers raised the height of the sea by seven and a half metres.

A group of us yachties hired Colin, a local man with a 1929 Chevrolet bus, to take us on a tour of the island. We packed a lunch and piled aboard to ride over steep volcanic ridges to Longwood Lodge, the place where Emperor Napoleon spent most of his years of exile. He had arrived on October 15, 1815, in HMS *Northumberland*, and died on May 5, 1821, at the age of fifty-one. His remains were buried in Sane Valley, one of his favourite walking places, although they were exhumed in 1840 and conveyed to Paris, where they were entombed with great ceremony under the dome of Les Invalides.

France maintains Longwood Lodge and the burial site, considering it to be a part of French soil.

We sailed on only five days after arriving, running with the southeast trade winds towards the island of Fernando de Noronha, about eighteen hundred miles distant.

"What on earth is that?" I exclaimed to Fiona as I took over watch from her at 0500 one sea morning.

I was still sleepy, and struggling into my safety harness as I peered over the dodger to see a bright orange light at the horizon.

"I was about to tell you," said a retiring Fiona, "that if you hurried you could see moonset."

278

With that and a short laugh, she went below, leaving me to watch the last few seconds of that night's full moon.

It is the constancy of the trade winds that allows us peripatetic sailors to plan a season's voyaging months, even years, in advance. We know the direction the wind will blow, and the strength will hardly vary for months on end. With *Lorcha* dressed in nearly full sail, the windvane self-steering gear controlling her direction, I need only sit comfortably in the shaded corner of the lee side of the cockpit. I am rocked by the waves just enough to make my handwriting scrawl as I make notes, and I feel like I am on a magic carpet. I am carried along with little effort, needing only to hang on, to share and enjoy our good humour and sense of adventure with the rest of the family as we make for our next landfall.

It is strange how the waves break more as the wind moderates, suddenly dumping in a welter of foam and a hissing crash just at the transom as they are disturbed by *Lorcha*'s wake. *Lorcha*, bow up, surges down the wave front like a child on a sled down a barnyard hill.

Lorcha loves to surf down the waves, and I let her, as she has never shown a tendency to bury her bow or let the waves overwhelm her. Her buoyant shape rises to the lift of the surge with an easy motion, not a quick jump.

On the afternoon of our fifteenth day at sea, still about thirty miles away from landfall, we sighted the distinctive Finger Rock of Fernando de Noronha rising above the horizon. It was just after sunset when we rounded the off-lying islands to motor into Bai de St. Antonio. This was a special place for us; we had been here before.

FERNANDO DE NORONHA TO BERMUDA **29**

Many images of our travelling years stand out in each of our memories, but etched indelibly on the minds of both Penny and Peter is the sight of leaping, spiralling, playful dolphins coming out to meet us as we sailed into the Bai de St. Antonio on April 30, 1984. Our two youngsters, only five and seven at the time, were even more enchanted because gliding between the adult dolphins were hundreds of tiny white newborns. I can still hear Penny crying out, "Look at the babies! Look at the babies!" And I can still see Peter stretched flat on the bow with his hand in the water, yelling, "I touched one!" as his trailing fingers skimmed caressingly over the back of a dolphin who seemed to arch his body in anticipation of Peter's contact.

We had thought it was our own special exhibition, and it was not until we went ashore that we learned that Fernando de Noronha is a breeding ground for the spinner and bottlenose dolphin, and, being highly playful and curious animals, hundreds and hundreds of them make a point of coming out to greet all the incoming yachts.

Now just five miles off the island and sailing slowly through the moonlight towards the familiar Finger Rock, Penny and Peter were at *Lorcha*'s bow eagerly scanning the rippling waters. We were all

But where are the dolphins? . . . crossing our track . . .
Brazil . . . shopping and a medical . . . sailing north . . .
Peter is ill! . . . we make for Cayenne . . . crisis over, we head
north again . . . Peter's birthday . . . Bermuda, the end of our
longest passage.

---

thinking that it was a wonderful landfall on which to celebrate our circumnavigation, for it was at this small, remote
island that we would actually cross our outbound track.

But celebrate though we did, it was without the dolphins.
Nary a one did we see, though four pairs of eyes ceaselessly
searched the dark, moonlit waters. The children were almost
in tears as they asked again and again, "But where are they?"

When we went ashore the next day, the islanders told us
sadly that there had been a problem with too many tourists,
tourist boats, and scuba divers in the coves where the dolphins nurture their newborns. They estimated three thousand dolphins had left over a period of three years – to end
up where, nobody knows. That nursery area is now protectively buoyed and small boats are prohibited to enter, but
could the limited tourism on this remote island have really
caused the attrition? I couldn't see it.

The romance of visiting a one-time pirate's lair was somehow diminished. Even being able to get safely ashore by taking our dinghy around the new jetty (last time we had
overturned in the heavy surf, and had had to rescue Peter,
who had been trapped in the dinghy) didn't brighten our
spirits. Perhaps the building of this jetty (soon to be
expanded) had contributed to the disruption that made the
dolphins flee.

But it was when we sailed away from Bai de St. Antonio that
a more logical answer to the dolphins' departure presented

itself. As we made our way down the coast, headed for mainland Brazil, I noticed a freighter coming up behind us very fast. The ship was powering so close that even though we were only about a hundred metres off shore, Paul tacked even closer inshore and asked me to talk to the vessel on the VHF to ask her intentions. We were very near Dolphin Bay, the main and most publicized breeding ground. Though the freighter did not respond to our call, I surmise it had come in that close to see the dolphins. It was throwing up a huge bow wave and travelling at about 20 knots. Wouldn't it just smash up a curious playful dolphin which wanted only to cavort in that enticing turbulence? The freighter roared destructively by, with Penny and Peter screaming and shouting uselessly at it to slow down.

"I don't think we'll see any dolphins today. They'll be too frightened," I said quietly as we drifted slowly past Dolphin Bay. It was calm and eerily silent. There was no sign of life.

The three buoys across the mouth of the bay will warn the tourist boats and yachts not to enter these deep waters – but who will stop the freighters from roaring by so close?

It was a silent crew that made its way to mainland Brazil, just three days' sail away. We couldn't forget about the dolphins, and we were apprehensive about our destination – Fortaleza. The town is a major port of call for westbound yachts as it is both interesting and a good stocking-up place, but boat robberies and growing violence were an unpleasant factor on our last visit. We were much relieved when the four yachts at anchor assured us that all was calm, both in the city and in the anchorage.

This was to be a short stop, laying-in supplies for what we knew would be another long passage and getting a medical exam for Peter, who had been running an early morning low-level temperature for a couple of weeks.

Any planned short stop in Brazil has to be tempered by the fact that this is a country with some splendid handicrafts, and anyone with an interest in lace, crochet, linens, rugs, and handmade clothes (as Penny and I have) will find it very difficult not to plead for one more day of market meandering.

Doctors or hospitals in foreign countries are as conscientious and professional as their North American counterparts, though usually at much less cost. Peter was given a thorough examination at the local hospital and I was assured he was just fine for travel – yes, even for twenty days at sea.

There was no more reason to linger, and when a brisk southerly started blowing a week after our arrival, the captain was ready to leave. By noon, we were sailing out of the anchorage, passing many of the *jungada* sailing rafts which the local fishermen take many miles out to sea.

We had set a course due north, crossing the doldrums at a right angle to lessen the number of miles we might have to motor in calms, but the brisk wind held. We were still sailing when we crossed the Equator (our fourth crossing of the trip) on our third day at sea. The next day the wind shifted from southeast, through east, and into the northeast. We had found the northeast trade winds, having somehow managed to sail right through the Inter-Tropical Convergence Zone, the normally dead flat band which separates the counter-clockwise South Atlantic trade wind system from the clock-wise North Atlantic trade wind system, and where one can expect to motor for at least twenty-four hours.

By our sixth day at sea the northeast trade wind was blowing hard, 20 to 25 knots and more in the gusts. This doesn't bother us going downwind, but we were taking it forward of the beam, at about 65° off the bow. *Lorcha* would give a lurch as she rose up to the top of a wave, then a quick fall as she went over the top to drop into the trough. Each time she did this, several bucketsful of water would fly over the boat, some cascading down the deck and some flying over the dodger. We wore our foul-weather gear all day when we were in the cockpit, and at night as well. But we were careering along at over 120 miles a day, knocking off the miles.

Our pleasure in our roaring ride came to an abrupt halt on our ninth night at sea, when I was woken up by the sound of

Peter moaning in his bunk. As I ran my hand over his forehead and body I was shocked at the heat – he was burning! I took his temperature – 40°C (104°F).

Though it was 0200 hours (and my watch), I woke him up and helped him into the cockpit where Paul and I doused off his limp and unprotesting body with cooling sea water. He seemed easier when we put him back in his bunk, but two hours later his temperature was still 40°C. I sponged him off again and asked Paul to check on him in another two hours. After twelve hours, six sponge-offs, and three doses of soluble Aspirin, Peter's fever was as high as ever. And now he was developing a deep cough.

I could feel my mind going into a panic which I tried to control by checking on the chart to see exactly where we were – hundreds of miles from anywhere – and by consulting Peter F. Eastman's *Advanced First Aid Afloat*. I suspected pneumonia. We did not have the antibiotic of first choice, but started Peter on a course of tetracycline.

I looked at all that blue water around us; no doctors, hospitals, or help. A temperature of 40°C is not life-threatening in itself, but I had been worried about Peter's health before we had started this passage. What could be the complications here? There was no way we could carry on. Barely thirteen hours after Peter had first become ill, we altered course to the southwest, heading for the nearest port, Cayenne in French Guiana, more than five days away, a long time for worried parents with a seriously ill child.

The following day we were a hundred miles nearer help. At 0600, Peter's temperature was down to 38.5°C (100.8°F), and we breathed a sigh of relief. But four hours later it was back up to over 40°C, and his cough was much worse. It had developed into a deep bark which left him breathless and hardly able to speak.

Peter was so good, not complaining as we took him again and again into the cockpit to sponge him down with the sea water that we regarded as cooling but which his burning body must have found icily cold. We administered his third tablet of tetracycline and some more soluble Aspirin. We had to get that raging fever under control.

We weren't succeeding. He'd cool down for an hour or so, but then his temperature would relentlessly rise again. Peter's neck and chest took on a bright red blush of fever. Both our children had gone through many high-temperature viruses, but I had never seen this before. He also complained of sore eyes. We put sunglasses on him to protect his eyes when we took him into the cockpit to sponge him off. I willed the boat forward.

With Paul or I always on watch, one adult was constantly available to check on Peter, and Penny hovered anxiously nearby. We tried to comfort him as best we could when he had a coughing spell. His breath was short and rasping in his throat, but we were thankful that there didn't seem to be any bubbling in his lungs.

It was a long and tiring forty-eight hours before his temperature got down to a manageable 39°C and stayed there.

That day and night were full of rain squalls. The wet clothes were piling up, with the boat beginning to be damp and musty, not very good conditions for nursing a sick child.

But Peter's condition was stabilizing; his temperature was now down to 38.5°C, and his cough was marginally looser. But he was listless, with sunken and circled eyes. That afternoon, however, he sat in the cockpit for an hour and ate some cereal, his first food in three days. Although we were much relieved and desperately wanted to turn the boat around to continue our passage, we were still wary and we continued to sail towards Cayenne for another twenty-four hours.

The next morning Peter was again much improved, with a temperature just above normal and ready for a large breakfast. It was time to make another decision. We were less than one hundred miles from Cayenne. It was the last day of May, and the hurricane season officially begins on the first of June. Peter's crisis seemed over, but should we stop for a check-up? Or should we turn north again, hoping to avoid being caught south of the hurricane belt?

We decided to head north. It was a calculated risk. We knew it could be as much as twenty more days before we reached Bermuda.

Because we had run downwind in the northeast trade winds to head for Cayenne, we now had to fight our way back off the coast. We brought *Lorcha* back on the wind, sailing as close to the wind as practical. We weren't laying our course and feared we might be driven too close to the Caribbean island chain. We wanted to keep well to seaward of all the islands, and to sail past without even sighting them.

And luck was with us. Peter's temperature went back to normal, and the wind shifted to the east, enabling us to easily lay our course. It seemed this passage was meant to be.

A couple of more days of good health and good sailing and our nightmare was over. We settled back into our seagoing routine as if there had been no interruption. Penny finished her Grade Five work, but went on with a regimented French-language program aimed at entering her in Grade Six French Immersion, the school program which she had started at the Kindergarten level before we left. I had bought an excellent book on advanced French grammar especially for this voyage, and Paul sat with Penny in the cockpit every evening using a French reader for oral French and discussion. On long passages we all need challenges, so out came the small chess computer. Peter became the champion of the family and Paul and I (only a notch above the beginning level ourselves) only rarely won a game from him.

One day Penny picked up one of Paul's woodcarving books, E. J. Tangerman's *Whittling and Woodcarving*, with the help of which he had carved many small animals. She was keen to try her hand at a little Scottie dog. Paul got out some straight-grained white pine scraps and cut a small piece for her, and she laid out the shape on the wood as per the directions. Paul gave her his razor knife with some hesitation; *Lorcha* was rearing over each passing wave as we once more beat our way against the brisk trade winds, but, he told himself, more fingers have been cut by dull knives than by sharp ones. Peter

286

had to start a whittling project, too, and he began with a fish. Wood shavings covered the cockpit, but we weren't bothered. What didn't get swept up would get flushed down the large cockpit drains.

Peter's ninth birthday was one of three he has had at sea where a party with other children was obviously out of the question. Nonetheless, we made an occasion of it, and a large chocolate cake was baked in the pressure cooker.

"Shall we have the cake for lunch or for dinner?" I asked the children.

"Lunch *and* dinner," they chorused.

And who could deny such charming little moppets on that long and difficult passage?

We were angling for a position due south of Bermuda at about 20° north latitude. North of that position, the trade winds could fail at any time. We would be in the variables, or Horse Latitudes, as they are sometimes called. In the olden days of sailing ships, the crews often found themselves becalmed here, and out of water to give to the horses they had on board. When that happened, the luckless animals would be pushed over the side.

Twenty-nine days at sea and we were listening to Bermuda Radio. Our SatNav showed us about twenty-five miles away at sunset. We wouldn't attempt a night entrance.

At 2000 we hove-to. Paul called Bermuda Radio on the VHF and gave them our position. "I have BA#334 chart of Bermuda, but not the chart for the entrance of St. George Harbour," he told the radio operator. "Can you tell me if the channel is well marked and what the depth is?"

"We have passenger liners drawing eight metres coming in almost daily," he replied laconically. "I don't think you will have any difficulty."

We entered harbour at 0600 the following morning, 3,328 miles and thirty days out of Brazil, our longest passage yet.

BERMUDA TO THE UNITED STATES

30

After spending only four days at friendly and welcoming – though very expensive – Bermuda, we checked with the U.S. Navy base about any possible tropical depressions forming in the North Atlantic. It was now late June and there had already been a hurricane further south which had rushed off towards the Gulf of Mexico. The forecast was a good one for sailing towards the United States' east coast. Armed with the helpful naval sheets showing the current axis of the Gulf Stream (which can run at two knots or more between Bermuda and the coast), as well as projected weather maps for the next few days, we set sail for Atlantic City, New Jersey.

We experienced typical summery conditions for these latitudes; the wind shifted about, and we alternated between sailing slowly and motoring for the first few days.

"Thar she blows!" we cried, sighting a pod of whales, in imitation of the cry of the whalers of that bygone era when whales were hunted in these waters. We saw many pods of whales spouting in the distance, as well as a few fairly close alongside *Lorcha*. It is thrilling to get a nearby view of these huge mammals, but not too close! We were also surrounded by dolphins several times, as schools of them swam past us, so many that we wondered if

Across the Gulf Stream . . . whale sightings . . . Peter hauls in the last fish . . . rain before wind . . . the last night watches . . . boardwalk ahead . . . culture shock.

---

any of them were from Fernando. A few would break off from the main group to come for a closer look at us and to play in *Lorcha*'s bow wave and wake, but they soon left to catch up with their rapidly disappearing companions.

"Fish ho!" cried Peter on our fifth day at sea. "Dad, can I pull him in by myself?" We had enjoyed good fishing on this passage, with both tuna and dorado having taken our lures. I haul in the larger fish, but let our ever-eager young fisherman pull in the smaller ones. This fish was leaping spiritedly out of the water and we could see he was a good-sized dorado.

This would likely be our last full day at sea, and our last ocean passage; we expected to make Atlantic City the following day, so this would also be the last large pelagic fish on our trolling line.

"Keep tension on the line, and pull in fast if he makes a run towards the boat," I told Peter, handing him a pair of cotton gloves to protect his hands and making room for him at the side deck where he could best fight the fish.

Peter's face took on a look of fierce determination as he felt the weight of the fish on the line. He smiled slightly every time he gained line, pulling the fish closer to the boat, but his face screwed to a worried grimace when he lost line in the tug-of-war with his adversary. Fiona and Penny cheered Peter on, and I hovered over him whenever he hung precariously over the rail, ready to intervene if necessary, yet reluctant to do so.

It was a fierce twenty-five-minute struggle before Peter had

289

the fish alongside where I could gaff it. I wasn't sure whether the fish or Peter was the more exhausted, but Peter had won. After the fish was brought on board we hung it under the boom for photographs. The sinewy golden creature was as long as Peter was tall.

As we ate our dorado steaks for dinner that evening, sailing with a moderate southeast wind coming from right behind us, I nervously watched a low dark bank of clouds moving towards us over the horizon. Severe thunder storms were forecast along the coast, about seventy miles distant, with a strong northwest wind behind the frontal system. That coming wind would be right on our nose, preventing us from sailing directly to our destination.

Fiona cleared away the dishes as I donned my foul-weather gear and safety harness. The southeast wind died with a last puff. The first rain pelted down like bullets during an eerie lack of wind as I ducked under the cockpit dodger to shelter from it. I dismally thought of the old sailors' weather-forecasting rhyme:

When the rain's before the wind,
Strike your tops'ls, reef your main.
When the wind's before the rain,
Shake'em out and go again.

I dropped several panels of our Chinese sail to reef just as the first gust hit *Lorcha* a sledge-hammer blow. I let the bow fall away from this strong wind, only concerned with riding out these first gusts before worrying about our course. For the next half-hour, rain squalls pelted us from every direction; the wind blew first from one dark cloud then another as the squalls swirled around us. Terrible crashes of thunder and flashes of lightning added to the confusion of the wind and seas. I lost track of our direction, concentrating only on trying to keep the wind coming from just forward of blowing across our beam, a good tactic to prevent damage to sails or rigging.

The wind steadied to blow strongly from the northwest. With the Gulf Stream also trying to sweep us away from the

290

coast, we were making no headway. I sheeted our small reefed sail area in flat along *Lorcha's* centre line and started the engine.

We motored through the night, some hours making only 1 knot towards our destination as *Lorcha* leaped over the wind-driven waves to bury her bow on the other side. Spray flew over the boat, and at the end of my watch I was soaked in spite of my foul-weather gear. Fiona and I traded watches through the night, taking turns hand-steering to make as much headway as possible. The presence of several fishing vessels around us made us nervous, as visibility was down to a hundred metres in the continuing rain squalls.

Dawn brought a clearing sky, and the rain gradually ended. The wind eased, but remained brisk from the northwest. It was only as we got nearer shore that the wave height decreased, and *Lorcha* began to make some speed.

"I can make out the tops of the hotels in the haze along the horizon," I told Penny and Peter as they huddled under the dodger, avoiding the spray. The sun rising behind us glinted off the gambling casinos which line Atlantic City's famed boardwalk.

Atlantic City is located on an island, really just a sandspit, which, like almost all the remainder of the 201 kilometres of New Jersey coast, is low and flat; a breakwater for the salt-water marshes which lie behind them. In 1852, Richard Osborne, a Philadelphia engineer, along with some backers, bought most of the sandspit known as Absecon Island. They punched through a railroad and laid out Atlantic City, a resort town for the working man of Philadelphia, about 96 kilometres away. By the Gay Nineties there were 570 hotels and boarding houses here. Atlantic City claims to have built the first beach boardwalk in the world, laid in 1870 to help those headed for the surf to get over the sand dunes to the water. The current boardwalk, dating from 1896, is twelve metres wide and six and a half kilometres long.

In 1976 the New Jersey State Legislature legalized gambling in Atlantic City, and the first casino opened to long line-ups in

1978. There has been a constant increase in gambling casinos since then, each competing with the others to be foremost with glitz and glitter.

By 1130 the sun was bright and we could make out the steady stream of people parading along the boardwalk. Charter vessels cruised along the water's edge giving tourists an oceanside view of the city. We slipped between the red and green markers into Absecon Inlet and were hardly able to find the Absecon Lighthouse, built in 1857, located amongst the tightly packed high-rise buildings. We headed towards the basin where the Senator Frank S. Farley State Marina is located. Fiona and I had spent a few days in this marina in 1977. Then it had been a somewhat rustic municipal marina; now New York multi-millionaire Donald J. Trump's Trump's Castle Hotel and Casino overlooks the site, and Trump has a lease to operate the marina and is advertising the first phase of a "multi-million-dollar expansion" making the marina "the largest and most luxurious marina in the northeast."

Accustomed to looking after ourselves in lonely anchorages, we hardly knew what to do here. We radioed the marina control requesting a transient slip, and a young woman in fashionable nautical attire appeared to guide us into our slip and to help us make fast to the planked floating docks.

Our neighbours on the boats in the slips nearby were mostly couples on flashy power boats there to spend a few days seeing the floor shows at the casinos and to try their luck at the gaming tables. We were back in North America – and this was true culture-shock!

HOMEWARD BOUND 31

"Where have you come from?" people would ask, eyeing our well-travelled-looking boat.

"From Canada," I'd reply.

"Which route did you come down by?" would be the next question.

"The long way," I'd tell them.

I wasn't trying to be coy, but I was finding it difficult to blurt out that we'd just come from sailing around the world. As word got around the marina, however, people started dropping by to ask if we had really circumnavigated. We were surprised at the reaction from these local sailors, because for so long we had been part of a community where *everyone* was a long-distance sailor. Though we thought our experience was far from extraordinary, we began to realize how fantastic our story sounded to sailors who were rarely more than a day's sail from their home port.

"Who wants pizza and ice cream on the boardwalk?" I asked Penny and Peter on our second day in Atlantic City.

As we walked along the boardwalk the kids were fascinated by the hucksterism and seaside souvenirs, the likes of which they had never seen before. Wide-eyed, they pleaded for some salt-water taffy or some of the "World's Best Fudge."

From Canada – the long way . . . Atlantic City . . .
sailing through fog . . . Horseshoe Cove . . .
we meet Jell-o . . . beautiful polluted beaches . . .
through the Narrows . . . New York, New York.

Despite multi-million-dollar casinos sprouting like mushrooms, much of Atlantic City is a slum. Whole city blocks are crumbling and abandoned, with sagging roofs, broken windows, and doors falling off their hinges. Since about 1940, Atlantic City's population has been in decline, though the surrounding waterfront communities amongst the coastal sand dunes are thriving.

Lorcha lay at the marina berth for two weeks while we cleaned her up, washed the sea salt from our clothes and our boat's interior, and rested after all those long ocean passages with too little time between them. Looking through our log books I calculated we had sailed 15,500 miles and across 205 degrees of longitude in the eleven months since we had left Australia, more than half way around the world.

"It's a bit thick out here," I announced to the rest of the family as we neared the sea buoy off Absecon Inlet and headed north for Sandy Hook and the entrance to Lower New York Bay. We had sailed out the inlet at about noon into thick fog. Visibility was a scant two hundred metres. I am nervous about sailing in fog, having sailed in enough of it to know I don't like not seeing where I am going, but not in so much that I feel comfortable doing it.

"We're not going back now," quipped my determined mate. "The SatNav will be giving us position fixes along the way, so what does it matter?"

The fog would lift for a while, then close in again as we

295

sailed through the afternoon and evening on this ninety-mile overnight passage. We were approaching one of the world's busiest shipping channels, with tankers servicing the New Jersey chemical plants around Raritan Bay, heavy traffic headed for New York harbour, and the vessels heading up the Hudson River for Albany. Fog, darkness, and lots of shipping: a nasty combination.

Fog horns moaned mournfully in the distance, then, as the fog momentarily lifted, I would see the lights of cargo vessels, tugs and tows, or fishing vessels not far off.

"There's a cargo vessel of more than 65 metres southbound towards us," I told Fiona at our change of watch, reading the pattern of navigation lights which indicate the direction of travel and type of vessel. "There's a fishing fleet shooting their nets to seaward of us, and a tug with a tow of more than 200 metres coming up behind and slightly inshore from us. The last SatNav position puts us about three miles off the coast, more than enough for safety. I'm going to get some sleep, but don't hesitate to call me if you get confused by the lights."

I'd rather be out in the middle of the ocean than sailing along a busy coast. The waves of the ocean won't hurt you, but the land around the edges brings all kinds of hazards.

Just before dawn the following day, in a drizzle of rain, I sighted the strong flashes, five seconds apart, of the Ambrose Channel light. That channel was gouged out of the sea bed into the submerged continental shelf by the outflow of the Hudson River and extends one hundred miles into the Atlantic Ocean.

With the faint outline of Brooklyn to the north, we rounded the four-mile-long sandspit known as Sandy Hook and headed south to wend our way around wooden-staked fish traps to the solitude of the anchorage at Horseshoe Cove, part of the Gateway National Recreation Area established in 1972.

At 0730 *Lorcha*'s anchor was firmly planted in the tidal ooze from the outflow of the salt-water marsh, a stone's throw away. No sounds of man reached us, only the quarrelling of the terns, gulls, oyster catchers, and ruddy turnstones as they searched for breakfast on the emerging sandbar a few metres from *Lorcha*.

The drizzle had stopped, but the poor visibility continued, and we sat in the cockpit to eat a hearty breakfast of fried eggs and toast, topped with mugs of steaming tea. One of the most densely populated urban areas of the world was only a few kilometres away, yet we were once again in a lonely anchorage, just the four of us, enjoying the sounds of nature.

"Dad," asked Penny, knowing her parents' habit after an overnight sail, "can we launch the dinghy so Peter and I can row over to the sandspit before you lie down for a nap?"

We spent only one night in Horseshoe Cove before moving to the marina at Atlantic Highlands on the southern shore of Sandy Hook Bay.

"What are those boats for?" asked Peter, pointing to about fifteen vessels of up to eighteen metres long as we walked along the docks at the municipal marina.

"They're head boats," I replied. "They take out people who want to go fishing for $15 per person."

"You have to *pay* to go fishing?" asked Peter in disbelief.

"Your children have unusual accents," said our helpful waitress at a waterside restaurant at Keyport, where we had sailed *Lorcha* a few miles along the shore in Raritan Bay. "Where are you from?"

"From Canada!" she exclaimed, as if it were some exotic place. "Sounding like that, I didn't think you could be from America. Now, what will you have for desert? We have ice cream, fruit cup, apple pie, or Jell-o."

"What's Jell-o?" asked Peter. The waitress did a double take.

"You don't have Jell-o in Canada?" she asked in amazement. "Listen," she said to the other waitresses, "these people have never had Jell-o! Are you having me on?" she demanded of our innocent son, looking at him very hard.

Amidst much laughter we explained that Peter had spent more than half his life on a boat with no refrigeration and had never tasted that common dessert.

"You've made my day," said the waitress. "One double order of Jell-o coming up."

We headed for Staten Island, originally settled as part of New Netherlands in the early 1600s and named for the States-General, the legislature of the Netherlands. We were easing ourselves into the urban density of New York City. We sailed for the entrance to Great Kills Harbour, half-way along the southeastern shore of the island, and were surprised to see all the trees. Crookes Point forms part of the outer arm of the harbour and is also one of the five units of the Gateway National Recreational Area. Every year, thousands of monarch butterflies go to the wooded area near the point to lay their eggs on milkweed plants. When Henry David Thoreau lived there in 1843, he wrote: "The whole island is like a garden and affords very fine scenery." A century and a half ago the Vanderbilts ran a 110-hectare (270-acre) farm on the island to provision the family mansions in Manhattan and elsewhere. Viewed from seaward there is still an amazing amount of greenery on this island, and it is often referred to as a workingman's suburb of Manhattan.

The summer of 1988 broke records for heat and drought all over North America, and we were travelling through this area during the height of that heat. On the outside of the arm of Great Kills Harbour was Great Kills Park, with a long sandy beach. Beaches are for building sandcastles and swimming, right?

"Why can't we go in the water?" complained Penny and Peter. "The beach is deserted."

The beach was deserted because that July the Atlantic beaches of upper New Jersey and Long Island, as well as the beaches of Sandy Hook, Raritan, and Lower New York bays were closed because of the medical wastes washing up on them. It was a health hazard never anticipated. Contaminated syringes, bandages, and dressings of all kinds were being collected on the sand. It was assumed that some unscrupulous company with disposal contracts with local hospitals was illegally dumping the material into some tidal creek rather than paying the fee for proper disposal.

The Algonquin Indians called the Hudson River "the river that flows two ways." It is tidal, ebbing and flooding for all of its uncontrolled 240 kilometres. At Great Kills Harbour we were about ten kilometres from the Narrows, where the waters of Upper New York Bay and the Hudson River come rushing through headed for the sea. Successfully heading a low-powered craft such as *Lorcha* through the Narrows, to continue through the Upper Bay into New York Harbour and past Liberty Island, and then to find a marina in daylight hours, all on a rising tide, takes some planning and patience. I made the calculations with my tide and current tables to find that if we left at 0500 a few days hence we should catch the tide just right.

The sun was up, but it was still and cool as we left the marina to motor along the shore to our first milestone, the Verrazano Narrows Bridge connecting Staten Island to Brooklyn. The Narrows and the bridge are named after Giovanni da Verrazano, who sailed into the Lower Bay in 1524 searching for the Northwest Passage to Asia. Cars, trucks, and trains passed overhead, their roars, honks, and beeps blending in a din which made *Lorcha*'s steel deck reverberate.

Henry Hudson, an Englishman in the employ of the Dutch, sailed along this coast in the summer of 1609 on his ship *Half Moon*, hoping to find that elusive passage which would take him to the Orient. Hudson traded axes and knives to the Indians for corn and squash when they paddled their canoes to the side of his ship. But when the water of the river turned fresh and gradually shoaled, Hudson disappointedly realised he was on a tidal river and not a strait. His name was bestowed upon the river. The following year, commissioned this time by the English, Hudson was equally unsuccessful in his search for that passage when he explored Canada's Hudson

Bay. No, perhaps he was *more* unsuccessful, since his crew mutinied and set him adrift in a small boat, nevermore to be heard from.

We were trying to keep out of the way of huge cargo ships coming up the channel behind us, staying to the right of the main channel, yet far enough into the stream to get a lift from the flood current now gaining strength.

As we rounded the bend of Anchorage Channel, we were in the busiest part of New York Harbour. Black-and-orange Staten Island Ferries, their many decks lined with passengers, came at us from up and down river. Tugs with barges in tow headed across our bow for Constable Hook Reach and the industrial area which lines the passage behind Staten Island. Ships waited at anchor, ready to take on or off-load cargo, some getting their anchors up as pilot boats bumped alongside. Tugs guided their charges along the channel, manoeuvring vessels too cumbersome to manage on their own.

My head felt as if it was on a swivel as I tried to judge the course and speed of those ships which would pass close to us, while simultaneously trying to do some sight-seeing.

New York City looked old-fashioned from mid-harbour. The ships and quays have a grimy, early-industrial-age look about them with the Meccano-set-like derricks and cranes. Tugs and barges haven't changed shape in more than fifty years and most appeared not to have been painted for at least half that long. Cubist high-rises lined the Brooklyn shore.

"There's the Statue of Liberty dead ahead," I told the children; each had a pair of binoculars to scan the cityscape around us.

"I can't see it," said Penny impatiently, sweeping her binoculars along the line where buildings meet sky.

"You're looking too high. It's not that big," I told her. "Look just past the stern of that white passenger liner coming towards us."

Dwarfed from a distance by all the monuments to commerce on the shores around her, the Statue of Liberty gathers her majesty only as you approach. As we were swept past by the current, we gazed in awe at this elegant creation shining her torch with a brightness easily perceived even in the sunlight.

Ellis Island lies just beyond, remarkable for its story-book buildings with their coloured stone and brick and tidy courtyard. Thousands of immigrants landed here, welcomed by the inspiring statue just down-harbour.

The cannons of Battery Park were trained on us as the tip of Manhattan Island came abeam. And Brooklyn Bridge over the East River was hidden from view by the modern glass and steel of the World Trade Center.

We eased toward the western shore, the New Jersey side, as the Empire State Building came abeam. The tidal stream was slackening, and would soon turn against us. We ducked into the Port Imperial Marina at Weehawken, opposite the Jacob Javits Convention Center, and were guided to the most expensive marina berth we have ever rented.

It was still before noon, but that summer's excruciating heat was upon us. *Lorcha*'s sun-scorched crew worked as fast as the heat allowed to get the sail cover on and the sun awning up as the heat haze blurred Manhattan's skyline on the opposite side of the river.

In 1624 the Dutch established a small settlement on that island as headquarters for the colony of New Netherlands. They called the island "Manhattan" after the Indian tribe that lived there, with the settlement designated as "New Amsterdam." Peter Minuit, Director General of New Netherlands, was sent out by the Dutch West India Company to make this province produce a profit. He landed on Manhattan on May 4, 1626, and bought it from the Indians for some cheap finery worth sixty guilders – usually translated to an amount of $24, probably the most astute real-estate deal in the history of the United States.

It seems Dutchmen were not too eager to head for the uncertainties of New Netherlands, so the Dutch West India Company began accepting settlers from anywhere in Europe. In 1643, a Jesuit priest reported counting eighteen languages spoken on the streets of New Amsterdam, thus the island's polyglot character was established early. New Amsterdam became New York in 1664, when a fleet of British ships outfitted by the Duke of York sailed into the harbour and demanded its surrender. Peter Stuyvesant, governor at the time and in his seventies, was willing to fight, but could rally no nationalistic fervour from his multi-cultural population, so surrendered without resistance.

"We'll take the ferry across the river to Manhattan this morning," Fiona told the children at breakfast the following day, "and stay in the city as long as we can stand the heat. We'll see some of the sights, then go to an art gallery or museum."

We joined the line-up of commuters at the ferry docks at 0830, all dressed in well-worn shorts and light shirts, sandals and sun hats, perhaps looking out of place beside the smart business and office-worker garb the other passengers sported.

"Empire State Building, please," I told the taxi driver, as he charged into the traffic on West 38th Street. The ride was mostly a slow creep through the rush-hour traffic, punctuated by whip-lashing acceleration as the driver changed lanes.

"The building is closed because of repairs to the elevators," said Penny when we got there, pointing to a sign on the door.

We were in the heart of the most elegant shopping district, so we lackadaisically ambled along Fifth Avenue, Avenue of the Americas, Madison Avenue, and Broadway, window-shopping. We eventually went into Bloomingdale's but felt out of place. It wasn't that we were intimidated by all these goods out of our financial reach, but that these symbols of conspicuous consumption now had no meaning to us.

After lunch at a Chinese restaurant, we dodged the heat by spending a few hours in the air-conditioned Metropolitan Museum of Art. Later we watched a police chase through Central Park, with both marked and unmarked cars as well as uniformed officers on little motor scooters dashing every which way. We had most fun bargaining for a wrist-watch each from the street vendors on Canal Street.

I began to wish I could turn back the clock three-hundred-and-some-odd years, to before the melting pot of Manhattan began to bubble. I would have enjoyed meeting those primitive people who once populated this island. Could we have anchored *Lorcha* off a village and rowed the family ashore in the dinghy to be made welcome by a people as peaceful and generous as those we had met in the South Pacific?

INLAND WATERS   32

"I'm ready for some countryside," I told Fiona as I finished my tidal calculations after dinner. "We'll head upriver at 0630 tomorrow morning when the tide should be turning."

As we sailed north we noted the Dutch place names. In 1629 the Dutch took measures to encourage immigration and instituted the "patroon" system, under which men who brought over more than fifty settlers to the new colony were given large tracts of land along the Hudson River; sixteen miles along one bank or eight miles along both banks. It was a semi-feudal system which allowed the "patroons" near-sovereign rights over their land and people. Jonas Bronck settled just north of Manhattan – the area is called the Bronx; and a little further along a Dutchman known as a *jonker*, meaning "gentleman" or "esquire," settled in the area now called Yonkers.

As we neared the George Washington Bridge near the northern tip of Manhattan, we saw the site of Fort Washington. During the American Revolution in 1776, George Washington and his army were being pursued by General William Howe of the British Army. Washington feared a direct engagement with Howe's superior force and retreated, allowing New York City to fall. Washington retreated again, and Howe overran Fort Washington, capturing three

The "patroon" system . . . Fort Washington . . . Tarrytown and
the ghost ship of the Tappan Zee . . . pollution . . . salt-water
fish; fresh-water fish . . . Hudson Highlands . . .
Esopus lighthouse . . . François and Daniel . . . pulling off
the mast . . . six waterways . . . the first lock . . . the Erie Canal.

---

thousand men and a large quantity of supplies. On the opposite side of the river, later that same year, the British scaled
the cliffs to surprise the Continental Army at Fort Lee, capturing that vantage point, too. This whole area of the Hudson
River and on up the valley was the scene of many battles of
the Revolutionary War.

The western bank, with steep cliffs resembling the walls of
a fortress, becomes the Palisades Interstate Park. The Palisades were formed 200 million years ago when lava boiled up
into an immense crack in the sandstone. The lava cooled and
crystallized, and through the ages the sandstone along the
river has eroded to reveal the 60-kilometre-long diabase wall,
standing up to 240 metres high. The preservation of the walls
as a park is attributed to the patronage of several wealthy
conservationists, including John D. Rockefeller.

Near the end of the Palisades we saw the stone marker near
the cliff edge indicating the New York/New Jersey boundary.

Here the river widens to form the shallow and lake-like
Tappan Zee. We had a good weather forecast and kept a sharp
lookout, as an old Dutch legend has it that when gale force
winds blow, a ghost ship sails the Zee, running down any
mariner so imprudent as not to grant her right of way.

On the right bank, Tarrytown lies at the foot of the hills
rolling to the water's edge. This was the home of Washington
Irving and the setting for his *Legend of Sleepy Hollow*. One can
easily imagine Brom Bones, carrying a Hallowe'en pumpkin
on his pommel, riding down from the wooded hills just

305

behind the town to give schoolmaster Ichabod Crane the fright of his life.

We sailed on with care, as Washington Irving wrote about sailing upriver to Albany, then called Fort Orange: "A prudent Dutch burgher would talk of such a voyage for months and even years beforehand; and never undertook it without putting his affairs in order, making his will, and having prayers said for him in the Low Dutch Churches."

Another eight kilometres along on the same eastern bank, we saw the infamous Sing Sing Prison, built in 1824, the guard towers and high walls easily visible from mid-channel.

It was a scorching 30°C, and we were glad to reach our destination for the day, Croton Point, projecting half-way across this wide stretch of river. We anchored off the north side, opposite the beach and picnic grounds of the state park, amid a fleet of local pleasure vessels. Fresh from the scare of medical-waste contamination in the Lower Bay and having just ridden the flood tide, we were concerned about water pollution. But this was obviously a popular swimming spot and, although we were all too cognizant of the fact that the Hudson River had epitomized the nation's problem with water pollution in the early sixties, the heat drove us into the water.

Each summer throughout the sixties the dissolved oxygen level of the water around New York City sank towards zero, oil slicks were left by tankers, dead fish surfaced near power plants, and a noxious blend of raw sewage and paper-mill wastes flowed down from the north. A presidential council called the river "an open sewer."

The clean-up began in 1966, when the Hudson River Fishermen's Association pressured the government into using the Federal Refuse Act of 1899 to stop the dumping in navigable waters and as a vehicle to take individual industrial polluters to court. Environmentalist groups formed all along the river, and folksinger Pete Seeger, a long-time resident of Beacon, became the catalyst. He and other environmentalists built

306

Clearwater, a thirty-two-metre-long replica of an 1800s Hudson River cargo sloop. They sailed the engineless craft up and down the river promoting its clean-up, and established "sloop clubs" for local residents to use as pressure groups against river pollution.

Industries and power plants have cleaned up their discharge after several dramatic court cases and hefty fines. But it is the residue of PCB's – polychlorinated biphenyls – a proven cancer-causing agent, which causes most concern. Though PCB's have been banned now for ten years, it is estimated that 230 tons of that chemical lie in Hudson River sediment.

"Make it a quick dip with no swimming to the bottom," we warned the kids.

The river's composition – fresh-water run-off originating in the Adirondack Mountains mixing with the Atlantic Ocean salt water brought up by the tides – complicates the ecology of the Hudson River. In the spring, up-river run-off brings fresh water down as far as Yonkers. Blueback herring, shad, sturgeon, and striped bass race up from the sea to spawn. In the summer months, the salt water is the stronger force, and it flows into the Tappan Zee, where the shallow warm waters become a perfect fish nursery with plenty of food from growing microscopic organisms. In the winter months, salt water reaches Newburgh, one hundred kilometres up-river from the southern tip of Manhattan, and such fresh-water species as catfish, yellow perch, carp, and eels mingle with young marine fish in the warmer salt water.

Peter especially would have enjoyed coming up this stretch of water in the spring. The banks are lined with commercial fishermen who set their nets at the sides of the river for the spring runs of shad, taking as much as five tonnes of fish per day. Then, from May to July, the Atlantic sturgeon, ranging along the Atlantic coast from Maine to the Carolinas, takes centre-stage. Females with egg-sacs weighing up to twenty-three kilograms follow smaller males up to the fresh water to spawn. There was once an active sturgeon-fishing industry along the Hudson; caviar was salt-cured by the barrel and the smoked flesh was so common that it was called "Albany Beef."

Past Croton Point, the Hudson narrows to about five hundred metres in width, pinched by the hills and cliffs of the Hudson Highlands. Three-hundred-and-thirty-five-metre-high Dunderberg Mountain, "thunder mountain" in Dutch, supposed home of the goblins which cause the thunderstorms of the area, set the tone for what lay ahead. We followed the snaking path of the river towards West Point, where the United States Military Academy opened in 1802, and the sharp bend at World's End where the changing direction of the current creates the whirlpools that terrorized those burghers of old. This is also the deepest part of the river, with holes up to sixty metres in depth.

The Highlands end at Storm King Mountain, where pirate treasure is rumoured to lie buried at the foot of a nearly sheer 150-metre cliff falling into the river.

An offer of a free slip from boaters vacationing further south took us to the friendly Marlboro Yacht Club. The club is a small one, based around a waterside restaurant with a floating dock accommodating about twenty-five boats. We met a few members along the dock, one of whom drove us to the nearest supermarket, then to his home to load us with his surplus garden fruits and vegetables. In the evening we talked well into the night with club members curious about our extensive travels.

This section of the Hudson Valley remains very rural. The steep river bank slopes prevent large-scale farming and are lined with small family truck gardens, orchards, and vineyards. The terraced hills and the soil resemble those of the Rhine Valley, with lots of sunlight and a climate tempered by the river, and some of the earliest experiments in viticulture in the United States took place here. Though many vineyards were converted to apple orchards during the prohibition era, an active group of vintners still paint their barns with replicas of their labels, and we made a game of spotting them as we steamed along.

Next day, high in the hills above us on the eastern shore, we saw the well-manicured lawns of Franklin Delano Roosevelt's home, now a national historic site and open to the public. Roosevelt was one of three New York governors who became American presidents: Grover Cleveland and Theodore Roosevelt were the other two. Just beyond, other gracious mansions were visible through the trees.

The spring of 1958 was a bad year for ice and much damage was done during the break-up. One of the few lingering traces is the Esopus lighthouse, which leans at an alarming angle due to the pressure of an ice pile-up. It warns the mariner from heading across the shoal area of the Meadows. Penny and Peter cheered this tiny house with light tower attached, looking like a leaning gingerbread house with a baby's bottle beside it. Up to this point, navigating the river had been only a matter of staying away from the banks. From here on, mud-flats, parallelling the river's sides, are revealed at low tide. The main channel switches from side to side, and one has to pay attention to the marker buoys.

In late afternoon we ducked into Esopus Creek, marked by another old lighthouse, this one being restored by a local historical society. We motored about one kilometre up the creek to where both banks are lined by waterfront cottages, and anchored off someone's lawn at a widening bend.

"I'm having problems with my engine," called a man with a heavy French-Canadian accent from the cockpit of his home-built 9.5-metre sloop. "Is there an anchorage near here where I can stop to repair it? I don't have very good maps for the river."

Motoring along at our usual sedate pace, we had gained steadily on this yellow-hulled vessel, puttering along for a while, then stopping on this windless day.

"There's a nice anchorage behind Coxsackie Island, about two miles from here," I shouted back. "That's where we will stay for the night, as the tide will turn against us in about one hour. Do you want a tow?"

"No, we'll make it," he replied, showing the independence of a long-distance sailor. "If need be, Daniel can tow me with our outboard-powered dinghy," and he pointed to a boy who looked about twelve. We remained near them as the boat stopped and started, its engine belching black smoke. Soon Daniel got into their dinghy and towed the boat slowly along, following us into the anchorage.

Daniel came over to swim and play with Penny and Peter, and told us their voyaging story, while his father, François, worked on their engine.

François had built the boat over the objections of his wife, who had no interest in voyaging. Determined, François and Daniel had sailed on their own to the Bahamas the previous September. There, Daniel's mother and two sisters had joined them for a month. After they flew home, François and Daniel began heading north again.

"It was too short a time to really enjoy the voyaging," said François, when he joined us later for a coffee. "After three years preparing for the trip, always being in a hurry, and all the trouble with my wife, plus not having the whole family together, it hardly seems worthwhile."

The river began to narrow past this point, letting us know that the end of our Hudson River travels was nearing. We stopped at the picturesque little town of Hudson, the unlikely home port of more than twenty whaling ships brought there by Nantucket and Martha's Vineyard whalers hard hit during the American Revolution.

We pulled *Lorcha*'s mast at the Castleton-on-Hudson Boat Club, ten kilometres south of Albany. From there until we reached Lake Ontario, 320 kilometres away, a clearance of six metres under low bridges dictated that *Lorcha* travel under power.

Ocean-going ships continue to the Port of Albany, at the southern edge of the state's capital, and one of the busiest inland ports of the United States. It was to this port that Robert Fulton's steamboat, *Clermont*, made its first run, sailing from New York City to Albany in thirty-two hours, a distance we had covered in five days. We tied up at the Albany Yacht Club at Rensselaer (named after the founder of the patroons system), on the opposite bank of the river from Fort Orange, the fur-trading station which became Albany at the same time New Amsterdam became New York. The chateaulike capitol building, which took thirty-two years to build, dominates this historic site.

Fifteen kilometres north of Albany, at Troy, six waterways converge: the Hudson and the Mohawk rivers; the old Champlain Canal, now abandoned; the modern Champlain Waterway which follows the upper Hudson; the old Erie Canal, now used only as a spillway; and the modern Erie Canal. The latter and the Champlain Waterway are now part of the New York Canal System. As we neared the first lock at Troy I radioed the lock-keeper to ask how soon we would be going through. "In about an hour," he told me. "Some southbound traffic will enter the lock in about fifteen minutes, and you'll go after that."

We drifted over to tie up temporarily to the wall along the bank. You can't hurry through the canal; the locks are operated on a first-come-first-served basis for pleasure craft, with the commercial barges which ply these waters taking precedence.

Eventually we could see the barge in the lock. The water rushed towards us as the barge was lowered the four metres to our level. The gates opened slowly, and it steamed past us. The light at the lock changed to green, and it was our turn to ease into the lock chamber, its rough concrete walls wet and dripping and covered in a green slime. We motored to a steel ladder inset into the walls, and looped our bow and stern ropes through the rungs. Penny held the boat hook at the bow to prevent *Lorcha* swinging into the wall, with Peter manning the stern to push off with his foot. We inched our way up as the water gushed in from the bottom of the lock until *Lorcha*'s

311

deck was level with the well-tended lawn which surrounded the working mechanism. As the level of the water in the lock reached the level in the canal ahead of us the turbulence diminished, and the lock gates swung open for us to continue on our way.

Three kilometres further along we turned left into the Erie Canal. We were nearly home.

CANALS AND LAKES   33

I ndigenous people were using the rivers and lakes to criss-cross the area which would become New York state and to travel to the Great Lakes long before European settlers arrived to travel up the Hudson River and head west along the Mohawk River Valley. In 1783, George Washington travelled to Fort Stanwix, now Rome, then on to Oneida Lake via Wood Creek, 210 kilometres from the Hudson River. He urged the improvement of the "vast inland navigation." This began a continuous drive to add canals and locks and to link up lakes, rivers, and creeks with the west-stretching Mohawk River.

In 1796, the first short canal with five locks was completed at Little Falls, 115 kilometres from the Hudson along the Mohawk. Because of the isolation of this outpost in the wilderness, labour was hard to find, and dozens of men fell ill from – of all things – malaria. Short sections and locks were added annually, but it wasn't until 1803 that New York's Governor Morris called for an overall plan for the Erie Canal, tapping Lake Erie and "leading its waters across country to the Hudson River." From an engineering viewpoint this scheme for an artificial river across the state was a fantastic idea for its time. On October 8, 1823, the first boats from Lake Erie reached Albany via this 1.2-metre-deep, six-metre-wide ditch. The canal had seventy-seven locks to handle boats up to ninety-five tonnes. Traffic along the Erie Canal built rapidly. In 1830, 12,890 boats arrived or departed from Albany during the season. Canal boats carried passengers and cargo and were towed along by two or three mules or horses walking in single file along the tow path, the driver often riding on the back of the last animal. The horses were changed at six-kilometre intervals, and, according to *The Canal Courier*, a historic journal about the canal, "the packets get along at about 4½ miles per hour" – about the same speed we were travelling on *Lorcha*.

It was the "Great Western Canal" that made New York City, of all the cities along the Atlantic Seaboard of the United States, the most important gateway to the west. Through the canal, the Great Lakes region had access to a major metropolitan trading and manufacturing centre.

Then came the railroads, often following the waterway routes up the Hudson and along the Erie Canal. During the 1850s this new mode of transportation started grabbing the larger share of most freight, and in 1869 the tonnage carried over the New York Central and Erie railroads surpassed that carried by the New York canals.

The trains still follow the canal cut, and our nights on *Lorcha* were often disturbed by freight trains rattling down the tracks.

In 1903, advocates of an improved barge canal based on the European canals system, capitalized on a strong anti-railroad sentiment to modernize the New York Canal system. Improve-

315

ments completed in 1918 gave the Erie Canal a depth of 3.6 metres and a bottom width of 23 metres, with thirty-five locks to lift boats 175 metres. Only a few minor changes have been made since that time.

Today the New York Canal system is setting records for traffic again, but the traffic is pleasure boaters. In 1986, over 121,000 pleasure boats transited the system, with most of that traffic on the Erie Canal. The system was in the midst of a $50-million refit to provide new and improved parks, marinas, restaurants, and shopping areas when we passed through.

We travelled the Erie Canal along the Mohawk River to Oneida Lake, crossed the lake, and made a right turn past Lock 23 to head down the Oswego River to Lake Ontario. (The Erie Canal continues from Lock 23 to Tonawanda and the Niagara River.)

When we had turned off the Hudson River, we were immediately faced with five locks in less than three kilometres. It took more than two hours to go up the fifty-metre staircase. After motoring a short distance between steep rock walls cut for this canalized section, we were in the Mohawk River.

We anchored out in the river overnight rather than tying to one of the barge terminal or park walls; these were often noisy with nearby road traffic or party-goers who had driven to the river's edge. At river anchorages, we always tried to find a spot behind an island or below one of the dams, where we got more of a breeze and could enjoy a quick swim before making supper and turning in for the night. Penny and Peter could no longer see the star constellations as clearly as they had at sea because of the lights around us now that we were well inland, and that was a disappointment, but the beauty and variety of the countryside was some consolation.

As we approached Schenectady, the tree-lined banks gave way to houses overlooking the river, followed by the industrial area with its crumbling barge terminals. A little further on we reached the city proper, with its riverside parks and older buildings lining the banks.

We liked travelling in the cool hours of early morning when

we were often rewarded by the sight of wildlife along the banks. Woodchucks might dash to their burrows, then stand on their hind legs at the entrance to watch us, ready to dive for cover. Squirrels would run down tree branches towards us, chattering noisily. Many mornings we saw white-tailed deer grazing at forest edges in the slanting sun. Their heads would pop up as they heard *Lorcha*'s quiet engine, ears swivelling as they searched for danger. Then with a bound and a wave of their white flag, they would be enveloped by the surrounding bush. Egrets stood stock-still, surrounded by riverside reeds, their beaks pointed skyward and one beady eye trained on us, hoping we wouldn't notice them. Their resolve would hold until we were alongside, when they would burst into flight, swooping along on wide wing-spans to alight further down the river, and *Lorcha* would begin a fresh pursuit. Kingfishers had a similar flight pattern, but they landed on riverside branches, leading us past their territorial boundary, when they would turn back and fly to a perch behind us.

The most dramatic part of the canal we travelled was through the steep rock cuts near Little Falls, and the highest single lift was twelve-metre Lock 16, with its "guillotine" lifting gate which threw water down on us as we passed under it into the vertical walled chamber. Penny and Peter's favourite stop was Rome's restored eighteenth-century Fort Stanwix, complete with stockade and a film recreating the battles which took place there.

Lock 21 is the first of the "down" locks, and after we turned onto the Oswego River it was downhill all the way to our last lock at the town of Oswego. Ahead lay Lake Ontario, our home waters. We had sailed out of Lake Ontario five years previously, and now it was as dramatic and emotional a moment for us to head out of that small canal to those familiar waters as it had been to leave Panama for the vast Pacific Ocean.

"Are you the people who sailed around the world?" asked Dawn Martin. She and her husband Ted and four-year-old Leo had been walking along the Oswego dock from their summer

317

home, their 9.5-metre sailboat. "We're from Toronto, too," she said, shaking our hands, "and we've enjoyed reading your articles."

"Sailing the rivers and canals must seem pretty tame after all that ocean sailing," said Ted.

"It's pleasant enough," I replied swiftly. "And I don't have to stand night watches."

The following day we stepped *Lorcha*'s mast in the morning, had a picnic lunch, and got the sail rigged in the afternoon. We day-sailed along the south shore of Lake Ontario, stopping at Rochester, Olcott, Wilson, and finally Youngstown, from where we could see the Toronto skyline, dominated by the distinctive CN Tower, across forty-five kilometres of water.

We had been preparing Penny and Peter for our return to Toronto by talking about what our lives would be like back in the city. Now, at the sight of Toronto's skyline, Peter, who had no memory of the city as "home," or any recollection of our house (which we had rented out), burst into tears. "I don't want to move off the boat," he sobbed. Fiona and I tried to console him, surprised by his outburst, although we shouldn't have been. After all, our small boat had been Peter's home for more than half his life. To him that skyline symbolized the end of the only way of life he knew.

"When will I be able to go fishing?" he sniffed. Shore-based children watch early-morning cartoons on TV while they wait for the rest of the family to wake up, but Peter would begin his day by baiting a hook with whatever food scraps he could find and hanging one or two fishing lines over *Lorcha*'s side. He knew how to organize his time for his interests while afloat, but was having difficulty imagining what he would do living ashore, especially if he couldn't go fishing.

"Welcome back to Lake Ontario," called Dwight and Carol Hamilton from the decks of *Mopion*, owned by Clive and Julie Smith, in Youngstown that evening. Dwight and Carol had been two of the handful of people who had waved good-bye

318

to us when we had sailed away from Toronto five years previously. We had written to them telling them that we would be in Youngstown for the weekend, and they had sailed over to meet us and escort *Lorcha* back to Toronto.

"There's quite a reception planned for you in Toronto," said Dwight, Harbourfront's marine manager when Fiona had worked there. "I hope you're ready for all the attention."

The next morning, aboard their Nonsuch 30, fellow Torontonians Ray and Rachael Souch handed me a small packet.

"We would like to give you this new Canadian flag," said Ray. "I know your old flag looks well-travelled," he pointed to the faded and dishevelled flag flying from *Lorcha*'s stern, "but we would like to see this well-known vessel sporting a new flag for her return to her home port."

We hadn't thought the old flag we had flown in so many countries would be a discredit to us (it was the third flag we had flown during the trip), but if the Souches were concerned, perhaps others would be too, so we accepted with good grace.

Clad in her bright new Canadian colours, *Lorcha* crossed the Niagara River to clear into Canada at the customs dock at Niagara-on-the-Lake. The formalities over, we rafted alongside another vessel for the night, planning to make an early-morning start to the last day of our voyaging.

"Is anybody awake?" was the loud hail at 0700 the next morning. I'd have known that stentorious bellow anywhere! Ed Pursey, from Cobourg, Ontario, had been one of the skippers of the celebratory fleet of boats we had sailed with to Newfoundland at the start of our voyaging in 1983. With him aboard his 11.5-metre *Pursea* were Art Andrews and Keith Whalen, Newfoundlanders who had hosted us, along with that Ontario fleet, when we had arrived in their province. Now, five years later, they had gotten together to welcome us home. "I thought you were supposed to be sailing for Toronto this morning," our former Canadian Forces drill-sergeant friend shouted for all to hear. "Is this what long-distance sailing is all about – just lying around all day?"

Ed brought *Pursea* alongside for a few minutes to give us all a big bear hug before we prepared to cast off. We sailed in company out the mouth of the Niagara River with a light wind, in a drizzle of rain, feeling very warm towards all these special friends who had taken the time to sail across the lake to meet us.

When we got to the middle of Lake Ontario, we were amazed to see a huge fleet of boats headed towards us.

"They wouldn't all be coming to meet us!" gasped Fiona in disbelief.

"Are we that important?" asked Peter.

"I guess the people of Toronto really have heard of us," said Penny.

We sailed on, basking in the glow of our fame until Ed Pursey's voice crackled over the VHF: "We'd better lay off the course a little or we're going to sail through today's Canada Cup race."

Our welcome to Toronto Harbour was noisy – about twenty boats began tooting, with crews waving and shouting greetings to us as we approaching the Eastern Gap. More vessels joined in as we entered the inner harbour, including several large charter vessels, their rails lined with people. Looking like a duckling leading a full-grown flock, *Lorcha* sailed proudly to Harbourfront's Queen's Quay Terminal against a background of arcing streams from the water-cannons of the Toronto Fire Department's fireboat *William Lyon McKenzie*.

As we neared the terminal, we could only shake our heads in amazement at the number of Torontonians who had made the trek to the waterfront on a summer Sunday to welcome us home. There were perhaps four hundred people there, as well as press and television people, and a barrage of congratulatory calls was jamming the VHF. The fenders squeaked against the quay and helping hands made our mooring lines fast as the crowd whistled, cheered, and shouted a welcome, and pressed forward to look at *Lorcha* and to shake our hands.

We stepped ashore prepared to sing a silly song we had

made up about our travels for the TV cameras – Fiona's public relations background was no doubt responsible for this – but Fiona was so choked up she could hardly get the words out, especially when we got to the line "and who knows when we'll go sailing ever again."

We also showed the crowd some of the equipment that had been useful to us during our five years of travel. "And in this pressure cooker I've baked 340 loaves of bread," said Fiona, holding our six-quart pressure cooker aloft. She took off the top and a newly baked loaf fell out

"Oops – 341. Did you make that, Penny?" Fiona turned to our laughing daughter.

Bob Brown, one of Harbourfront's directors, presented us with a plaque which read: "Presented to *Lorcha* and her crew. Welcome Back 'Round the World Sailors. August 28, 1988."

Then Doug Gibson, our editor and publisher, handed us the first copy of the book we had written about our initial twenty months of voyaging in the Atlantic Ocean. Dorothy LeBaron of The Nautical Mind Bookstore had had the foresight to bring down half a dozen boxes of books and we happily signed and dated flyleafs till the very last book was sold. There was still a huge crowd of well-wishers, and we welcomed at least a hundred people (only a few at a time!) onto our floating home and talked ourselves hoarse until the setting sun reminded us that we should be looking after that first priority of all sailing voyagers – a safe mooring for the night. Willing hands helped throw off the lines, and we sailed slowly along to Harbourfront's Pier 4 Marina to tie up, one slip away from *Lorcha*'s first berth after her launching in 1980.

We had indeed come full circle.

EPILOGUE

"Are you the family that sailed around the world?"

We were surprised how many people knew of us and our voyaging. We felt we were an ordinary family, yet people would stop to speak to us on the streets of Toronto, picking us out of a population of more than two million.

There was a dizzying number of interviews for newspaper articles and radio and television shows, as if we were the only people to have voyaged extensively in their own boat. Only we seemed to understand that in the community we had just left, *every* boat was an ocean voyager. We wrote to D. H. (Nobby) Clarke of Ipswich, England, consultant to Guinness Superlatives Ltd. (publishers of the *Guinness Book of World Records*), to ask how many small boats had sailed around the world. He told us that *Nancy Dawson* was the first pleasure boat to have done so, in 1850, and since then approximately 450 pleasure boats with amateur crews such as ourselves had circumnavigated.

"How are you settling in?" and "How have the children adjusted?" were the questions people most often asked us. Lurking behind them was the unasked question: "Can a family that has had such an extraordinary life experience for so many years, return to function under the stresses of city living?" Perhaps, worded in another way the question would have been: "How high is the personal cost for having lived so unconventionally?"

As the inhabitants of the only yacht anchored off an uninhabited island, we had been completely at ease. We had

323

visited some of the major cities of the world. We were used to change; we adapted and made our own way. Could our home city be so foreign to us that we couldn't cope? Surely not.

Four days after arriving back in Toronto we moved into our house. Two days later, Penny and Peter started school. Penny rejoined the same French Immersion class she had attended at Senior Kindergarten level, now at Grade Six. Peter went into an unstructured English-language Grade Four at the same school, Dewson Public School.

"You just came back from sailing around the world?" Peter's classmates would say. "So what! Our family went to Canada's Wonderland this summer."

Our children's biggest complaint was that school took so long. They had done their correspondence classes in two to three hours a day working with Fiona on *Lorcha*, but now they had to be in school for almost seven hours.

Eighteen months after our arrival in Toronto we are all just fine. Penny is now in Grade Seven at the University of Toronto Schools, an academically demanding institution, and Peter is doing well in Grade Five, where he is part of the gifted program. Their interest this past summer was in learning to sail a 3.4-metre Mirror dinghy.

I have joined experienced cruising sailors David and Carol Ladell, who own Meridian Marine. Meridian specializes in outfitting cruising boats and has expertise in charts and guide books. I feel I have found a place where I can put my sailing experience to practical use. Fiona seems to miss our cruising life most, but she's slowly adjusting and becoming more involved in free-lance public relations and publicity work for various clients.

We still own *Lorcha*, but we didn't sail her very much during our first summer back in Toronto. Perhaps she would be better off with new owners ready to accept the challenge of piloting her over the oceans of the world.

We have been much in demand for slide shows and lectures about our voyaging. If a decade ago, when we began to plan our trip, there was a trickle of people who dreamed of

324

such a life, today there is a torrent of would-be long-distance voyagers outfitting their boats, saving their money, and thirsting for knowledge on how to voyage as we did. There is an even greater number of absolute non-sailors who simply want to hear our stories.

Joseph Conrad once described sailors as "the grown up children of a discontented earth." We are proud to have been part of that band.

APPENDIX A:
Description of *Lorcha* and Equipment

KM-30
Designed by Frans Coblens of Amsterdam in 1977
Double-chine steel construction
Hull and decks built by Karmac Yachts, Hamilton, Ontario, Canada, 1979
Converted to junk rig and fitted out by Paul Howard
Launched in 1980

Principal dimensions

Length overall 29'3"
Waterline length 23'7"
Beam 9'7"
Draft 4'3"
Displacement (weight) 5 tonnes
Registered tonnage (a measure of interior volume) 7.19
Sail area 440 square feet
Mast, yard, and battens of aluminium

Equipment

Hydrovane self-steering gear
Engine
    Two-cylinder Yanmar diesel of 15 h.p.
    200 litres of fuel
Standard Horizon Maxi 88-channel VHF
Sestral Moore compass
Dinghy
    7'8" × 3'8", fibreglass construction, built by John Bain of Sault
      Ste. Marie, Ontario, to the Phil Bolger "Puffin" design
    Dinghy outboard: Seagull 40 featherweight 2 h.p. outboard

326

Anchors

    Main: 7.5 kilo Bruce on 200 feet of ⅜" chain, with Simpson
        Lawrence Hy-Speed windlass

    Others, in order of most often used:

        35-lb. fisherman anchor

        Viking 5000 aluminium dismountable "Danforth" type
            anchor

        35-lb. Southwest Marine Factors plow type anchor

Galley

    Two-burner with grill propane stove with 20 lb. of gas in two
        tanks

    340 litres of water in tanks and jerry cans

APPENDIX B:
Lorcha's Interior Layout

We bought a hull built by a professional builder of steel yachts. *Lorcha*'s hull had had all the steel work done before she arrived in our back garden. The ballast had been poured into the keel, and the hull was primer-painted inside and out.

I covered the hull with a tarpaulin, installed a wood-burning stove (it was January), and began by insulating the hull with bead-board foam. I attached 1" x 2" (17mm x 34mm) wood strips to the steel framing to support the plywood liner, then began in earnest to build in the wood interior.

The first layout shows how *Lorcha* was outfitted when we left Toronto. The cockpit lockers had hatches on either side, with the centre portion used as the propane gas bottle locker, as it had pipes to drain any leaked gas out through the transom.

Peter's quarter berth was on the port side, with some lockers for his clothes and toys along the hull. The sides were straight fore and aft so he could curl up and sleep comfortably no matter how the boat rolled. There was two feet (sixty centimetres) of space over the cushion to the deck liner, and a corner of the head of the bunk was open to the main cabin. Peter would crawl into his bunk over the engine box, which was just under the companionway and the same height as his bunk.

Penny's bunk was opposite and similarly arranged.

Just forward of Penny's bunk was the head (short for

"head rope," the rope the sailors of old grasped as they leaned over the side to relieve themselves). *Lorcha*'s head was a telephone-booth-sized compartment with standing headroom.

Opposite was the galley, occupying four feet (1.2 metres) fore and aft and coming out to the centre line. We had a sink and a two-burner-plus-grill propane stove. Dishes and a skillet were kept in racks under the deck lining, and under those, at counter level, were some divided spaces and a screened drawer.

We ate at a drop-leaf table. With the table leaves down, the back rest for the settee closed the space between settee and table support for a harbour double berth. We sometimes used this as a play area for the children when at sea, as there was no fear of them tumbling out.

Opposite was the settee berth where Fiona and I slept on our watch-and-watch-about system at sea. Its inboard edge had a canvas lee cloth to help hold the sleeper in when the boat was rolling heavily.

A two-foot-square (sixty-centimetre) chart table was hinged to the bulkhead at the head of this berth. A removable leg held the inboard forward corner up. The chart table was chest high, high enough so the off-watch could sleep with his or her head under it. When the navigator was braced against the galley bulkhead behind him, he could work at the table with both hands. It also could be hinged at the foot of the bunk at a level convenient for writing while sitting.

The three shelves and a locker forward of that berth were where we kept most of our clothes and linens.

Forward of the mast was the hanging locker for the foul-weather

329

Layout of Lorcha when leaving Toronto

A. Lockers
B. Cockpit/Lockers
C. Cockpit/Footwell
D. Qtr. Berth/Peter
E. Qtr. Berth/Penny
F. Companionway
G. Dishes in Racks
H. Galley
I. Sink
J. Cooker
K. Toilet
L. Backrest/Shelf
M. Shelf
N. Shelves
O. Settee/Berth
P. Hinged Table
Q. Hatch
R. Mast
S. Hanging Locker
T. Anchor Chain Box

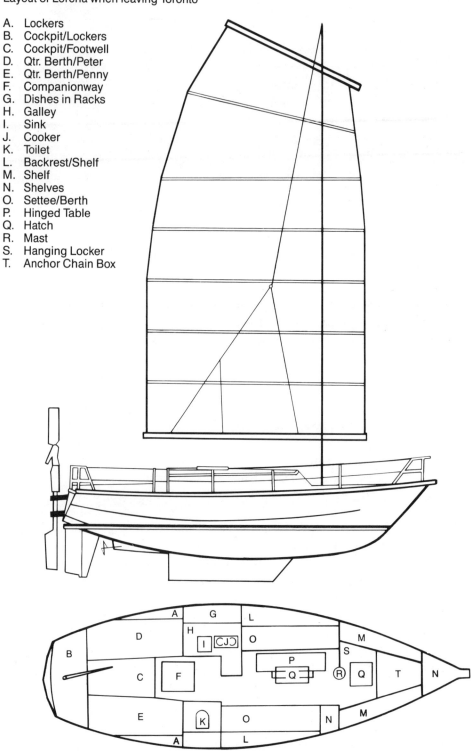

Layout of Lorcha when returning to Toronto

A. Lockers
B. Seat
C. Cockpit/Footwell
D. Berth/Peter
E. Berth/Penny
F. Companionway
G. Dishes in Racks
H. Galley
I. Sink
J. Cooker
K. Toilet
L. Shelf/Backrest
M. Shelf
N. Shelves
O. Settee/Berth
P. Table
Q. Hatch
R. Mast
S. Hinged Hatch
T. Anchor Chain Box
U. Desk

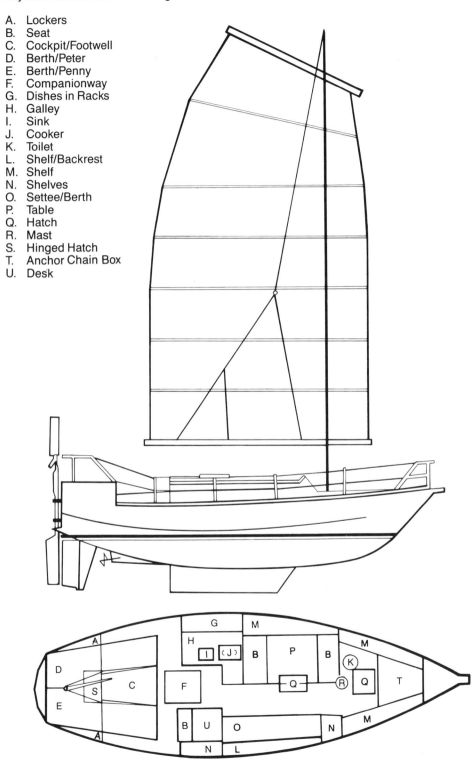

gear. A shelf ran along either side of the boat, and there were shelves in the bow. The top of the anchor chain box served as a platform for baskets of fruit and vegetables.

By the time we returned to Toronto, *Lorcha*'s interior had undergone major changes. In the Canary Islands, Fiona decided she wanted more stowage space for staple foods. We took the head out of its compartment and shifted it forward of the mast to the former hanging locker. There was only sitting headroom here, but as I was the only one wanting standing headroom in the head, I was outvoted.

Where the head had been became a stowage area for six plastic, screw-top, ten-litre containers filled with flour, rice, sugar, oatmeal, and cornmeal. Tinned goods and other things were also stowed here, and so was the hanging foul-weather gear.

In Brazil, we decided to change the dinette arrangement, installing an athwartships table and bench seats. The children now were able to have one side of the table each to do their school work on. This eating area could be made down to a double berth by lowering the table to the level of the seats, and using the back-rest cushions over it as a mattress.

The biggest change was the aft cabin we added in New Zealand. The children now slept with their heads towards the transom. They had three and a half feet (1.1 metres) of space over their bunk cushions for sitting headroom, four and a half feet (1.4 metres) from cabin sole (floor) to ceiling. Food was now stowed in the heads of the quarter berths, and one side became the hanging locker. The head-turned-food-stowage area enjoyed a third incarnation as I installed in it a desk with a lifting top and a built-in seat for an office space for Fiona.

APPENDIX C:
Itinerary

Times given for passages are from secure-in-harbour-of-departure to secure-in-harbour-of-arrival.

Miles listed for passages are the accumulated sea miles sailed over the bottom from daily positions. There would be some disparity with the miles sailed through the water because of tacking, meandering from the desired course, or adjustment for currents.

1985

April 14
Cristobal, Panama, through the Panama Canal to Taboga Island, Panama, in the Pacific Ocean – 14 hours.

April 20 – May 1
Taboga Island to Academy Bay, Santa Cruz Island, Galapagos Islands – 940 miles: 11 days 1 hour.

May 18 – June 15
Academy Bay to Pitcairn Island – 2,776 miles:
29 days 7 hours.

June 21 – June 27
Pitcairn Island to Mangareva Island, Gambier Islands, French Polynesia – 350 miles: 5 days 2 hours.

July 10 – July 23
Mangareva to Papeete, Tahiti, French Polynesia –
935 miles: 12 days 14 hours.

August 18
Papeete to Moorea – 10 miles:
3 hours.

August 26
Moorea to Papeete – 10 miles:
3 hours.

September 6 – September 7
Papeete to Huahine –
110 miles: 23 hours.

September 18
Huahine to Raiatea – 20 miles:
4 hours.

September 26
Raiatea to Bora Bora –
40 miles: 9 hours.

October 4 – October 9
Bora Bora to Aitutaki Island,
Cook Islands – 465 miles:
5 days 7 hours.

October 19 – October 21
Aitutaki Island to Palmerston
Atoll – 220 miles: 2 days.

October 25 – November 2
Palmerston Atoll to Neiafu,
Vava'u, Tonga – 642 miles:
7 days 13 hours.

November 22 – November 24
Hunga, Vava'u Group to
Nuku'alofa, Tongatapu –
170 miles: 1 day 22 hours.

November 30 – December 14
Nuku'alofa to Whangarei, New
Zealand – 1,135 miles:
13 days 11 hours.

1986

May 27 – June 10
Whangarei to Vila, Efate
Island, Vanuatu – 1,248 miles:
13 days 20 hours.

June 24 – June 25
Vila to Lomuda Bay, Epi Island
– 80 miles: 20 hours.

June 27
Lomuda Bay to Paama Island –
10 miles: 2 hours.

June 28
Paama to Port Sandwich,
Malekula Island – 28 miles:
6 hours.

July 2
Port Sandwich to Crab Bay –
28 miles: 5 hours.

July 3
Crab Bay to Norsoup –
10 miles: 2 hours.

July 5
Norsoup to Palikula Bay, Santo
Island – 38 miles: 6 hours.

July 10 – July 11
Palikula Bay to Waterfall Bay,
Vanua Lava – 110 miles:
24 hours.

July 13
Waterfall Bay to Dives Bay,
Ureparapara – 23 miles:
5 hours.

July 15 – July 16
Dives Bay to Ndende Island,
Solomon Islands – 191 miles:
1 day 15 hours.

July 19 – July 21
Ndende to Port Mary, Santa
Ana Island – 192 miles: 1 day
19 hours.

July 27
Port Mary to Tavanapupu,
Marau Sound, Guadalcanal –
135 miles: 1 day 13 hours.

July 30
Tavanapupu to Neal Island –
25 miles: 6 hours.

July 31
Neal Island to Honiara –
26 miles: 6 hours.

August 8 – August 9
Honiara to Mbili Pass, New
Georgia Group – 115 miles:
24 hours.

August 15
Mbili to Matai – 10 miles:
2 hours.

August 17
Matai to Talina – 8 miles:
2 hours.

August 19
Talina to Seghe – 16 miles:
4 hours.

August 20
Seghe to Mbareho – 6 miles:
2 hours.

August 21
Mbareho to Viru Harbour –
28 miles: 6 hours.

August 23
Viru to Egholo – 22 miles:
6 hours.

August 26
Egholo to Rendova – 10 miles:
2 hours.

August 28
Rendova to Lambeti – 20 miles:
5 hours.

August 29
Lambeti to Rovorovo Lagoon –
20 miles: 6 hours.

August 31
Rovorovo to Mbasroko Bay –
14 miles: 4 hours.

September 2
Mbasroko Bay to Bailakolo Bay
– 4 miles: 1 hour.

September 4
Bailakolo Bay to bay beside
Ringgi Cove – 12 miles:
3 hours.

September 6
bay beside Ringgi Cove to Gizo
– 21 miles: 5 hours.

September 9
Gizo to Vella Lavella – 14 miles:
4 hours.

September 14
Vella Lavella to Gizo – 14 miles:
4 hours.

September 17
Gizo to Simbo – 26 miles:
6 hours.

September 20 – September 23
Simbo to Misima, Papua New
Guinea – 201 miles:
2 days 20 hours.

September 29
Misima to Deboyne Islands –
28 miles: 6 hours.

October 2
Deboyne to Conflict Group –
49 miles: 9 hours.

October 3
Conflict Group to Slade Island
– 48 miles: 9 hours.

October 4
Slade Island to Basilaki Bay –
8 miles: 2 hours.

October 6
Basilaki Bay to Samarai –
24 miles: 6 hours.

October 7
Samarai to Dagadagabonalua
Island – 3 miles: 1 hour.

October 9 – October 13
Dagadagabonalua to Samarai
for clearance, then on to
Cairns, Australia – 493 miles:
4 days 3 hours.

1987

June 9 – June 24
Cairns to Mount Adolphus
Island inside the Great Barrier
Reef, day-sailing with over-
night anchorages at Low Isles,
Hope Islands, Cooktown, Cape
Flattery, Howlick Island, Cape
Melville, Flinders Islands, Han-

nah Isle, Night Island, Portland
Roads, Cape Grenville, Hanna-
bal Islands, Escape River –
approximately 450 miles:
15 days.

June 26 – July 2
Mount Adolphus Island to
Cape Hotham in the Van Die-
men Gulf – 717 miles:
6 days 4 hours.

July 3
Cape Hotham to Fannie Bay,
Darwin – 45 miles: 9 hours.

July 23 – August 10
Darwin to Cocos Keeling Atoll
– 2,029 miles:
17 days 22 hours.

August 21 – September 13
Cocos Keeling Atoll to Port de
la Nievre, Antsiranana, Diego
Suarez Bay, Madagascar –
2,913 miles: 23 days 1 hour.

October 3
Port de la Nievre to Ampanasina Bay – 36 miles: 6 hours.

October 4
Ampanasina Bay to Baie d'Andovohouka – 46 miles: 9 hours.

October 5
Baie d'Andovohouka to Baie
Ampamonty – 16 miles:
5 hours.

October 7
Baie Ampamonty to Nosy Mitsio – 22 miles: 5 hours.

October 8
Nosy Mitsio to Hellville, Nosy
Be – 41 miles: 8 hours.

October 11
Hellville to Nosy Komba –
6 miles: 2 hours.

October 12
Nosy Komba to Hellville –
6 miles: 2 hours.

October 19
Hellville to Nosy Kisimasy –
16 miles: 3 hours.

October 20
Nosy Kisimasy to Rivière Baramahomay – 23 miles: 4 hours.

October 21
Rivière Baramahomay to Nosy
Valiha – 29 miles: 6 hours.

October 22 – October 23
Nosy Valiha to Mahajanga –
110 miles: 1 day 7 hours

November 10 – November 24
Mahajanga to Richard's Bay,
South Africa – 1,310 miles:
14 days 2 hours.

1988

February 5 – February 6
Richard's Bay to Durban –

95 miles: 19 hours.

February 22 – February 24
Durban to East London –
250 miles: 1 day 16 hours.

February 25
East London to Port Elizabeth
– 140 miles: 19 hours.

February 29 – March 2
Port Elizabeth to Mossel Bay –
190 miles: 1 day 16 hours.

March 7 – March 9
Mossel Bay to Capetown –
260 miles: 2 days.

March 23 – April 8
Capetown to St. Helena –
1,758 miles: 16 days.

April 14 – April 30
St. Helena to Fernando de
Noronha, Brazil – 1,806 miles:
14 days 12 hours.

May 6 – May 9
Fernando de Noronha to Fortaleza – 340 miles:
2 days 20 hours.

May 17 – June 16
Fortaleza to Bermuda – 3,328
miles: 29 days 21 hours.

June 21 – June 27
Bermuda to Atlantic City, New
Jersey, U.S.A. – 660 miles:
6 days 2 hours.

July 11 – July 12
Atlantic City to Atlantic Highlands in Raritan Bay –
90 miles: 19 hours.

July 13 – August 23
Atlantic Highlands to Youngstown, New York, on the Niagara
River – approximately 500 stat-
ute miles or 804 kilometres:
37 days of lazy day-sailing in
inland waters.

August 27
Youngstown, New York, to
Niagara-on-the-Lake, Ontario –
2 miles: 1 hour.

August 28
Niagara-on-the-Lake to Toronto
– 30 miles: 6 hours.

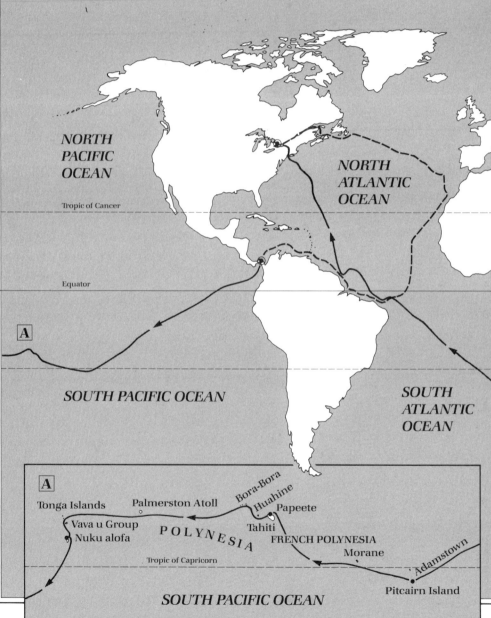

$\mathbb{S}$TILL IN THE SAME BOAT

–––––– *Lorcha's* route described in *All In The Same Boat*
––◄––– *Lorcha's* route described in this volume

SCALE

0   1000   2000   3000 km
0   1000   2000 miles

NORTH PACIFIC OCEAN

NORTH ATLANTIC OCEAN

Tropic of Cancer

Equator

A

SOUTH PACIFIC OCEAN

SOUTH ATLANTIC OCEAN

A

Tonga Islands   Palmerston Atoll   Bora-Bora
                                        Huahine
Vava u Group   P O L Y N E S I A   Papeete
Nuku alofa   Tahiti
                          FRENCH POLYNESIA
Tropic of Capricorn   Morane
                                              Adamstown

Pitcairn Island

SOUTH PACIFIC OCEAN